# THE INTEGRATED ACTOR

# THE INTEGRATED ACTOR

## IMAGINATION, BODY, BREATH, VOICE

*Alex Taylor*

*methuen* | drama
LONDON • NEW YORK • OXFORD • NEW DELHI • SYDNEY

METHUEN DRAMA
Bloomsbury Publishing Plc, 50 Bedford Square, London, WC1B 3DP, UK
Bloomsbury Publishing Inc, 1359 Broadway, New York, NY 10018, USA
Bloomsbury Publishing Ireland, 29 Earlsfort Terrace, Dublin 2, D02 AY28, Ireland

BLOOMSBURY, METHUEN DRAMA and the Methuen Drama logo are trademarks of Bloomsbury Publishing Plc

First published in Great Britain 2026

Copyright © Alex Taylor, 2026

Alex Taylor has asserted his right under the Copyright, Designs and Patents Act, 1988, to be identified as Author of this work.

Cover design: Ben Anslow
Cover image: Winter tree branches in the shape of human lungs
(© Mike Hill / Getty Images)

All rights reserved. No part of this publication may be: i) reproduced or transmitted in any form, electronic or mechanical, including photocopying, recording or by means of any information storage or retrieval system without prior permission in writing from the publishers; or ii) used or reproduced in any way for the training, development or operation of artificial intelligence (AI) technologies, including generative AI technologies. The rights holders expressly reserve this publication from the text and data mining exception as per Article 4(3) of the Digital Single Market Directive (EU) 2019/790.

Bloomsbury Publishing Plc does not have any control over, or responsibility for, any third-party websites referred to or in this book. All internet addresses given in this book were correct at the time of going to press. The author and publisher regret any inconvenience caused if addresses have changed or sites have ceased to exist, but can accept no responsibility for any such changes.

A catalogue record for this book is available from the British Library.

A catalog record for this book is available from the Library of Congress.

ISBN:  HB:    978-1-3504-4133-0
       PB:    978-1-3504-4132-3
       ePDF:  978-1-3504-4134-7
       eBook: 978-1-3504-4135-4

Typeset by Integra Software Services Pvt. Ltd.
Printed and bound in Great Britain

Online resources to accompany this book can be found at:
https://www.bloomsburyonlineresources.com/the-integrated-actor

For product safety related questions contact productsafety@bloomsbury.com.

To find out more about our authors and books visit www.bloomsbury.com and sign up for our newsletters.

# CONTENTS

| | |
|---|---|
| List of Figures | vii |
| Foreword | viii |
| How to Use This Book | x |

| | | |
|---|---|---|
| **Introduction** | | 1 |
| 1 | Some Science | 5 |
| 2 | A Discussion about Truth | 9 |
| 3 | Imagination, Imagination, Imagination | 13 |
| 4 | Breath 1 | 17 |
| 5 | Habitual Use – Old Habits, New Habits | 23 |
| 6 | Alignment and the Larynx | 43 |
| 7 | Working in Semi-Supine – Floor Work 1 | 47 |
| 8 | The Concept of Centre – A Physical Centre | 55 |
| 9 | Pitch 1 | 61 |
| 10 | Language and Text 1 | 71 |
| 11 | Working in Semi-Supine – Floor Work 2 | 77 |
| 12 | More about Breath – Breath Capacity | 87 |
| 13 | Language and Text 2 – Phrasing and Meaning | 93 |
| 14 | Semi-Supine – Floor Work 3 – Whispered 'Ah' | 97 |
| 15 | Freeing the Body to Free the Voice | 105 |

## Contents

| | | |
|---|---|---|
| 16 | Support | 111 |
| 17 | Resonance | 123 |
| 18 | Range, Pitch and Stress | 143 |
| 19 | The Channel for Sound | 149 |
| 20 | Language and Text 3 | 157 |
| 21 | Language and Text 4 – Shakespeare | 169 |
| 22 | Other Aspects of Iambic Pentameter | 181 |
| 23 | Language and Text 5 – Shakespeare Sonnets | 189 |
| 24 | Punctuation | 199 |
| 25 | Integration: Imagination, Body, Breath, Voice | 209 |
| 26 | Working with Energy – Character Exercise | 217 |
| | Conclusion | 231 |
| | Further Reading | 233 |
| | Index | 235 |

# FIGURES

*All diagrams created by Jade C. Arvis.*

1 **Head and Torso**   19
This diagram shows the following features of vocal anatomy: the tongue (one of the key articulators), the hard palate and the soft palate, the vocal tract, the location of the larynx and the vocal folds, and the location of the diaphragm.

The muscle known as the diaphragm is attached to the bottom of the ribcage, from the bottom of the sternum at the front to the bottom of the lower back ribs at the back.

2 **Organs of Speech**   160
This diagram shows all of the articulators involved in the formation of speech sounds.

To be clear, the tract called the oesophagus has no role in the production of sound. This is the passage way that carries food and fluids to the stomach. Note that when we ingest water, it bypasses the vocal folds, situated in the larynx, as it travels down the oesophagus.

3 **Chakras**   222
This diagram indicates the general location of the various chakras, or energy centres, in the body. This is to enable you to visualise them if you wish to explore the work in the final chapter of the book. A colour version of this diagram is available in the website that accompanies this book.

# FOREWORD

Actors sometimes say to me, 'I need to find the way to be a better actor …' or, 'the way to use my voice …' or, 'a better way to use my body'. I think it is important to say from the outset that I don't believe in 'the way'. In my experience, there are many ways to approach a creative use of the self – there is no one way.

I first thought, when I began writing this book, that I was going to share with readers my approach to accessing the imagination, the body and the voice in order to harness their power in such a way that an actor is capable of utilizing themselves to their fullest extent. Once I had begun the task of writing the book, I realized that such a goal was far too ambitious. At any rate, this is not, now, what this book is attempting to be. (If I live long enough, perhaps one day I will write such a book, but that is not this book.) Rather the pages that follow will share a range of insights about the imagination, the breath, the body and the voice that I have found can be useful to the actor in training.

Throughout my career as an actor, director and a teacher, I have sought ways in which it might be possible to integrate the use of oneself in the execution of the challenges that face the actor. What follows are a series of insights to the kinds of processes I have found to be involved.

When I began my own journey, which I suppose was in my teens, when I first had an opportunity to act, and which then came into focus in the years of my own actor training, I little realized that a large part of the work I needed to do was on reintegrating aspects of myself that had become disparate and somewhat disconnected. My sense of this disconnectedness only became clear to me through the struggle of attempting to become a better actor, and I only really began to discover ways to address these issues as I became a teacher. This book offers insights, I hope, to this process.

I am going to spend time in the pages that follow encouraging you to go within and, to begin with, you will spend a good deal of time focusing on your spine, and for two main reasons. Firstly, the spine supports the whole of your body and is central to the physical experience of yourself. Secondly, the spine channels and supports the core of your central nervous system. For both reasons, it is very important to you. From this initial work on the spine and the body, you will then focus on your experience of the breath and its relationship with your imagination, which is your key resource as an actor. (That is to say, both the imagination and the breath are key resources.)

Much of the discourse, and the work, that follows focuses on simple physical/imaginative exercises designed to assist in the reintegration, physically and imaginatively, of yourself. Many of the exercises are simple but require focus and concentration. Some of you may find you have little patience with this approach, in which case this book is not for you though, perhaps, the insights shared in this book may be of greater value at a later stage in your own creative journey. However, if you think you have a genuine interest in exploring a psycho-physical approach that may help you arrive at a different understanding of yourself and enable you to become a better actor, please read on.

# HOW TO USE THIS BOOK

This book aims to introduce different areas of work designed to facilitate integration for the actor, between imagination, breath, body and voice.

You will find quite a number of sections within the book that discuss the philosophical underpinning of the work or which enter into discourse about the nature of acting. These sections may not be of interest to you; if so, you are welcome to skip them. I have highlighted in **bold** type aspects of theory that I think are especially important or relevant.

Feel free to dip in and out of this book, sampling as you wish, and if you are more interested in engaging with exercises, you will find that these appear, usually laid out in stages, in boxes within the text. However, I have attempted to lay out the philosophical underpinning, the discourse and the practical work in a clear, progressive way, if you wish to start where the book begins and work your way through to the end.

I would say, though, that the ideas and the work that are outlined in this book only represent the beginning of the work the actor needs to do.

Online resources to support this book can be found at: https://www.bloomsburyonlineresources.com/the-integrated-actor

# INTRODUCTION

### What is an integrated actor?

Put simply, it is an actor for whom mind (imagination), breath, emotional response, physical embodiment and expression are interconnected and seem to function as one. This is, essentially, what I understand by the Stanislavskian term 'psycho-physical': that what originates in the mind has a corresponding physiological response and that anything the actor does will be as a result of a psychological (or it may be, imaginative) stimulus.

One of the issues that arises within traditions of actor training is that crucial aspects, such as practical studies in movement and voice work, often do not seek to make experiential connections between the actor's experience of the physical skills work and the ways in which these skills need to be integrated within the actor's creative process so that they become a fundamental part of the way in which the actor works. In many approaches to actor training, I think it is assumed that the actor will strive to make connections between the various disciplines for themselves and that they will find ways to integrate voice and movement skills within their own acting practice.

This book, then, is principally about **how you use yourself as an actor – about how imagination, imagined experience, body and breath must work together.** The aim of this book is to share insights into both the imaginative and physiological processes of acting through an exploration of practical exercises in body and voice work that have grown out of my own practice.

I think that many actors experience a disconnect between their imaginations, their breath and their bodies that means that they will not be able to embody, in the fullest sense, the characters they play or connect in the deepest imaginative way with a dramatic text. This is very often not as a result of the training they may have undergone, which seeks to redress this unbalance, but is more frequently a result of the way they have lived, and the way they have been educated. The simple truth is that many individuals – not just actors – experience this disconnect which I believe is a result of the way in which we have been educated in childhood and young adulthood. Education in my own time, and still today, values the ability to develop the intellect, and our examination system in the UK is focused towards the development of intellectual prowess. It is our abilities to analyse and to reason as well as to 'know', in an intellectual sense, that are valued and tested. These skills are also tested at the point when we commence our professional careers if we want to work in most branches of society, though they are less valued and less valuable in the Arts. However, we are also physical, spiritual and sentient beings, and I would argue that our education, and the way we live, should pay attention to the development of all of our self so that mind and body, thought and feeling, can become reintegrated.

I believe that we find it difficult to function in an integrated way now because we have been taught to separate thought from feeling – we have been taught that rational thought can be trusted but our feelings cannot. We have also been taught that thinking, and writing about what we think, is of more value than doing something.

I daresay that many of us think we are more advanced now – in terms of thought, scientific knowledge and philosophy – than people who lived in a more distant time: Elizabethan England, for instance, or the ancient Greeks. In some ways, that may be so, but perhaps we are less in touch with ourselves, our imaginations and our bodies, and less in touch with the physical world in which we live.

This book is for anyone interested in approaching the job of acting with their whole being and, I would argue, this book is also for those who may wish to explore another way of being in their everyday life. However, it is written, principally, with the actor in mind.

It has taken me some years to come round to the notion of writing a book about body, voice and acting and their relationship to the imagination. My intention here is to share some key elements in my way of working along with the philosophical and aesthetic principles that underpin my practice. This book does not seek to be a complete approach to actor training, or to voice or movement work. It seeks to provide opportunities for you to explore a philosophy, and a range of approaches to imaginative/physical work in relation to acting, that enable 'integration' in which mind, body, breath and voice function holistically and as one.

Part of what this book seeks to do is to explore and to reinforce the fundamental, organic nature of the actor, and of acting processes, and to explore ways in which the actor's imagination, which I would suggest is at the core of everything an actor might achieve, can enable the actor to stimulate, to access and to harness their body and voice as a means of embodying, expressing and communicating their acting choices.

I have been fortunate to collaborate with many exceptional teachers, practitioners, actors and performers, so the way I work now has been hugely influenced by these colleagues. These influences will be acknowledged in this book – I believe it is of paramount importance to pay tribute to the work of others that has influenced one's own practice. However, there are elements within my own way of working that are original, too, and it is my intention to try to share these with you as you work your way through this book.

In my own early training, the Alexander Technique was a key component and the foundation of the approach to voice work. The Alexander Technique has impacted on my creative life at various stages since, so that whilst I have at times moved away from Alexander work to explore other practices, particularly in the area of voice work, the influence of the technique through working with practitioners, such as Niamh Dowling (Manchester School of Theatre, now director of RADA), Carolyn Serota (The Juilliard School) and Charlotte Okie (Hong Kong Academy, now at the Juilliard School), has been part of my working life and, in recent years, I have come to realize that the principles of the Alexander Technique and the application of these principles to the physical and creative processes of the actor are important and a means of opening doors not just in terms of physical use and vocal function but also in relation to embodying the creative processes of acting. **So, Alexander principles, combined with an exploration of our relationship with our breath, are at the core of the approach to both voice work and acting within this book.**

I fundamentally believe in a practical way of working that encourages the actor to explore an organic approach to acting but, as part of that approach, it is necessary to identify why some imaginative or physiological approaches may be more helpful than others. Whilst, traditionally, actor training has focused on what actors may need in order to gain employment within the industry, I think there is something to be said for the acting studio being a place where the actor and the teacher can, together, strip away the demands and pressures of the profession in order to get to the heart of the various aspects of the creative process.

With this in mind, this book does not offer you a magic formula that will make all your acting problems vanish. In order to become an integrated actor, there is a good deal of physical and technical work that needs to be undertaken, so this book does not offer any kind of 'quick fix'. You may find many of the exercises in this book quite simple. **I believe in simple, straightforward exercises that need to be repeated in order to result in embodied practice, and that such exercises need to be re-explored constantly, in order to be of lasting value and for skills to be spontaneously available to the actor.**

If you were a pianist, for instance, **there is nothing especially entertaining about the regular practice of scales, yet musicians engage in practice up to eight hours a day and, do indeed, regularly have to practise scales in order to develop and maintain the flexibility, dexterity and consistency of contact of their fingers with their instrument. Only when the musician has complete mastery over their technical skills can they then allow their imaginations to work within the music they interpret. Why, when an actor practices, should the process be more entertaining or any less rigorous than that of the musician?** Of course, as part of their eight hours of practice a day, a musician will play and interpret music but an actor, too, can also work with text, with partners and with scenes as part of their daily practice. However, I would maintain that the actor, like the musician, does need to develop the discipline to practise and to exercise.

## *The nature of acting*

What does good acting require of the actor? To state it very simply, at a fundamental level, **the actor must be able to be as available, as responsive and as expressive when acting as they are, when relaxed, in their everyday life** – arguably even more available, responsive and expressive as the actor must be 'switched on', that is to say, alert and aware, but available, at all times when they are working.

In the execution of their craft, many actors constantly get in their own way. Stanislavski, the practitioner who, over 100 years ago, wrote the most thorough and detailed books about the acting process, which we still draw upon today, refers to the ways in which this can occur in the opening chapters of his first book (*An Actor's Work*, Jean Benedetti, Routledge Classics, 2016.)

Very simply, but for any number of reasons, **the actor may become tense and inhibited when attempting to act. Sometimes this is just out of sheer nervous funk, sometimes it is a result of a desire to do well, to achieve one's best work or to please the audience, and sometimes it is a result of becoming self-conscious, aware that they are being observed.** Acting is scary – the feeling of excitement many actors feel just before a performance is, in fact, part of that fearful response. In the act of performance the actor lays themselves open to all kinds of potential failure and to the fact that, however good they are, the audience may just not like them. So when they are standing in the wings waiting to go on (or they may be in a film studio just before the moment that the cameras roll), the actor is likely to experience something of a classic fight or flight response. Does the actor stay and 'fight' or do they run away, 'take flight'? The vast majority of actors – though not all – decide to 'fight', which is to say they commit to the performance and make their way onstage when their cue comes. If we stay locked in a fight or flight response, however, in order to meet the demands of the performance, we are likely to put on some or other kind of 'armour', which is to say that we hang onto habitual tensions in the body that help us feel 'safe' or we acquire a way of meeting the performance situation that involves locking joints or over-engaging musculature which, again, makes us feel protected but which gets in the way of an ability to explore the natural, organic, psycho-physical responses that result in honest and expressive acting.

Patsy Rodenburg writes about the result of one of the external responses we may have to fight or flight in *The Actor Speaks* and describes what she refers to as 'Bluff' as a means of defence when meeting situations that might cause anxiety – the chest lifted and puffed out, combined with a voice that may be over-loud and falsely confident. Essentially, this is the result of tightening and holding in the lower back and of pulling in and tensing in the abdominal area, and this may also include locking the knees. 'Bluff' may also include lifting and holding in the chest area, a raised chin, and a head that is held rather than poised, and all of these kinds of tension will inhibit and restrict potential healthy and expressive psycho-physical experience (imagination, body and voice).

What follows next is some scientific evidence to support what I am asserting. The science may not be of interest to you – you may be willing to take on trust that mind and body are intrinsically interconnected and mutually dependent, in which case do skip the following sections, but if you like scientific evidence do read on.

# CHAPTER 1
# SOME SCIENCE

### Fight or flight

The fight or flight response was first described by Walter Bradford Cannon. His theory states that animals react to perceived threat with a general discharge of the sympathetic nervous system, preparing the animal for fighting or running away. More specifically, the adrenal medulla produces a hormonal cascade that results in a series of defensive reactions. This state of hyperarousal results in several responses beyond fight or flight. The wider array of responses, such as freezing, fainting, experiencing fright and/or fleeing the scene, has led researchers to use more neutral or accommodating terminology such as 'hyperarousal' or the 'acute stress response'.

The autonomic nervous system is a control system that acts largely unconsciously and regulates many basic physiological functions. This system is the primary mechanism in control of the fight or flight response, and its role is mediated by two different components: the sympathetic nervous system and the parasympathetic nervous system. The sympathetic nervous system originates in the spinal cord, and its main function is to activate the physiological changes that occur during the fight or flight response. The parasympathetic nervous system originates in the sacral spinal cord and medulla and works in concert with the sympathetic nervous system. Its main function is to activate the 'rest and digest' response and return the body to homeostasis after the fight or flight response. This system utilizes and activates the release of the neurotransmitter acetylcholine.

For many actors, the fight or flight response kicks in as part of doing the job – some of us experience this as the excitement we may feel at the thought of meeting an audience, and some of us experience this as stage fright – sheer nervous funk that something might go awry in the act of performance. Either way, the autonomic nervous system may tell us to stay and 'fight' and it is this response that leads to our being overly protected, and muscles and joints may lock and 'defend' in response.

### Polyvagal theory

If you are the kind of person for whom scientific evidence for the interconnectedness of mind and body is helpful, then you may find an investigation into polyvagal theory also of interest. Stephen Porges introduced the polyvagal theory in 1994. Rooted in neuropsychology, this theory is based on the vagus nerve's role in the regulation of emotional responses and the 'fight or flight' response. The vagus nerve is a long nerve that originates in the brain stem and extends through the neck and into the chest and abdomen. It is tasked with regulating critical body functions such as heart rate, blood pressure, breathing and digestion. There are, in fact, three nervous system states relative to the vagus nerve, activated in a particular order. I don't believe it should be necessary here to go into greater depth in relation to polyvagal theory, except to say that it emphasizes the importance of the vagus nerve in the way that brain, heart, lungs and gut are inter-related and connected. If you have further interest in knowing more about the vagus nerve and polyvagal theory, Deb Dana has published a number of books focused on the theory and its application to our understanding of trauma and recovery. Published in 2020, *Polyvagal Exercises for Safety and Connection* (W. W. Norton and Company, 2020) may be of particular interest to those wanting to understand psychophysical processes at a deeper level.

**What this scientific information makes very clear is that there is a crucial and fundamental relationship between mind and body which, to all intents and purposes, work as one. It follows, then, that the actor must find ways to stay at ease, access an appropriate balance of tension, and meet the space and the audience without feeling the need to equip themselves with protective 'armour' but to remain available and open. The key to this, then, may lie within the actor's ability to focus the mind and imagination in such a way as to be able to free the body and facilitate creative freedom.**

## Fascia

Other evidence of the interconnectedness of all parts of the body lies within our understanding of the role of the fascia. The fascia is a layer of connective tissue below the skin. This is, in fact, multi-layered and supports tissues and organs. It also helps the function of our bloodstream, bone tissue and musculature. The fascia can be identified in four main layers: superficial, deep, visceral and parietal. All these layers contain nerves that render our fascia almost as sensitive as our skin. Superficial fascia lie right under our skin and can include muscle fibres. Deep fascia cover bones, muscles, nerves and blood vessels. Visceral fascia go around organs such as lungs, heart and stomach, and parietal fascia are tissues that line body cavities, such as the pelvis.

In the latter part of her life, Kristin Linklater became fascinated by the existence of fascia throughout the body. I recall in one workshop with Kristin that she produced a photographic image of the fascia and the way they interconnect throughout the body. For Kristin the fascia provided evidence of the way everything within our being and experience is interconnected.

## Mind and body

These are just some of the ways in which scientific research supports the notion that mind and body have a powerful inter-relationship. I have absolutely no doubt that there may be multiple other ways in which we, as human beings, may experience this interconnectedness. It is my lived experience that helps me to feel confident about this – scientific evidence merely supports what I already know.

At this point, it may be worth saying that whilst, from time to time, I will cite scientific research in support of some of the key elements of the work explored within this book, I think the experiential knowledge that comes from the day-to-day practice of working with actors in training, and within the industry, is another important and valuable form of research.

As you will see, the emphasis in my work lies in the power of the imagination to direct and release the body, as well as in a mindful exploration of simple physical exercises that can free the actor (or speaker, or singer) and enable the actor to access all of themselves in performance. Put in simple terms, when we are able to feel free, to be at ease, the mind (imagination) is connected to the body through a variety of organic means and an exploration of thought and imaginative stimuli can enable us to be available, to tap into our imagined experience and to express and communicate this freely with other actors and with audiences.

# CHAPTER 2
# A DISCUSSION ABOUT TRUTH

I'd like to spend a moment to talk about truth in acting. It's a word that is frequently bandied about, one that has long been used in actor training, often as a shorthand to encourage the actor to produce work that is honest and direct, without artifice or mannerism. The word 'truth' itself is extremely powerful and suggests something that is timeless, all-encompassing and irrefutable. In art, though, truth is rooted in a particular time and place and resonates within the parameters of societal and moral concerns of its own time and can be moulded by fashion. So, 'Truth' in acting is an artistic construct.

For example, we can see films of stage performances given by Laurence Olivier that, at least on an initial watching, can seem, by our standards today as overblown, theatrical and mannered. We can watch performances by actors such as Bette Davis in black-and-white Hollywood movies of the 1930s and the 1940s in which the acting, by contemporary standards, can appear to be melodramatic and full of mannerisms. However, these are performances by actors much lauded in their own time and whilst some of them can seem old-fashioned or overly dramatic, even external, by our own standards now, they are truthful creations within the contexts within which they were originally created. These contexts include the practices, fashions and expectations of the time, its moral compass, and the limits of the technology both in the theatre (no microphones, the limits of the lighting, for instance) and in movie making (in early sound films the camera is fixed and the microphones not very sensitive). I would argue, if we can see past some of these elements, that there are still truths within these performances from other times that can still resonate for us today. What is the element, then, within these performances that we can identify as 'truthful'?

I would argue that truth in acting may reside in several elements. The most superficial of these, but nonetheless difficult to achieve, is an ability to behave in a physically free and spontaneous way – to embody physical responses that appear to be human and natural. **Relaxation and freedom within the musculature of the body are key here. As part of this ability to be spontaneous, the voice must be relaxed and at ease, and expressive. The more difficult aspect of truth in acting for discussion is the actor's ability to work imaginatively and emotionally from themselves, from their lived and imagined experience, in a direct and honest way. In this sense, everyone's truth is different for the simple reason that everyone's lived experience is different.**

Truth, in acting, is achieved when the actor is able to work authentically, from themselves, in response to a number of contributory factors. These include the text; the other actor or actors; an ability to live, imaginatively, within the world of the play; and the demands of the space (or the medium) within which the actor is working.

### The Integrated Actor

In the UK a great deal of emphasis in actor training can be placed on the concept of transformation. I take this to mean that the actor appears to transform themselves imaginatively, physically and vocally into the character they are playing. If this is possible, then I believe that the most important 'transformation' lies, principally, within the actor's imagination, but I would like to suggest that, if the work is to be truthful, then the actor must work, authentically, from themselves. **In the end, the actor only has themselves, their lived experience and their imagination, to work with.**

I also believe that the first 'transformation' is for the actor to inhabit their body **and their voice from a place of ease and openness, relinquishing habitual patterns of tension, if possible, in order to be able to use themselves freely and be at their most expressive.**

### No quick fix

It sometimes seems to me that actors in training want the practitioners they work with to provide an insight or an exercise that will suddenly make their work easy for them so that their problems magically melt away. I think there are occasions when this can happen as the result of an exercise but, in my experience, if an actor is able to achieve creative freedom in performance this is the result of a considerable amount of regular practice and a great deal of personal homework. So, whilst I hope this book will provide insights into the creative and psycho-physical processes of acting, it does not provide anything by way of being a 'quick fix'.

### Intuitive elements within the acting process and performance

I'd like to touch on this aspect of acting, briefly, before moving on. Most of us experience, from time to time, a sense of what someone is thinking without their having to speak, or we might have sensed that something is about to happen just before it does, or we simply pick up what someone else is feeling without their having to put their feelings into words. Perhaps it is easiest to label this 'intuition'. I would like to say now, at the start of your journey through this book, that I think that the actor's ability to be intuitive, to tap into their intuitive sense, is a key element within their development and within their ability to communicate with other actors and with an audience: a sixth sense, if you like. I also believe that through the exploration of imaginative and psycho-physical exercise, the actor begins to develop their intuitive abilities. These can be difficult to name and to describe, and for some of you, this will not be an aspect of acting that interests, but I would simply ask that you try to keep an open mind.

One of my best friends, someone who enjoyed a lengthy career as an actor who has now, sadly, passed, used to talk about what she called 'attunement'. What she meant by this was an ability to be so 'attuned' to the other actors on stage that you knew where they were, what they were feeling, or what they were about to do without having to see, or speak directly to, them This sense of 'attunement' can equally be applied to the actor's relationship with the audience – that through sensing the quality of an audience's attention, their 'energy', it is then possible to make adjustments within the performance in order to engage and involve them. This is, also, not something an actor does alone but can be brought about through the cast being 'attuned' to each other, to the space and to the audience. I don't know how my friend learned this – I suspect it was something she developed as a result of many years of experience, working in repertory theatre, on tour and in the West End – but I do believe it is possible, both from my own experience as an actor and as someone who works with actors within a studio environment.

**Judi Dench speaks about this ability to be attuned in an interview with Richard Eyre that has been broadcast by the BBC. She speaks about it in a very practical way – about an ear that is listening to the other actors on stage but that is metaphorically also turned towards the audience, picking up their responses, and about an additional eye that is monitoring what is going on in the space whilst her real eyes are seeing the stage and the other actors. I am not sure that all actors have, or utilize, these abilities but I think developing these intuitive skills is desirable and important.**

In further illustration of the importance of intuitive abilities within the work of the actor, there is an exercise that is conducted at the Moscow Arts Theatre School, where a group of actors – perhaps twenty second-year acting students – are arranged in a simple formation, perhaps two lines of ten chairs arranged to face each other. The actors might start the exercise sitting on the chairs. They then are asked to perform a sequence of activities in unison: for instance, to stand, to turn to the left, to walk in line until they are behind their chair, to lift the chair, to turn to the right, to walk to form the line opposite where they began, to put down the chair to form another row of chairs, and then to sit back down upon the chair. All of this sequence must be performed by the group as if they are thinking and moving in synchronicity with each other – action, rhythm, pace, spacing, timing, all of these elements are executed in a synchronized way. To some of you reading this book, this may seem far-fetched, but in fact, not only can second-year actors at the Moscow Arts Theatre School achieve this, they are able to execute such a sequence over and over in complete synchronicity. You might like to think that this is due to the senses being acutely aware, and I am sure that this is one set of skills that is being drawn upon, but I feel also sure that this is an exercise that develops a sixth sense, which my friend, above, described as 'attunement', and as a result of being both available and relaxed.

If you are interested in, and ready to explore some of these ideas and practical exercises, read on.

# CHAPTER 3
# IMAGINATION, IMAGINATION, IMAGINATION

When Ellen Terry, perhaps the most famous actor of her generation along with Henry Irving, with whom she regularly acted at The Lyceum Theatre, was asked what were the three most important attributes that an actor could possess, she stated, 'Imagination, Imagination, Imagination'.

I have spent some time in the introduction to propose the notion that the processes that occur in the brain are simultaneously experienced in a variety of ways in the body: a thought stimulates a psycho-physical response. This may also be experienced as an impulse which may lead to physiological responses being activated, and this in turn might also be identified as an emotional response.

In acting the actor must possess the skill of allowing their imagination to work within the given circumstances of the scene, and as part of the inner life of the character they play. **I believe that the actor's imagination should be fertile and must be able to be given free rein as this is the main source of their creativity but, again, when we are anxious, unduly nervous, self-conscious or when we feel defensive, the imagination tends to shut down.** I suspect that this is owing to the fact that self-consciousness and anxiety lead us to focus on the external – put simply, the 'fight or flight' response, for instance, makes us unduly aware of the audience and of the impact we may have upon them (and they on us), so we stop the processes of the creative imagination and become too aware of the things that might go wrong or of the negative response the audience may have towards us: the elements that lie outside us. I also think that exploring the imagination is not something that our educational system encourages, nor is it encouraged by the contexts in which we interact with other people everyday. For many of us, the ability to allow our imagination free reign begins to be lost as we begin our schooling and, certainly, by the time we find ourselves in secondary education, developing our intellectual, rather than our imaginative, capabilities becomes paramount.

Perhaps it is useful, then, to focus on the moments in our everyday lives when we know our imaginations are working. For many of us, now, the main stimulus is a visual one: we spend so much of our time looking at screens and the images we see on them stimulate us in various ways. **However, all of our senses stimulate imaginative responses which frequently also become physiological and emotional responses.** So, the smell of a meal as it is cooking stimulates us to anticipate the meal on the plate and can trigger a whole series of physiological responses, such as salivating and possibly recognizing that we feel hungry. Reading a piece of fiction can frequently stimulate our visual sense – we may see the places and the people described, we may sense the atmosphere, we may even seem to enter these scenes and become part of the story, in our imagination. Our aural sense can also be a powerful imaginative stimulus – listening to a piece of music can be particularly evocative of our emotional responses – and the sensory experience of taste and touch can also trigger a series of physiological and emotional responses. So, for most of us, memory is triggered by any and all of these senses.

**I'd like to touch on the fact, now, that we are all different. Traditionally, I think it has been assumed that the actor will rely largely on the visual sense to spark their imagination but, in fact, any of the senses may stimulate imaginative responses within us and for some of us it may be the senses of hearing, taste, smell or touch, rather than the visual sense, that provoke psycho-physical responses. I would also say, if we are inclined to rely on the visual sense, that if the things that we conjure up through the stimulation of our visual sense do not provoke other sensory responses then it is not much use to the actor. For instance, when we imagine our favourite meal, we should seem to smell it or taste it or imagine the textures in our mouth when we start to eat it, or if we visualize a favourite place we should seem to start to sense the temperature of the air around us, or start to smell it, or recall what it feels like to touch some of the surfaces or the objects there.**

I'd also like to suggest that, as we are all different, our imaginations may work in very different ways, too. Let me offer a simple illustration of what I mean.

When I began my own actor training we spent time attempting to visualize our spines. We were asked to imagine our vertebrae and see them in relation to each other, to see one vertebra, a space between this vertebra and the next vertebra, and so on. To an extent, I felt I could do this, but then I would become frustrated as my ability to visualize a series of vertebrae seemed to become impossible – I felt as if I lost count and as if my ability to imagine failed me by the time I reached the centre of my spine. Owing to this, I would essentially give up trying to imagine my spine, just hoping that it would take care of itself. Many years later, when working with an Alexander Technique teacher, I found myself imagining my spine as a shaft of light and imagined that light shooting from the base of my spine right up to the occipital joint just inside the base of my skull. This was not something suggested to me: the Alexander practitioner was cradling my head and my neck and focusing on that relationship, and asked me to allow my spine to lengthen out along the therapy table. My imagination then came into play <u>of its own accord</u> and I suddenly saw what I can only describe as light, somewhat like electricity, shooting along the length of my spine.

I share this one experience not because I think that, if you are reading this book, you should be seeking the same kind of imaginative and psycho-physical responses, but to illustrate that there are many ways in which our imaginations can work within us when we are relaxed and focused and that there is no, single, right way for us to imagine an experience whether that be physiological or psycho-physical and emotional.

I began working on imagining my spine in a somewhat literal way, but later found that by allowing my imagination free rein something more powerful and, perhaps, more efficient, could be achieved. **So, the actor does need to be able to tune into and to access their imagination, in whatever way it chooses to work, as this triggers psycho-physical responses within that enable the actor to live in the imaginary given circumstances, to initiate action, and to begin to experience the inner life of the character.**

In life, I would also like to suggest that our thought processes are frequently random and that multiple thoughts can be firing within our minds, all jostling for pre-eminence, at any given moment. It is often tempting for the actor to create thought processes for the character they play that are simple and linear. Perhaps this is, indeed, a good starting point and helps the actor to map out the journey they will undertake as the character during the course of the creative experience of acting the play. **However, I would suggest that if we are able to be at ease within the rehearsal studio or the performance, then our imaginations will not be working linearly – we may find ourselves thinking, 'in the moment' – and that the imagination may be stimulated by any and all of our senses as well, of course, as by the other actors we are working with in that moment.**

To begin with I am going to encourage you to engage your imagination as a means of developing self-awareness and of exploring your relationship with your own body. To become aware of yourself in simple activities, such as standing, sitting, and walking, and to notice your breath and your relationship with it, and then to explore potential change in all of these manifestations of being. Later, I will ask you to focus on text and explore how the responses that language stimulates within you, both sensorily and in terms of thinking and feeling, can be harnessed and, in turn, this work with language will lead to scene study.

**Sensory exercise**

Try a couple of simple exercises which are to do with our relationship with our five senses.

> ### Simple sensory exercise
>
> Imagine a slice of lemon in front of you and place this imaginary slice of lemon in your mouth. The chances are, even as you start to imagine this, that your salivary glands start to react.
>
> Similarly, imagine a large container of water is set in front of you – it's very large and, perhaps, just above the height of your waist. Dip your arm into this imaginary container of water and move your arm backwards and forwards in the water. The chances are that you will seem to experience the texture of the water and the way it resists the movement of your hand and arm, and some of the sensations of the water on your skin and as it moves through your fingers.

These are elements that relate to your sense memory, and this is very important to you as an actor in terms of imaginatively embodying the character you play and their experience.

## The Integrated Actor

### Muscularity

Before I move on to outline different areas of work, I'd like to mention that, whilst the actor needs to be free and at ease in order to achieve work that can be seen as truthful, the work of the actor is necessarily muscular – especially if you intend to work in theatre spaces where being present and being heard are activities that engage both your imagination and the musculature within your body which needs to work in response to your imagination.

I am often surprised today at how unmuscular some younger actors can be, particularly when they speak, or, they may, at times, be sufficiently muscular and then let that all go at other times and become both not present and inaudible.

At the moment of reading, you may not be clear about what I mean – hopefully, this will become clearer as you make your way through this book – but **if you are to have energy as a performer you need to develop a deep, experiential understanding of the ways in which your body, and the muscularity within it, needs to engage with your imagination in order to breathe, to speak, to be a dynamic presence, and to have the sustained energy it takes to inhabit a large space and keep an audience engaged and interested in what you do.**

If you are to be heard in a large theatre space, this is a matter of imaginative engagement, physical presence, muscular work and energy. I would argue that much of this work is also required for the camera but, of course, you can be much more intimate in the way you speak for a microphone. However, I would argue that your voice still requires some physical engagement, even when speaking quietly, if your spoken thoughts are to be clear and if the words you speak are to be picked up by the microphone.

**Let's be clear, though, that when I speak here about muscular engagement I am not talking about overworking. Many actors misunderstand this – and indeed many voice and acting coaches do, too. If you have a tendency to overwork then it is very likely that your body and your voice will become tired, and if overworking this can occur quite quickly.**

Right now, you may not have a clear sense as to what an appropriate level of muscular engagement is. **Let me be clear, here, however, and say that anything you do will require some level of muscular engagement in your body but that what the actor is working for is the appropriate balance of tension that is required for a particular activity whether that be standing, sitting, walking, running, speaking, singing and so on.** I am going to spend a good deal of time early in this book to emphasize the importance of relaxation and freedom in the body in order for you to be able to communicate what is in your imagination through your body and through your voice, but with freedom there must also be a balanced muscular engagement that relates to the particular task at hand.

**Perhaps the best way to sum all of this up for now is to say that to be fully present and expressive in what they do actors must be free, yet at the same time acting is muscular.**

# CHAPTER 4
# BREATH 1

'Breath is life onstage' (Michael Langham)

I had the great good fortune to work with director Michael Langham during the early 1990s when I was one of the master teachers at the Julliard School in New York and he was the Director of the Drama Division. When I raised with him some of the issues that actors in his production of *Romeo and Juliet* were having in relation to their breath, he said to me, 'But don't they know that breath is life onstage'.

That statement had a profound effect on me and is, in fact, multi-layered. To state it simply, at a fundamental level our relationship with breath is the key not only to the way our voice functions but also to the whole experience of creating a performance. Hopefully, some of the discussion that follows here can help to clarify why, 'Breath is life onstage'.

*Concepts of breath*

What is breath? It is, of course, a need, a fundamental physical need – along with food, breath keeps us alive. Breathing is something that we, generally, take for granted. It is not something we think about because the business of breathing is a response to a reflex that kicks in as we are born, and after that moment it, more or less, takes care of itself.

**The nature of the breathing reflex, though, is such that it responds to our physiological and emotional state. For instance, the rhythm of our breath changes depending on whether we feel calm or we feel elated or excited, or whether we feel anxious or fearful. So as well as being necessary to life, breath, and the way we breathe, is a fundamental physiological response to our thought processes and to our inner emotional experience.**

Breath is also a form of energy. I sometimes think that it can be useful to the actor to imagine this. As the breath drops in we take in some of the air that surrounds us, and that air is full of particles of energy.

> Simple exercise for breath as energy
>
> Standing, with your feet under your hips and with easy knees, allows your spine to align with your head simply poised on the top of your neck. Now imagine that the energy in the air, surrounding you, fills you through the simple act of allowing

a breath to drop in. As the breath drops in, we harness that energy and can then channel it.

Find a way to imagine the particles of energy that surround you – the air is filled with thousands of tiny atoms, jiggling about and bouncing off each other. Sense, as the breath drops in, that the air that falls into you fills you with energy. Sense it moving through your body from your centre: down your legs and into your feet, up your spine and into your head, arms and hands. Sense how you harness this energy as the breath drops into you, and how you radiate this energy as you allow breath to fall out of you.

The word 'inspiration' (which most of us take to mean the moment of having a creative or imaginative idea, the moment when our imagination is fired up so that we suddenly understand something or feel we know what to do in the moment) actually means 'to breathe in'. So breath can also inspire us, and in the moment that breath comes into us that, alone, can enable us to feel energized, ready and in charge.

### *Some facts about breath*

When we are at ease, the physiological response to a breath is a similar experience for all of us. In the moment that we need a breath there is a response in the breathing reflex, located in the diaphragm. The diaphragm is a dome-shaped muscle that is attached, all the way round, to the bottom of the rib cage. As the centre of the diaphragm contracts downwards, the lungs begin to expand and air is drawn into them. The oxygen that is drawn in then stimulates and enlivens our being, and the air that has filled us also becomes fuel that we can utilize in order to express ourselves through sound or speech. We may have no need to speak, however and, assuming that we don't wish to express anything, we then, simply, allow the air to fall out again. When the body then feels the need for it, the breathing reflex within the diaphragm will then initiate the next breath to drop in.

**When a natural and efficient breath takes place, and when the dome of the diaphragm contracts downwards to initiate the intake of a breath, the organs below the diaphragm need to be slightly displaced. In order for this slight displacement to take place, the muscles of the lower abdominal area need to release and, thus, respond to the breath dropping in.** In our everyday lives, when we are relaxed, this happens automatically and without thinking about it. Interestingly, in preparation for sleep, our mind and our body need to be completely at one with this organic process which is part of our internal experience of being relaxed and at ease. If we are not able to be in touch with a natural breath or if there is anything psychologically or physiologically that interferes with it, quite simply, we will not be able to fall asleep.

Breath 1

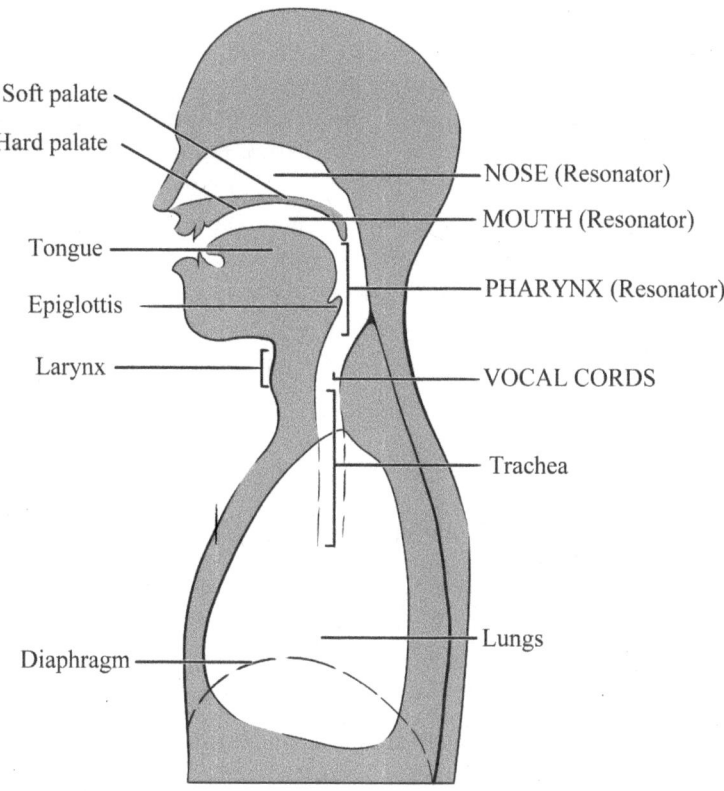

**Figure 1** Head and Torso
This diagram shows the following features of vocal anatomy: the tongue (one of the key articulators), the hard palate and the soft palate, the vocal tract, the location of the larynx and the vocal folds, and the location of the diaphragm.

The muscle known as the diaphragm is attached to the bottom of the ribcage, from the bottom of the sternum at the front to the bottom of the lower back ribs at the back.

This natural and organic breath, then, is a crucial element to the easy and expressive function of the body and the voice and, if we accept that in the moment before we fall asleep the breath is at its most relaxed and organic, then there is a paradox here for the actor who needs to access this kind of an organic breath but who definitely does not want to feel sleepy or to fall asleep.

I think there are two things to be aware of in relation to this, then. First of all, when we ready ourselves for sleep, the breathing rhythm falls into a particular pattern that is very much slowed. Also, as part of this pattern, the amount of breath we take prior to and when we sleep is quite small. If we are breathing in order to do something, or to express ourselves, then we will not wish to replicate this slowed down pattern essential to sleeping – though, when we exercise the breath in a relaxed state, we may find that we come close to this pattern. Secondly, **the actor needs to have an awareness of the fact** that the breathing reflex naturally responds to our thoughts and our feelings. In life, it naturally speeds up or slows down, or may even become erratic, as we respond to our thoughts and inner emotional experience. So, as an actor, the breathing reflex needs to be responsive to our thoughts and feelings so that our bodies and our voices can express not only our emotional responses but also our thoughts and our intentions.

If we take a moment to remind ourselves of the fight or flight response that can take over at the point when the actor has to meet the audience (or the camera), it becomes important to consider how this may impact on something as fundamental and organic as the experience of breathing. **If the actor's response to going onstage is to defend themselves in some way, then the likelihood will be that they will interfere with their response to the need to allow a breath to drop in,** either by interfering with the breathing reflex itself (for instance, holding the breath) or by inhibiting the natural physical responses that take place as a response to that breath (for instance, holding in or clenching the stomach so that the actor is not able to allow for the natural low belly release that is a response to the breath dropping in). As a result, the healthy and expressive function of the voice, and the body, may be compromised and other elements of the actor's performance, e.g. natural and spontaneous physiological responses, may also be inhibited.

## *More facts about the breath*

The psycho-physical act of breathing is far more complex than I have described it above. If you are minded to know more about what happens when we breathe, if the science of it is of interest to you, by all means undertake further research. There is a very useful description of what happens to initiate a breath in Kristin Linklater's *Freeing the Natural Voice* (Nick Hern Books, 2006), and even more detailed descriptions are available in theoretical and anatomical reference books such as Meribeth Bunch Dayme's *The Performer's Voice* (W. W. Norton and Company, Inc, 2005).

**From the actor's experiential perspective, however, the need to allow a breath to drop in is a response to an impulse that we sense within us, and it is this reflexive response that needs to be tapped into and allowed to respond freely in order to access the voice and to be able to act freely and expressively.**

Further groups of muscles may be involved in the act of breathing – certainly there are a large number of muscle groups that have been identified as possibly playing a role in initiating an intake of breath but there are a number of traditionally held concepts in regard to breath, as the performer experiences it, that I believe are not useful and that I would like to dispel.

**First of all, it is not in the actor's best interests to 'control' the breath. Breath control is a phrase that has been used, traditionally, in the teaching of voice for actors for many years, and a number of concepts have been put forward as a means of establishing this control: for instance, the notion that breath is directed by the actor from the diaphragm, or that the outflow of the breath through the vocal tract is directed by a slow, controlled, movement of the ribs.**

It is my belief that consciously trying to exercise these concepts is simply not useful to the performer and that practising exercises that are a response to these beliefs creates tension within the physiological system and may lead to overwork. In time, overworking leads to vocal tiredness, voice loss and, at worst, vocal pathology. If there is an element of control, it lies mainly with our ability to allow the breath to drop in, allowing the lower abdominal area to release as this occurs.

Some practitioners of voice are insistent that the oblique muscles play an active role in the outflow of the breath and assist in its control. Actually, vocal science does not support this theory. I have seen evidence of a singer exercising their voice in a clinical trial, where electrodes were attached to various muscle groups, including the obliques, so that information could be gathered through visual images on a video screen. It was clearly demonstrated that when the singer engaged the oblique muscles to 'assist' the outbreath, the voice instantaneously cut out, i.e. the larynx became unstable and the voice either stopped functioning or 'flipped' into falsetto. When the obliques are left alone, i.e. not actively engaged, and when the breath is left to move freely through the vocal tract, the resulting sound, as breath meets the vocal folds, is stable, healthy and expressive. (Anne Marie Speed, *The Voice Explained*.)

**Another phrase that is commonly used and has been used for decades (if not centuries) by some practitioners is 'breath support'. I would like to suggest that there is no such thing as breath support and that thinking of breath as a form of support may be counterproductive and, potentially, dangerous.** It is true, of course, that we are unable to make a sustained or energized sound without breath being present and accessed. Breath, then, is fuel and, indeed, is necessary in the production of sound. However, the notion of 'breath support' can lead us to believe that if there is some kind of problem with vocal function that this can most likely be solved by increasing the amount of 'breath support'. This is a fallacy – a completely misconceived idea – and will most likely lead to vocal difficulties in the shorter or longer term.

The simple fact is that, in order to produce a sound, we do not need a great deal of air. It may be that to speak or sing a long, sustained phrase we will need more air in the system but the speaker or singer should not make assumptions about this as the amount of air needed for a particular phrase will vary from person to person, and this is related to the need to speak (or sing) and the nature of the thought itself. **It is actually how the breath is managed at vocal fold level that determines how efficiently the breath may be accessed and the phrase may be sustained.**

I'll explain further. The note we speak or sing is made as breath meets the vocal folds within the vocal tract, and the vocal folds resist the air. Air then, as it tries to make its way through the vocal folds, vibrates the folds and a sound is produced. The quality and efficiency with which that sound is produced are a direct result of the way the vocal folds function. Quite simply if we make it difficult for the vocal folds to resist the breath – for example, if we drive or push too much breath at them – then the vocal folds will quickly become tired (because they have to work too hard to resist the air), or their function may be compromised, i.e. there is some kind of problem with the quality of the sound we produce.

This, then, brings me back to the fact that it does not help us to focus on breath as a means of 'supporting' the sound we make. The speaker or singer probably won't solve a problem to do with vocal function by driving more air at the vocal folds or, more simply put, by taking more breath.

I think it is comforting to know that, in life, we are normally able to take the air we need in order to speak the phrase we next intend to speak – and we do this automatically: we don't consciously think about it. So, if you are relaxed and at ease as an actor so that a reflexive breath is able to drop in, you will find that you can work to the end of the thought you are singing or speaking with relative ease. If this is not the case, then it is likely that the issue does not lie with the breath itself, but more likely at vocal fold level, i.e. in the way the vocal folds are functioning in their attempt to resist the air in order to make the required sound. So, for instance, if the breath is running out before the end of the phrase you are speaking, the likelihood is that the sound itself is not being efficiently produced; for example, there may be a lot of air in the sound resulting in a breathy tone as a result of the vocal folds not making clean, firm contact. It may also be that we are not imaginatively prepared for the thought we are going to speak or sing, i.e. we have not imagined it, not received it, before we commit to communicating it.

## *The approach to breath*

How then should you think about your relationship with your breath? Put simply, it is a reflex that responds to a physical need, to a thought and/or to an emotional response. If you are sufficiently at ease and relaxed, breath drops in, in response to an impulse (which may be a physical need, or a response to a thought or a feeling) and it is then able to be expressed through sound. When breath drops in, there should be a small amount of low belly release in response to the small downward contraction within the diaphragm, and there may also be a degree of movement in the bottom of the ribcage. (More about the ribcage later.)

In so many ways, an organic breath is really natural but it can be one of the most difficult things to achieve for the actor for the simple reason that it may be difficult for the actor to let go of performance habits – possibly associated with fight or flight, or the way they live on a day-to-day basis – which get in the way of this organic process.

# CHAPTER 5
# HABITUAL USE – OLD HABITS, NEW HABITS

The vast majority of us have them, and the habits that we develop through our lifetimes feel not only familiar but necessary to us. Many of these habits, however, get in the way of natural, healthy function. It isn't just the 'fight or flight' response that gets in the way of being a free and expressive actor, but our own habitual use.

Some of our habits are a response to traumatic experience in our lives – some of these experiences may have occurred when we were very young. The mind may think it has resolved these experiences or may indeed appear to have 'forgotten' that they ever took place, but the likelihood is that they will be locked within our bodies and that one or other sets of muscle groups will remember them and be inhibited or locked as a means of protection or defence. **I do not advocate using psycho-physical work in acting – acting, movement or voice exercises – as a means of releasing or attempting to reintegrate these traumatic experiences. In my view, this is not the job of the acting tutor nor is it the role of actor training.** I believe that when actor training touches on these areas it becomes dangerous and, at the very least, acting tutors who engage in this kind of psychological approach are irresponsible. Unless you are a qualified therapist or psychologist, this is none of your business.

However, having said this, I do believe that the work that actors undertake can, by its very nature, be therapeutic. Working on elements such as grounding and alignment, which necessitates the letting go of habits, or working in semi-supine in order to release in the lower abdominal area so that an efficient breath can drop in and be experienced, can have therapeutic benefits, as this work aids in the reintegration of the physical self, and can stimulate the relationship between the imagination and the body. However, the goal of the tutor is not a therapeutic one – rather, therapeutic benefits may occur as a by-product of the work the actor does in order to make themselves open and available to the character they play, the text they have to speak, the other actors they have to listen and respond to, the world of the play they must inhabit imaginatively, and the audience who participate in the performance process.

**If the actor is to address their habits and relinquish any that are not useful they must become aware – or I could say mindful – as a necessary step, in order to learn how to let them go. And they must have a willingness to do this.** As our physical and vocal habits can feel very much part of who we are, some actors can seem unwilling to let them go – perhaps because it feels as if they are being made to feel that something about themselves is 'wrong'. I can only say that this should never be the goal of the acting tutor.

## The Integrated Actor

### Self-image

Another aspect that can get in the way of being an authentic and expressive actor is the actor's own self-image. If you really wish to be a versatile and complete actor, then you must be able to let go of any preconceptions you may have about yourself in order to lend yourself to the character you play. Society, of course, has its role to play in helping to fashion our self-image. The notion that a stomach must be flat, for instance, may seem a small thing but if that is something the actor has bought into then they are unlikely to be willing to allow a deeper breath to drop in because this would necessitate a low belly release, and so the organic impulse to allow a natural breath to occur is likely to be inhibited.

I shall simply say that it is my belief that if you want to be a complete actor then you need to have no pretensions about how you are viewed or the image that you may seem to present when you are acting.

### Being grounded

Being grounded, the act of grounding, is important to an actor in so many ways. For physical skills teachers it is usually the very first port of call, although often not much time is given over to establishing what the experience of being grounded is.

**Working on becoming grounded, which should involve experiencing what this state of being, and these words, may mean, is the first opportunity for an actor to start to become aware of their body, themselves, their breath, and their relationship to the ground and the space they inhabit.**

**I mention above that it is of crucial importance to an actor, particularly in relationship to healthy vocal function, but also in relation to how the actor inhabits the space and in terms of their presence.**

Being grounded is fundamentally about your relationship to the earth and to your centre of gravity. When we are grounded we are more likely to access the musculature that supports vocal function easily and healthily, so in terms of working on your voice exploring grounding and what it might mean to you is of tremendous value and should be given due time and attention. Like so many aspects of acting, being grounded isn't something we should work on and then assume that we can forget about it. It is something that should be reinvestigated every time we prepare to undertake physical-vocal work.

### Alignment

Before we explore what it means to be grounded it is, perhaps, useful to be aware that early humans were not essentially designed to stand and move about on two feet, rather they were designed to employ four limbs, arms and legs, but could stand if they had a need to do so. Of course, over millennia humans have evolved and established the ability to stand and to move about principally utilizing only two of our limbs, so that we now think of this as natural for us, but this activity does place, potentially, a good deal of strain on our anatomy and physiology.

If we observe the baby as it crawls and then first learns to stand, we can see that this is not a simple or an easy matter for any child. Inevitably, there are many attempts at standing and many falls – it is not something that any of us succeed at the first time we attempt it – and when we have acquired an ability to stand we then have to learn how to walk without falling.

Learning how to stand should, essentially, be a balancing act. When the various component parts of our anatomy are aligned – principally the feet, knees, pelvis, shoulder girdle and the head, the one over the other – it is then possible to balance and to remain in an upright position. For many of us, though, in early childhood, it becomes an act of will, an effortful act.

I would suggest that, for some of us, tensions that we bring into the body in order to force ourselves to stand and to walk in early childhood may remain with us and be carried forward into the rest of our lives, becoming deeply rooted habits which may hamper us in various ways.

The torso, of course and the head is also supported by the spine, and it is a fact that many of the component parts of our body – the hips, the shoulders and, especially, the head – are of considerable weight. The weight of the head, in particular, can bear down on our spine if we allow it to do so, placing undue pressure on the vertebrae and when we allow this to occur, the spine begins to collapse in a subtle way: that is to say we, ourselves, may not be aware of it and others around us may not perceive it. However, this potential tendency to allow the weight of the head to bear down unduly upon the spine will tend to compromise function in our neck, which will shorten, the upper spine, which may then become more curved, our lower spine, which may become more arched, and so on. This process, in turn, will affect the free flexible movement of our larynx in the vocal tract – this movement is essential if we are to access range and achieve a useful balance of resonance – and the sense of openness in the upper chest area, and the freedom of movement within the ribs and the lower belly – all of which are useful in terms of an easily available, free breath. All of this, in turn, will affect how we sound.

Given that this is a section on being grounded, this long description of the perils of standing and learning how to walk may seem like a digression. **However, the relationship of the rest of our body to our feet, and to the tail of our spine, is crucial in our experience of being grounded,** and paradoxically, if we allow the weight of the head to bear down on the spine, if we slump a bit through the shoulder girdle by partially collapsing the upper spine, if we depress the chest and so on, we may feel as if we are more grounded simply because we are allowing more of the weight of the component parts of our body to give to gravity. As I hope will become clear as you move through this book, this would be counterproductive simply because it is not a healthy use of our whole being, particularly in relation to our breath and to vocal function, but we also become physically less expressive if we allow these things to take place.

The Integrated Actor

As I hope you will experience as we move forward, it is a sense of natural alignment through the spine that can reduce the stresses and strains of sitting, standing, walking and moving, working with our sense of being grounded, that enable us to function in a healthy and expressive way.

I mentioned, above, an old-fashioned notion of 'support' in relation to the voice but at this point, as you begin to think about what it means to be grounded and aligned, I would like to suggest that **the whole of your body is part of your support system** for the way you can access your breath, the way the breath functions, and in relation to the way your vocal folds function.

### Being grounded when seated

As you think about and explore your sense of being grounded, then, I would like to begin by exploring how you might experience this in a seated position first. You can undertake the simple exercise that follows with your shoes on or off, but you may find it beneficial to begin to work without shoes or socks so that the soles of your feet are fully sensitive to the ground. Wear footwear if you find that preferable.

#### Grounding exercise

**Stage 1**

Take a chair and sit upon it. Make sure that the soles of your feet are touching the floor. If this means that you need to sit forward on the seat of the chair, ensure that you do this. Articulate the soles of your feet, gently and subtly, against the floor exploring the ways in which the various surfaces on the soles of your feet can make contact with the floor. Take your time with this: it seems so simple but taking time helps to increase and develop your awareness and establishes now the ways in which you are going to approach the other exercises that will follow in this book. Once you have explored the potential nature of contact between the soles of your feet and the floor, remain seated with as much of the sole of each foot as possible in contact with the floor – principally, this will include your heels, the ball of each foot, and the toes.

**Stage 2**

Now turn your attention to your sit bones and to the tail of your spine. Placing your imagination in the tail bone – you should have a sense that the tail (the coccyx) wants to move directly down to the floor immediately below you. You may not have a clear sense of this to begin with, so focus on your sit bones and, keeping the soles of your feet against the floor, gently and subtly articulate your sit bones against the seat of the chair. (If you are unsure as to where they are, this will help you identify them.) As part of this process you will find that you move forwards and backwards in your hip girdle and your lower spine – this is fine and a natural part of this exercise. Once you have explored the potential contact between your sit bones and the seat, you should be able to come to rest on your sit bones in such a way that the centre of the sit bones makes firm contact with the seat and it will feel to you as if the weight of your upper body is being carried by your sit bones.

## Stage 3

Place your imagination in the tail of your spine now and, once again, visualize it wanting to move down directly towards the floor. It may help you to imagine a tail growing straight down out of your tailbone with the tip of this imaginary tail touching the floor. Think now of the rest of your spine lengthening away from the tail in the opposite direction. To help with this, drop the weight of your head onto your chest so that you are not holding in any of the muscles around your throat or in the muscles that run up and down the length of your neck spine behind you. Slowly and with maximum concentration, bring your head back to a poised position at the top of your neck spine. To do this, be aware that you are not raising the head by lifting your chin or by engaging muscles in the throat area, rather you are utilizing muscles in the back of your neck – try to use these muscles minimally, with as little effort as possible in the muscles on either side of your neck spine to raise the head. Also, as you do this, think of your lower face, particularly your chin, remaining relaxed and disengaged from the activity. As your head rises, you are looking for the point at which your head feels poised on the top of your neck – not held, not fixed – and your eyes should be looking directly ahead of you.

If you are used to raising your chin – and a good many people like to do this habitually, so that the head is, essentially 'held' rather than poised – you may need to repeat the head/neck manoeuvre several times: slowly, using minimal effort in the neck as possible. Once you have found the poised position of the head, you may notice that the way you see the world (your relationship with your eyeline) has shifted and that your eye-lids are more open than usual. If this is the case, embrace this new sensation for your eyes and your eye-line.

## The yes/no nod

You can also check whether your head is poised by exploring a simple and subtle activity. If you nod 'Yes' with your head – very subtly, and repeat this nodding movement quite rapidly – you should be able to change the 'Yes' nod into a 'No' nod (again, keeping the movement of the 'No' nod very subtle) without feeling any major gear change at your occipital joint. This is the joint that occurs where the top vertebra of the neck spine sits inside the space in the back of your skull. If you can feel any kind of significant shift or gear change here when changing 'Yes' into 'No' then you have not found the place where your head is naturally poised.

Once you have found this place – the head lightly poised at the top of the neck spine – imagine a cushion of air around the top vertebra of your neck spine so that you imagine that your head is floating on, or supported by, this cushion of air.

### Recap

So, as you sit, you are grounding through the feet, the tail of the spine, and the sit bones. The tail of your spine wants to lengthen in the direction of the floor, in your imagination – again, imagine a tail growing down towards the floor from your coccyx – and, conversely, your neck spine wants to lengthen away from the tail and, if your head is poised and not fixed, imagine that the head wants to move directly upwards off your neck spine whilst your forehead wants to move forwards to the wall opposite you. This final imaginative task with your head is difficult to achieve, but essentially the head (the head, and not the chin) wants to float forward and upwards off the spine. In sitting, this encourages your spine to release and lengthen and this, in turn, frees the ribcage, the breathing musculature and the breath itself.

### Mantra

There's a mantra that you can say silently to yourself: 'Let my neck be free to allow my head to float forward and upwards'. This is a classic direction from the practice of the Alexander Technique and we will revisit this repeatedly as we work through a series of physical/vocal exercises.

### Final stage

Finally, as you ground yourself through the sit bones, the tail bone and the feet, do you have a sense that your kneecaps also want to float forwards and upwards as you allow the weight of your lower body to give to gravity? (The soles of your feet remain on the floor.) I'd like to suggest that there is a sense of a forward and upward direction in your head and a similar sensation in your knees.

Take your attention, now to your breath. It is likely that you will find that your lower abdominal muscles are soft and not held and that the lower abdominal muscles are, subtly, moved when the breath drops in. Imagine, as the breath falls out of you, that it travels up your spine and as it arrives in your head encourages that feeling of lengthening through the spine and of the head wanting to float forwards and upwards as the breath moves through you and out of your mouth. Allow time for the next breath to fall in – it will do if you remain calm and focused and wait for it. When the breath falls out of you, you should allow this to happen with no sense of control – the breath simply falls out.

## Standing

You are now ideally focused to move into standing.

In an ideal world, standing is a balancing act with weight evenly distributed through the body – the head balanced over the shoulder girdle which, in turn, is balanced over the hips, the knees and the feet. However, for many of us this is not the case – rather, standing becomes an act of will and defiance. I believe that this goes back to very early childhood when we move from crawling on four limbs to a decision to stand and walk. This is the point at which we should learn the balancing act that would enable us to stand with relative ease, and I am sure some of us do learn this, but I think a number of factors encourage most of us to employ effort and tension in the act of standing.

There are two key factors here. One is the simple fact that in the child's first attempts to stand and to walk there will be many falls. This must be a cause of intense frustration for us and for some of us, in order to avoid falling, we will grip through the legs, the belly and the spine so that we force ourselves to remain upright. Locking in the lower abdominal area will lead to an inhibited or restricted, rather than an organic, breath and so even at this very early stage, the act of standing may lead us to inhibit our experience of breath and our access to our voice. The other factor that may lead us to inhibit is social pressure – the eager parent who aims to be supportive whose enthusiasm wills us to stand and walk, or the older sibling, already walking, who may have little patience with the younger child's constant falls in their attempts to stand. In our determination to please, or to defy, we may learn to stand through force of will and this may lead to locking knees and gripping in the abdominal muscles. In an ideal world, then, the child should be left to figure out the balancing act for themselves and, left to their own devices, they will.

We will explore some of these potential issues a bit later, but for now, from your seated, grounded position, let's explore the potential ease of moving up into a standing position.

At this point, I'd like to take the opportunity to say that I believe that the point of this work for you as an actor, performer, presenter, speaker is not that you are expected to go around maintaining this ideal physical usage in every aspect of your daily life, but that by exploring what is possible now, in terms of being grounded, aligned, easy and free, you will be able to access what you need later, when you need it and may be more aware of the source of other issues when they may occur.

So, let's explore standing from a grounded, seated position.

### Exercise for standing

### Stage 1

Remind yourself that your tail is moving down towards the ground below you. Your neck is lengthening in the opposite direction, away from the tail, while in your imagination your head wants to move forwards and upwards and lead the spine into standing. It is the sense of direction of the head (not the chin or jaw) moving forwards and upwards that will bring you to standing. But don't attempt to stand yet, rather stay where you are and visualize what you intend to do before you do it. As you do this, stay connected to your breath – by which I mean, allow the breath to drop in and out of you naturally, leaving your lower abdominal muscles available and responsive to the breath. Make a deal with yourself now that when you do move into standing you will leave your breathing alone – you will not hold your breath or grip in the belly muscles.

## Stage 2

Before you stand, play with the sensations of forward momentum that will facilitate you to stand. Keeping your feet about hips-width apart and grounded with the floor, maintaining the length and freedom through your back, rock your head and spine forwards, from the hips and tailbone, in the direction of your knees. Your neck remains long – it does not shorten – and also do not allow yourself to arch your lower back while you are rocking. Let your forehead lead the spine as you rock forward and backward, taking your head forward to the point where it is directly above the knees, and then allow yourself to rock back onto your sit bones into the grounded position you started from. Repeat this rocking motion several times and while you do this feed into your imagination the idea that your head (not your chin) wants to float upwards as well as forwards.

## Stage 3

After rocking in this way several times allow your head to move forward of the knees and in this moment let your head float forwards and upwards to lead your spine into a standing position. This actually feels a bit risky and in the very last moment, you may not believe that you are able to move into standing without locking or gripping something in your body. There is, if you like, a point of no return where, once you have rocked yourself to that place, you simply have to allow your head to float forwards and upwards into standing. Your spine will follow and, as you stand, imagine your sit bones wish to move directly towards the floor, keep your knees easy – don't allow them to lock – as this is crucial to your sense of balance and freedom once standing.

You may wish to explore this movement from sitting to standing several times, focusing on different aspects each time. For instance, as your head floats forwards and upwards and moves you into standing, it may be helpful to remember the contact between the soles of your feet and the floor and to know that there is strength in your relationship with the earth – very simply, the soles of your feet support this movement to stand, and they support the whole of your body once standing. Remember, too, that there is no reason to hold in your lower abdominal area (your belly) nor any reason to hold your breath – breath should drop in and out naturally as you move into standing. Nor is there any reason to arch your lower back or grip in this area as you attempt to stand. If you sense this is wanting to happen, as you rock, keep sending your sit bones into the seat of the chair and/or the tail of your spine in the direction of the ground. It may seem counter-intuitive but, as you stand, your sit bones and tail of spine should still want to maintain a relationship with the ground and still want to move towards it while your head takes you forwards and upwards.

### Final stage

Once standing, check that your knees are easy – for some of you this may mean that the knees feel slightly bent, if you are used to locking them habitually. The knees should not be locked. When they are – and many of us do tend to lock our knees (for many of us this locked position feels safe) – it is likely that we will begin to arch in the lower back and we will start to grip in the lower abdominal (belly) area. This, in turn, will inhibit the natural, organic response of the breath. (Just to clarify, we are aiming for a straight leg with the knees unlocked.)

## Sitting

As a corollary, you may also want to explore the experience of sitting.

### Exercise for sitting

From standing, your head continues to want to float forwards and upwards (not your chin) while the tail of your spine wants to drop down and back. Simultaneously, the knees want to move forwards and upwards as you allow them to bend so that you can send your tail, and your sit bones, back down to the seat.

Throughout the process of sitting, your head continues to want to move forwards and upwards, and your spine remains long – again, no need to arch in the lower back – and your breathing remains free.

## Being grounded when standing

### Exercise for grounding when standing

#### Stage 1

Your feet are hips-width apart. Your knees are easy – not locked – and it seems in your imagination (and indeed in your physical experience) as if your head wants to move forwards and upwards off the spine.

Your tail bone wants to move in the direction of the floor. If this is difficult to imagine you may find it useful to go back to sitting and then move into standing, simultaneously directing your sit bones to remain in the same position as they were when you were sitting on them. To do this, you may need to allow your knees to bend more as you stand. If you are able to manage this, you should now have a sense of the tail of your spine wanting to move downwards in the direction of the ground.

### Stage 2

In standing, you should sense, as your spine lengthens upwards and away from the tail bone, as if your shoulders are just hanging off your spine – the right shoulder wants to float away from your body and off to the right; your left shoulder wants to move away from your body and immediately to your left.

Notice that you are breathing and remind yourself that breath drops in when you are ready and then falls out.

### Stage 3

Shift your weight slightly forwards through your torso (the head leads you forwards) until you feel pressure in the balls of your feet and/or your toes. Shift your weight slightly backwards so that you now feel more pressure in your heels. Return your weight to the centre, and then shift your weight to the right so that most of your weight is now over your right foot. Then shift your weight to the left.

Again, you can explore this simple exercise several times. Notice whether you are more comfortable, or attracted to, a particular position – weight forwards and in the balls of your feet, or backwards and in your heels, or possibly to one side or the other. If you prefer being forwards or back or to the side rather than being in the centre, this is likely to be telling you that you have an attractor state – somewhere that seems natural to you when you are in a standing position but is, in fact, effortful.

### Stage 4

It's then worth exploring what happens to your breath when you shift your weight forwards, backwards and sideways. Go back to the place where you are balanced and aligned with your weight centred and let the breath drop easily in and out. Now, slowly, do the shifting the weight exercise, allowing yourself to remain in one position for a bit of time, and notice if anything changes in your experience of breathing in that position. Shift your weight again and then stay with the weight distributed in another position and, again, notice your breath. You should find

> that, whenever you return to the position where you are grounded over both feet, that it is easier to breathe here.

Bear in mind with this exercise that the shifts should be small and so the effect on your breathing may be subtle, but noticing these subtle shifts and changes can be interesting in itself, and whatever you sense in relation to your body and your breath, in giving yourself over to this simple exercise, you are developing your awareness of, and sensitivity to, your experience of the breath and yourself.

### Stage 5

Now repeat the same exercise sequence but this time, when remaining in a particular position, weight either forward or back or to the side, speak a short section of a text that you know: three or four lines are probably enough. Or, if you can't think of a text, counting from one to twenty will also work. (I'd recommend a text, though – something you know and like – and for future exercises in this book you will find it beneficial to be able to speak some words that you know.) Again, as with the breath, you should find that your voice functions differently when your weight is balanced differently. Hopefully, when you return to the place where you are grounded and your weight is centred, when your knees are easy and when the breath can drop in and out easily and naturally, you should find that your voice is more at ease or more relaxed and that the whole business of speaking is easier.

It's important with the exercise above that you speak in an engaged way. Right now, you may not know what I mean by this but if you speak quietly, but with commitment, and if you think of sending the sound away from yourself, perhaps to the wall opposite you, you will probably notice the kind of shifts in your voice that it is possible to experience. The important thing is not to whisper or use half-voice – a sound full of air – as you are likely to find that you will sound the same however you shift your weight or change your centre of gravity. For now, and for the future in working with your voice, a breathy sound is not very helpful to you. When we speak like this other people sense our lack of commitment to what we say, and an aspirated sound – half sound, half breath – doesn't communicate efficiently within a space or for a microphone. Also, as a point of information, an overly aspirated sound is not particularly healthy, as your vocal folds are likely to become dry, and dry folds become tired quite quickly. Similarly, if we are using a text that we know for the purpose of exercise, it is really important that you speak the text, to the best of your ability, as if you own it and mean it.

## The Integrated Actor

It's also useful to reflect that, if you feel your voice seems more full or even more expressive when your weight is forwards, or backwards and so on, that this may be because this physical stance and the way you sound is familiar to you, i.e. you've hit your attractor state and this is how you sound to yourself most of the time in your everyday life. If this is your perception when exploring the exercise above, I recommend spending time in the grounded, centred and aligned position, letting the breath drop in and out naturally, and exploring what may be an unfamiliar sound to you because this is a place where your voice can work most efficiently and most easily. When we place unnecessary pressure on the voice over extended periods of time, it is this that is likely to lead to vocal tiredness, voice loss and potential voice pathology.

## Simple experiments with sound

### Sounding exercise 1

When working on grounding in the seated position, it can be interesting to experiment with the idea that if you make a sound, the sound comes up from your sit bones. Try touching off a sound as if the energy of the sound originates only from your sit bones. (A simple sound, such as 'Huh', is a good starting point.) Remember, your head should be poised and not held or fixed and your lower jaw should be relaxed enough that there is a small space between your lips. What do you notice about the quality of this sound? How or what do you feel in your body when accessing this simple sound as if from the sit bones?

### Sounding exercise 2

When working on grounding in the standing position, imagine that you can touch a sound off from the soles of your feet – as if the sound could travel from your feet, up through your legs, into your torso and up through your spine to your head. Again, work with a simple, 'Huh', checking that the head is poised and the lower jaw at ease. Notice the quality of the sound.

If with either of these experiments the sound seems particularly 'dark' or swallowed, think of allowing the sound to travel away from you as it releases between your lips. Again, if you wish, you can move to speaking a short section of text that you know as you experiment.

## Being present

The kind of work you have now been engaged in is very much with, and for, yourself. As an actor, when you practice on your own, your focus is very much with yourself, but

## Habitual Use – Old Habits, New Habits

when you are in rehearsal or performance you are always working with, and for, someone or something else: with your fellow actors, for the space, with or for the audience. For now, having spent time exploring what it means to be grounded, aligned, and in touch with the breath, spend some time being present.

### Stage 1

You can be seated or standing, or you could be lying on the ground, if that's preferable. As you allow breath to drop in and out of you, see the space. Even in exploring this activity you can be general in your attention or specific – you can allow your gaze to roam, randomly, around the space or you can let your gaze pause, momentarily, on this detail or another. I'd like to suggest that when we are fully present we are able to see, and appreciate, the detail that is in the space around us.

### Stage 2

In exploring being present you can also engage your other senses – indeed, you may find it preferable to explore through one or more of your other senses. Draw in a breath through your nose – does the air have a texture or a fragrance? Take your attention to something in the space your gaze can focus on, and as you allow your gaze to linger there, do you hear anything – it might be the tiniest sound? Is there something you can touch – explore the sensations and the textures of it.

### Stage 3

If you have the time, you can move slowly around the space, spending time to see different parts of it, to pause and listen, to notice fragrances and textures with your senses of smell and touch. When you have satisfied yourself that you have explored the space around you as fully as you would like to, take yourself to a place somewhere in the midst of the space, ground yourself: as you now see the space, do you feel more alive to it and do all of your senses feel more engaged? I would like to suggest that this is part of what we mean when we refer to 'being present'.

## Energy and presence

At this point, I'd like to introduce you to the concept of energy. We are going to return to the notion of energy and of what it means for a performer at other points within this book and, hopefully, concepts of energy and how you experience energy will clarify as you return to explore them at various stages.

If you are generally healthy – eat well, take moderate exercise, and generally sleep well – you are well-energized. A number of things that we do contribute to the energy available to us, principally eating healthily, and breathing. If you miss a meal or have a bad night's sleep, this will affect your energy levels.

Many actors feel that in order to produce energy that they must 'work', that is to say, overwork by making themselves tense or by pushing or straining in order to appear that they are energized. However, it is very important that you don't engage in this kind of overwork which will result in your becoming tired more quickly and, more importantly, will lead to your being more restricted and less expressive, both physically and vocally.

There are many ways of tuning into your energy but for now let's focus on two particular concepts: that, if we are at ease, we draw energy into ourselves from the ground and the space around us, and that breath that enters us and falls out of us freely is also a source of energy.

### Energy exercise 1

In a grounded, standing position, then, and sensing the contact between the soles of your feet and the floor, imagine that you are like a plant or a tree, with roots going down into the earth below you, and that like a plant you can draw energy into yourself from the ground. You might find it useful to give this an image – water energy, or light energy, electricity or laser energy – and imagine it travelling up through your legs (energy arriving in your knees encourages them to feel that they wish to float forwards and upwards) into your centre, into the root of your spine and then along the length of your spine, to arrive in your head and move to your brow at the front of your head. The energy arriving here encourages you to find the sense that your head wishes to move forwards and upwards off your spine.

### Energy exercise 2

Another way of thinking about energy is that it is in the atmosphere all around you. The air around you, for instance, is filled with atoms bouncing against each other. Standing in a grounded and aligned position, imagine that you can sense the vibrations of energy all around you and that you draw upon this energy as the breath drops in and falls out of you.

Litz Pisk, an inspirational movement coach who worked at the RSC, and within the theatre and film industry internationally, offers a wonderful and imaginative way of tuning in to your energy. When standing in a grounded position she advocates that we should 'feel the sap rising'.

This first consideration of energy and what it might be is, principally, an awareness exercise and, hopefully reinforces the idea that there is always energy present within us and available to us and that this is not something we need to manufacture: energy is within us and is available to us – we just need to know how to tune our awareness of it.

## Breath and presence

We are always breathing. As previously explained, the breathing reflex kicks in as we are born and, for the vast majority of us, it takes care of itself throughout our waking and our sleeping lives.

**When we feel ourselves under pressure of one kind or another we tend to interfere with our breathing reflex. We can do this in any number of ways. If we feel some kind of performance anxiety when we go in front of the camera or when we go onstage, it is possible that our breathing reflex will become erratic in some way or that we may 'put on armour' by tightening muscle groups – tightening in the lower belly area is a common response to this kind of performance anxiety – so that the body's natural responses to breath dropping in are compromised.**

Performance anxiety brings with it a heightening of the senses – for instance, the eyes may open wider and then become glazed, the jaw and facial muscles may become tight, the knees may become locked, the upper body and the shoulders held and tense. When these phenomena begin to take place, the ability to allow the breath to move in and out of the body in an organic way becomes compromised and we lose the ability to be present. It is also likely that the throat may start to constrict so that, when we speak, we will sound unlike ourselves.

Stanisalvski identified that for an actor's work to be truthful they have to be able to remain at ease and relaxed. Without the ability to be relatively at ease in the mind and the body we are not able to be in touch with our imagination, nor available to respond and react, spontaneously, to our fellow actors, to the events taking place around us, to the space or to the audience. At the heart of the possibility of being at ease and available is the ability to be in touch with an organic breath and if you are able to allow a natural, easy breath to fall in and out of you when you are onstage or in the presence of the camera, the rest of your being will also begin to become more at ease.


## Simple body and breath exercise

If you prefer to explore this exercise from a grounded, seated position, please adapt it accordingly.

### Stage 1

Standing with your feet hips-width apart with your weight grounded and centred, place the palm of one hand on the back of your neck – gently stroke the back of your neck from the top of the back spine to the base of the skull with your palm. This is your neck. Relax your hand and arm down by your side, and now drop the weight of your head onto your chest. Now allow the weight of your head to give to

> the pull of gravity, start to roll down through your spine and allow your head to drop towards the floor. As you do this, be aware that you are undoing your spine, vertebra by vertebra, until your head and upper spine are hanging between (or over) the space between your knees.

It's important that you do this by releasing your spine down to the root (tail bone) – for instance, as you drop down, don't hold as you arrive at the area of your spine close to your waist and then find yourself hanging from the waist. It's important to roll down through the spine and undo it right down to the root in order to be fully relaxed, or released, through the spine. When you've done this, all of your torso will be hanging over (or between) the space between your knees from the tail of your spine. As you hang, notice that you are breathing.

> **Stage 2**
>
> Bring yourself back to standing. Start by thinking of a gentle push through the soles of your feet as the tail of your spine moves directly down towards the floor. This helps you to establish your sense of being grounded, and also helps to initiate the movement through your spine as you come back to standing. Uncurl the spine, vertebra by vertebra, to bring yourself back to standing, imagining the vertebrae uncurling one by one.
>
> When all of your back spine has aligned, your head should still be resting on your chest. Finally, slowly allow your neck spine to uncurl as your head returns to its poised position at the top of the neck spine. Try to be aware of bringing your head up through the neck and not through the throat area at the front – this area should stay relaxed and not engaged – and resist any desire as your head arrives atop the neck spine to lift the chin. The head should be poised, not held.

Before we continue, spend a moment or two to explore the idea of the head being poised on the top of the neck spine. Imagine that there is space all the way around the top vertebra of the neck – this vertebra sits inside a space in the back of your skull – imagine a cushion of air all the way around this vertebra, with your head lightly poised on this cushion of air.

When the head is not fixed – and, ideally, it is never really fixed – it is still and yet it has the potential to be active. This seems a strange concept but, very simply, if your head is poised, if someone were to tap the back of your head lightly, it would immediately nod gently as if saying 'Yes'. From this poised position, you should also be able to make a tiny 'No' movement with your head and you should be able to interchange the 'Yes' nod with the 'No' nod without feeling any significant gear change at the occipital joint, i.e. where the head is balanced at the top of the neck spine.

### Stage 3

Experiment with this – start with the 'Yes' nod and remember that you should not feel as if you have to undo something in the back of your neck to achieve it. If you do feel a moment where you have to unlock something to achieve the 'Yes' nod then you are holding and your head is fixed rather than poised. From here, move into a tiny 'No' nod, and then alternate between the two, allowing some time to be in both the 'Yes' state and the 'No' state before you change from one to the other. The movements are very small – tiny – don't exaggerate them. The movements should feel very easy. When you return to a position where the head is, once again, still be careful not to lock or fix the muscles in your neck in order to hold your head in place – allow it to remain easy and poised.

Immediately after this exploration it might be interesting to speak a text you know – or count from one to twenty – ensuring that you do not fix the head in order to speak. What does that feel like, and sound like?

### Stage 4

Now, begin to drop down through the spine and build up through the spine. You can start this process slowly if you wish to ensure that you are dropping down right to the root of the spine and then building up through the spine in an efficient way. The objective with this exercise, though, is to find a rhythm that reflects your organic breathing rhythm. As you familiarize yourself with the process of rolling down and building up through the spine you should find that you need to drop down through the spine quickly, allowing the breath to fall out of you with no sense of control. There should be a small pause as you hang over your knees as you wait for the next breath to want to drop in and, as the next breath drops in, you can then build up through the spine as you return to standing.

As simple as this exercise is, it takes some practice, and you should reinvestigate it each time you give yourself over to it. There should be a sense of complete freedom as you drop down through the spine and release the breath. You should notice that as you drop down through the spine you release in the lower abdominal area – the muscles here are not held at all. This happens naturally, but it is good to notice that this happens: that when you drop down through the spine, the belly releases. Also, when you are hanging over your knees, you should notice that your head is hanging off the neck and not held by it – there should be no effort in the muscles of the neck as you hang at the bottom.

As you begin to return to standing, leave your belly alone. You do not need the musculature here to assist you to stand. However, when the breath drops in as you start to return to standing, the breath needs your belly to remain relaxed if it is to drop in easily. As you arrive in the standing position, you should be at the end of your in-breath and ready to drop down through the spine again and release the breath.

When you have repeated the dropping down through the spine and the building up through the spine exercise, co-ordinating it with your breath, a number of times, you should find at the end of it that, as you stand, align and ground yourself, your breath is completely organic, i.e. that it falls in and out of you easily and that the lower belly muscles are available to respond to the breath as it falls in.

Some of you may prefer to breathe out when you return to standing through the spine – to gently pull your stomach muscles in, as it were, to assist you to stand. Of course, we can do this, but I would like to suggest that the stomach muscles should have very little to do with the business of standing. Remember, as discussed previously, that being upright should largely be a balancing act. There are muscles at our core that do assist the spine in standing but these are not located in the abdominal, or lower abdominal, area. The psoas muscle, located within the torso, for instance, helps with alignment but should be able to engage independently of the transversus abdominus (lower belly) musculature.

### Stage 5 – Sounding

Now, once you have thoroughly investigated this exercise, repeating it several times, you may like to add sound into it. As you drop down through the spine, freely and easily, release a sound imagining it falling out from the centre of your being. Don't think of controlling this in any way – don't anticipate the way you will sound – let the sound be unconscious: a kind of animal noise. Don't push this sound, or work for it, just let it happen – and aim for a full sound not something breathy.

As you return again to standing, ground and align yourself, and speak a text you know. How does that feel and what do you notice?

You should find, after repeating this exercise with and without sound, for a few minutes that when you are standing, grounded and aligned, that breath is dropping in and out of you with relative ease and that you are no longer holding in the belly area. I would say that, for all of us, this is a natural state when we are not feeling under pressure, and I would like to suggest that when we walk out on stage this is the state of being we should take with us.

As I indicate above, this sequence of exercises can be adapted and can be conducted in a seated position if preferred. If working from being seated, the torso will hang over and rest on the knees once you have rolled down the spine with the head hanging off the spine. When returning to seated alignment, send your tail of spine and sit bones towards the seat as you uncurl. In the same way as in standing, breath should fall out as you roll down and should drop in as you return to seated alignment.

## More about body and breath

If as an actor you are to remain free and available when acting, I would like to impress upon you that there is an integral and intrinsic relationship between the body and the breath. More than this, that there is an integral relationship between the mind (imagination), the breath, and our inner emotional experience. Key to this relationship is the freedom and flexibility of the lower abdominal muscles.

> ### Abdominal release exercise
>
> If you walk around the rehearsal studio, or across the stage, as you walk, do your lower abdominal muscles remain free and responsive to your need for breath? If you break into a jog, can you keep your lower abdominal muscles at ease so that they respond as your breathing responds to the demands of increased physical activity?

If you are able to achieve this freedom in the belly area you are more likely to remain available to all that is taking place around you, and you will find that, if you call out when you are jogging, or if you suddenly stand still and speak, that your voice is much more likely to be able to respond in the moment. Let me explain. In the moment when the breath drops in, if the belly is free to respond, the larynx, which lies in the vocal tract and is the place in the body where every sound is made, naturally returns to a neutral position. In this position, we are more likely to access our optimum pitch – the sound we make when the voice is not under pressure and is at its most relaxed. This part of the voice is extremely efficient. It tires less easily and other people listening to this part of the voice feel reassured, comfortable to listen, and are likely to trust the sound we make in this part of our range. I will come back to ways in which you can ensure that you access this part of your voice in due course.

# CHAPTER 6
# ALIGNMENT AND THE LARYNX

I have already mentioned that it is not necessary for you to think of alignment as some kind of physical 'holy grail' nor that there is an expectation that you will stand, move and behave maintaining some kind of ideal alignment throughout your working life as an actor. However, there is an aspect of alignment that is crucial to the easy and expressive working of your voice that does need to be maintained if you are to sustain your vocal health. This is the relationship between your head and your neck.

In his autobiographical book *The Year of the King*, Antony Sher (Nick Hern Books, 2004) recounts in some detail the creative processes he went through as an actor when preparing to play Shakespeare's *Richard III*. There is a section in which he recounts how, in physically attempting to transform himself to create Richard's physicality, he began to lose his voice in rehearsal. The extreme curvature of the spine that he attempted to adopt resulted, at first, in Antony Sher compromising the head/neck relationship and it was this that placed pressure on the voice and resulted in a loss of voice. Working with the RSC Director of Voice, Cicely Berry, he discovered that he could make a number of adjustments within his body in order to create the physicality he desired, as long as he maintained the intrinsic relationship between the head and the neck.

I have mentioned above that when a free and flexible breath drops in, the larynx usually relaxes to a neutral place. If the head/neck relationship is compromised, this will not occur. If the head/neck relationship is compromised, then the vocal tract, the channel in which the larynx is suspended, becomes squeezed or otherwise restricted and, when this occurs, undue pressure is brought to bear upon the function of the vocal folds which come together to vibrate in order to make the sound.

The larynx is made up of a number of structures formed of cartilage. These structures are ring-like, placed one on another, and house the vocal folds – which lie across the inside of these laryngeal structures – and protect them. The larynx, in turn, is suspended from tiny muscles and ligaments within the vocal tract and when the vocal tract is relatively free and not constricted, the larynx is able to move flexibly up and down within the vocal tract. In fact, if the voice is to have any range or expressivity, the free, flexible movement of the larynx is crucial. Broadly speaking, when the larynx moves up within the vocal tract, the pitch of the voice rises, and when it lowers, the pitch drops.

The free, flexible movement of the larynx can be compromised even by small adjustments made in the relationship between the head and the neck. You might wish to explore this.

### Exercise – Observation of larynx

#### Stage 1

You can be standing or sitting or lying down. With your head poised and your neck aligned, swallow: you will notice that the larynx bobs up and then down again, usually returning to the place where it was originally at rest, within the vocal tract. If you lift the chin slightly – and/or shorten the neck – and then slightly fix your head in position (we usually engage muscles in the back of the neck to 'fix' the head) and attempt to swallow you will find that you can do it, but that it does not feel very easy or comfortable. Return to the neck aligned/head poised position and you should find that swallowing is, again, much easier and that the larynx feels freer.

#### Stage 2

Fixing the head, then, has implications for vocal use. You can test this as you speak: keep this simple and attempt to count, from a lowish note up a short scale, speaking on pitch (i.e. not singing), from one to six or seven. You should find that counting aloud is easier when your head is poised and balanced and more difficult when the neck is shortened and/or the head is fixed. If the head is fixed, you may well find that you are unable to move up in pitch beyond a count of four or five, or that you can continue to move up in pitch but that you have to force or push to make your voice work.

This flexible movement of the larynx in relation to changes of pitch is entirely natural. It is possible that you may have been encouraged by a vocal coach to keep your larynx in one position as you move up and down in your range, for one reason or another – some singing teachers, for instance, believe this is desirable. However, if you are successful at maintaining the larynx in a fixed position whilst moving through the vocal range, it is worth saying that this is likely to foreshorten the range and, in the longer term, result in some kind of vocal stress as undue pressure is being placed on the larynx if it is not allowed to move in response to pitch.

#### Stage 3

If you find it difficult to sense subtle movements within the larynx and vocal tract, you can palpate by placing your thumb on one side of your Adam's apple (the front, and most prominent part, of the larynx) and a couple of fingers on the other side – just rest them lightly: you are not squeezing or pressing. This will help you monitor what may be happening in terms of movement when you explore the two or three simple exercises above.

## Alignment and the Larynx

Hopefully, as a result of this exploration, you will discover that it is easier and freer for your larynx to move and for you to cover a small range of notes easily and comfortably when the head is poised and the neck maintains its length and is not unnecessarily shortened.

Tucking your chin downwards or inwards is also potentially problematic, by the way, because this can force the larynx into an unnaturally low position. Whilst you may find, if you do this, that you probably will not really have a problem moving through a range of notes when you speak or sing, and you will probably still be able to feel your larynx moving fairly comfortably within the vocal tract (though not everyone will feel this and some of you will, again, feel distinctly uncomfortable with the chin tucked downwards), but you will probably notice that your voice has a somewhat heavy or sepulchral tone. This might, in some contexts, be a useful sound, but know that you are placing yet another set of pressures on the larynx – you are depressing it – and habitual use in this position will be tiring and could be potentially harmful if consistently sustained.

So, to conclude this section, the alignment of the neck and the poise and balance of the head are crucial in allowing the larynx to move freely and easily within the vocal tract, in exploring and developing your vocal range, and in maintaining your vocal health.

# CHAPTER 7
# WORKING IN SEMI-SUPINE – FLOOR WORK 1

I have started the exploration of imagination, body, breath and voice from both standing and seated positions for the simple reason that, as an actor, you will usually be standing, possibly in motion, or seated, for most of the time you will be working, but in training it is very common to work in the position known as semi-supine.

## F. Matthias Alexander

This position is directly taken from the practices of F. Matthias Alexander who developed the Alexander Technique, but the semi-supine position is commonly used by teachers and practitioners now without any reference to the man who originated physical/vocal practice in the semi-supine position. Many people think of the work of Alexander as, essentially, a means of re-integrating physical use – which it is – but the development of the technique grew out of his experience as a speaker and amateur actor and of his frequent experience of voice loss.

Working with mirrors, Alexander observed that when he was presenting or performing he had a tendency to pull his head down and back, so that the neck was short and the chin lifted, and that this was compromising vocal function. Over time he developed a way of working with 'directions' – a way of focusing thoughts to encourage healthier physical use – so that the head, rather than moving down and back on the top of the neck, would be directed forwards and upwards. In Alexander's thinking, the head leads the whole spine so, as the head is directed forwards and upwards, the spine simultaneously releases into length. (The tail of the spine is directed to move down towards the floor, but the rest of the spine lengthens away from the tail in response to the head, at the top of the spine, being directed forwards and upwards.) When you work with these directions and become familiar with them, you will notice a number of benefits in relation to your breath, your body and your ability to access your voice.

All of this, however, takes time, and I don't want to explain all of the benefits to you now – if I do, this will pre-empt your genuine experience of the work and any discoveries that you might make as a result of the exercises you undertake as you move through this book. I will happily be providing further explanation at key points as the work progresses.

## Why work in semi-supine?

As already mentioned, standing is frequently an activity that we maintain through adopting tensive or effortful physical habits that become second nature to us and, thus, can feel habitual and 'natural'. As I mentioned earlier on, human beings were not originally designed to go about on two limbs and the processes of learning to stand and to walk when we are small can establish ways of being that we will carry with us all our lives that may not, in the end, be efficient or useful.

Many other aspects of our lives, as we grow and develop, may also interfere with our ability to be grounded and aligned in a healthy and organic way. Some of these may be to do with fashion – the desire for a flat stomach, for instance – some of these may be to do with schooling or other kinds of training: concepts of 'standing up straight', for example. I remember myself being drilled in thrusting the chest out, the shoulders back, lifting the chin and pulling the stomach in throughout my own school days. I would hope that this draconian approach to what is desirable in a young person's physicality has now disappeared, but I suspect that vestiges of these ideas are still being inculcated in various ways within our lives.

Stated simply, if we work in the semi-supine position – lying on the ground with a support for our head and with our knees drawn up – we are much more able to relax, to let go of habitual tensions in the body, because the ground is there to support all of our weight (head, shoulders, back, pelvis). You can work with the legs down and completely supported by the floor, but I think there are two main reasons why the semi-supine position, with the knees drawn up, is preferable. Firstly, the semi-supine position replicates, broadly, a standing position – remember that when standing the knees should be released and not locked, and the feet grounded. Secondly, if the knees are up with the feet on the floor we are more likely to remain present as we direct our thoughts and work through the body in different ways.

However, if there are reasons why working in semi-supine is uncomfortable for you, then you should make adjustments to the exercise as the whole point is to find ease and relaxation in the body which you are not going to achieve if there is a physical reason why the semi-supine position cannot be a comfortable one for you.

## Imagination, body, breath, voice – Semi-supine exercise 1

When preparing to work in semi-supine, many people will just go straight down to the floor to lie on their backs. I prefer even this to be a thoughtful process.

Have a book or two nearby as you are going to need to use these as a support for your head. It is important to understand that in natural alignment the head is slightly forward of the spine. If we then lie in semi-supine with our head resting directly on the floor, this does not help us replicate the natural alignment of head, neck and upper spine. Using books to support your head when lying in semi-supine will help you in finding natural alignment. There isn't a formula for the number of books you might need: one or two books should be sufficient, but you need to experiment with the number of books – you may need more or less.

## Stage 1

If you are moving down to the floor from standing, have a moment of finding where you are grounded over the feet, remind yourself that your knees should not be locked – they should be released as if they already wish to move forwards and upwards – and without consciously doing anything, but working with your thought, remind yourself that your head also wants to move forwards and upwards off the spine. Notice your breath as it drops in and out of your body.

Allow your elbows to float up towards the ceiling. When your elbows have gone as far as they can, allow your wrists to float towards the ceiling, and when they have gone as far as they can, allow your hands and then your fingers to float upwards. You have, essentially, reached your arms and hands upwards to the ceiling but you have not stretched, so there is minimum effort involved. Let your arms remain extended towards the ceiling for a minute or two and again pay attention to your breath. It may seem quite difficult to breathe satisfactorily in this position but if you are able to allow your breath to drop in quite deeply, if you are able to release your lower belly a bit, you will find the experience of breath dropping in and out easier.

Allow a low breath to drop in and then drop and hang over your knees from the tail of your spine as you allow the breath to be expelled naturally from your body – the movement of your head, neck, and torso as they all are allowed to drop and hang over your knees will naturally push the air out of you. You may find that your knees need to bend more – they will certainly need to remain released – otherwise you will find yourself wanting to fall forwards: your legs are there to support you as your feet remain grounded.

Before moving down to lie on the floor, there are various small manoeuvres you can explore. You may find it beneficial to shake out your head, neck and spine as you hang by shaking your shoulders – left right, left, right – whilst allowing your head and neck to hang off your spine. If you choose to do this, notice how the shaking of the shoulders can free the head and the neck, and can help you stimulate and release musculature through the spine.

It's useful to spend some time simply allowing your head, neck, shoulders and torso to hang from the tail of your spine over your knees for a minute or two. Your feet and legs are working to support you but feel how the pull of gravity affects your head, neck and all of your spine as you let go and hang in the upper body. Really let yourself hang and sense the ground pulling you towards it – notice how the head hangs off the neck-spine, the neck hangs off the body spine, and all of the spine hangs off the tail. Imagine you can sense the spine lengthening towards the floor as you allow the weight of the head to hang off it – and this, indeed, may be happening.

Now give into the pull of gravity and find a way to move down to the floor.

Many people now just move down and lie on their back but, ideally, you need a support for your head which is where the books come in. As you move down to the floor, then, arrange one or two books to provide a support for your head. This is necessary because in standing alignment the head does not naturally line-up with the spine behind you but is slightly forwards of it.

### Stage 2

With the books supporting your head (not your neck, which should be free) lie on the ground. Your feet should be hips-width apart. You can begin with your legs completely down and supported by the floor, like the rest of your upper body, and then, allowing your knees to float towards the ceiling, draw your legs up so that the soles of your feet are in contact with the floor whilst your legs remain bent and your feet remain hips-width apart. You will need to find a position for your feet, close enough to your sit bones, that you find it easy to maintain this semi-supine, knees up, position – if you leave your feet too far away from your upper body you will find that you want to let your legs fall back down to the floor. Experiment to find a position for your feet and legs that is comfortable for you.

Part of the value of this semi-supine work is that in this position you are able to let go of habitual tensions many of which you do not really need for standing, sitting, walking and so on, or for speaking. However, the semi-supine position does replicate standing, so you are still grounding through your feet whilst your knees wish to float forwards and upwards and your spine lengthens, led by the head, which also wants to move forwards and upwards off the spine.

### Stage 3

Rest in this position and think of the weight of your upper body being able to completely give to gravity. The floor is there to support you – allow it to support you. You may already find, having drawn your knees up that more of your lower back is in contact with the floor.

It is not your objective to force the back down to the floor and nor is it desirable that all of your back will be in contact with the floor. There are two natural curvatures in the back spine – one in the area we often refer to as the small of our back and another towards the top of the back spine – you don't want to eliminate these as they are natural, but you do want to work with the idea that as you give your weight to gravity, your spine can make a fuller contact with the floor. You might find it useful to notice any sections of your spine that are not making contact with the floor and then imagine that you can relax these sections more fully, imagining the spine moving closer to the floor as the area you are focusing on relaxes more fully. The floor is there to support you.

Imagine the shoulders wanting to fall back towards the floor. Again, they may not make contact, but the weight of the shoulders is quite heavy and they, naturally, want to give to gravity and move in the direction of the floor. As you let the weight of your torso give to gravity, sense the area across your upper back, the space between the shoulders, spreading and widening across the floor. Then imagine that this spreading sensation is travelling into your upper and lower back, and into your pelvis, i.e. that your hips are also widening and spreading across the floor.

Sense your sacrum – the back of your pelvic girdle which forms the central part of your hips – sitting firmly on the floor and imagine this area is also spreading across the floor. Take your attention now to the tail of your spine. You may not have a strong sense of this but you can probably imagine where it is. If you would like a stronger sense of your tail bone, it may help you to gently push the area where you think it is back against the floor, and then release the pushing. Imagine the tail of your spine wanting to move in the direction of your heels – if it helps, you can imagine that you are actually growing a tail out of your tail bone in that direction. Then imagine the rest of the spine lengthening out along the floor in the opposite direction, away from the tail.

## Stage 4

If you can visualize that your spine is made up of individual bones – the vertebrae – picture the tail bone moving down towards your heals, or towards the wall opposite your feet, and then picture the bone above the tail bone wanting to float in the opposite direction away from the tail. Take your imagination to the next vertebra, and allow this to float away from the bone beneath it. Try to take your imagination through the whole length of the spine, picturing each vertebra floating away from the vertebra below it or you can imagine the spaces between your vertebrae gently opening up as you imagine your spine lengthening out along the floor. This can be a difficult process and takes a good deal of focus. Try not to be too literal about it – for instance, you don't need to count the bones to ensure that you are monitoring each of them one by one. Rather, trust your imagination to lead you through this process. There is a very strong connection between your imagination and your body and when we think something is happening it does, indeed, begin to happen – so try to tune into, and trust, that mind/body relationship.

You can think through your neck spine in a similar way – there are seven cervical bones in the neck spine. It's an extension of your back spine and it may be useful to imagine your neck spine lengthening naturally out of your back spine with the six spaces between the seven vertebrae gently opening up as you allow the neck spine to lengthen.

Then focus on the top vertebra of your neck spine which sits inside a space in the base of the back of your skull. Imagine a cushion of air all around this top vertebra so that in your imagination you picture your head floating on this cushion of air. It may help to remind yourself that the books behind your head are there to support the weight of it – let the weight of your head be supported by the books.

There's an interesting connection between the sense of lengthening in your neck and your jaw joint on either side of you – this is around, or just below, your earlobes. As you imagine your head floating forwards and upwards off your neck spine, notice that you do not need to clench your jaw and that, in fact, your lower jaw wants to float down and away from your upper jaw. If you relax the muscles in your lower face you'll probably find a small space between your lips as you allow your lower jaw to want to float down and away from your upper jaw. It may also help if you imagine tiny springs between your back molars on either side of the inside of the back of your mouth. The springs are gently pushing your upper jaw away from your lower jaw so that there is an increased sense of space here between your upper and lower back teeth on either side.

Remind yourself that while your neck is lengthening away from your tail, your tail is still lengthening down towards your heels or the wall opposite to it. Simultaneously, your shoulders are still spreading across the floor, moving apart in opposite directions: your right shoulder wants to float away to your right and your left shoulder wants to float away to your left.

You're lengthening and widening through your back with the floor supporting all of your weight and you can now take some of your attention into the musculature in the front of your body. If your torso is being supported by the floor, there is no reason to hold on to any of the muscles in the front. Think of your breast bone softening, the area of muscle sometimes referred to as your solar plexus softening, and your belly being looser rather than held.

## Stage 5

We will do some more detailed work on all of these areas in a moment but, for now, take your attention to the fact that you are breathing. Focus first of all on the breath falling out of you, and at the end of the out-breath allow yourself to pause for a moment so that you can find the moment when the next breath wants to drop in. Imagine that your torso is hollow, an empty space, and that when the breath drops in, it can drop deeply inside of you.

The area from your belly-button to your pubic bone in the front should be elastic and flexible. When the breath drops down within you, you should feel this lower belly area responding to the breath, i.e. there is some movement here when the breath drops in. Imagine that the breath could drop in as deeply as your pubic bone.

Do you have a sense of where the breath may touch down inside you? When the breath falls out of you, do you have a sense of it touching off from somewhere within you?

Feed in the impulse for a sound and imagine that you can touch this sound off from the place where you sense the breath touching down inside you. I'll suggest that you keep this simple and that the sound is a version of 'Huh' – touch it off from a place deep within your body and let it fall out of you.

### Stage 6

If you think you have experienced some success in touching a sound off from your centre, maintaining your sense of lengthening and widening on the floor and your sense of ease, try speaking a section of text that you know from your centre. What do you notice about what you feel or how you sound?

The touch of sound exercise described above may result in your experiencing a physical sensation as if the sound is connected, muscularly, to a deep place within you. However, it is more likely that exploring where the sound touches off within you will be purely an imaginative exploration. If you are finding the exercise difficult, can I suggest that the area where the sound may seem to touch off inside you is somewhere between your belly button and the tail of your spine. It may be as high and as far forward as your belly button or it may be as low and as far back as the tail bone, but it is likely that you will experience the sense of touching off somewhere between these two points.

# CHAPTER 8
# THE CONCEPT OF CENTRE – A PHYSICAL CENTRE

I would like to suggest that you will call the place where it seems to you that sound touches off, 'centre'. This concept first came to me from the work of Cicely Berry. I have incorporated this into my work over the years, and I will aim to clarify my understanding of it here. It is important that this should lie, as I describe it above, somewhere between your belly button and the tail of your spine, and not higher in the body.

I have been teaching the ability to centre the body, the imagination and the voice for many years, and early in my career when my pedagogy was less developed, teaching centring got me into trouble. I was Head of Voice for the BA Acting programme at Rose Bruford College in the early 1980s, and I used to refer to centre constantly in my voice work. Maxwell Shaw was the Course Director at this time – an inspirational theatre practitioner and acting teacher – and he took exception to my description of centre: 'Is this a concept or a physical centre?' he asked me.

That question has led me to reexamine what the concept of centre may be throughout my subsequent career, in the UK, in China and in America. Essentially, the 'centre' is a physical centre that you sense within your gut, and this centre is also located in the area where you may experience physical sensations in response to the strongest and deepest emotional responses. So it is the place within you where breath seems to touch down, where sound appears to touch off, and a place where our emotional experience can be located and anchored.

This centre is something that you can experience physically and if you do experience a physical sensation that seems to be the sound touching off within you, then this is helpful as it will enable you to identify centre and then trust that you can work from it. However, in my experience, not everyone has this physical experience of centre, at least not to begin with, but I believe (and it is my experience as a performer and as a teacher) that working from an imagined centre is still useful to you because it helps you to focus and harness your energy and also facilitates a relaxation and freedom in the vocal tract that enables you to be more expressive.

### Further explanations of centre

I would like to spend some time offering some explanations with regard to the concept of centre and what it is.

## The Integrated Actor

It's a term that has been in use in voice work for many years and the concept comes to the West from a range of spiritual practices such as Buddhism, Taoism and Hinduism, and you may have had some previous experience of centring if you have practised Yoga, or studied Tai Chi, or some form of martial art. However, in relation to acting, the term 'centre' has a range of different applications and may be conceived differently, depending on the practitioner. For instance, when Patsy Rodenburg refers to 'centre' she appears to mean the place, physically, where our weight is balanced evenly over our feet when we are aligned. In a section above, I refer to this as being grounded and aligned, although I would also assert that the centre is our centre of gravity which I understand to be at the heart of Patsy Rodenburg's concept.

However, centre, in my work, is many things: it is the place where we are physically centred (Patsy Rodenburg's meaning) but it is also the place where breath touches down and sound touches off within us, and is also the centre of our emotional experience.

I first explored the idea of centre through the work of Maggie Ross when I was training as an actor at Bristol Old Vic Theatre School in the 1970s. Maggie was Head of Voice at that time and we would work frequently in semi-supine within the classroom exploring the notions that breath touches down within us and that sound touches off. Maggie would say, 'The work we do is all in Cicely Berry'. Cicely's book at the time, which had just been published, was *The Actor and His Voice*, subsequently retitled some years later as, *Voice and the Actor*. I dutifully bought the book in hard back, and in a holiday period I started to work my way through it, reading a chapter and then practising the exercises described.

It was during this personal work that I had my first physical experience of centre. This was a definite physical sensation, deep within me, when I was attempting to touch off sounds. I found this to be revelatory and having had this physical experience of breath and voice, when I returned to the class room, and Maggie Ross would say during an exercise or when I was speaking a text, 'Think from centre', it was easy for me to do this because I knew, because I felt I had experienced it, where my centre was.

I share this personal experience as a means of trying to illuminate your own understanding of centre but, in doing this, I also accept that you may have a different kind of experience and that for some of you it may remain, simply, a concept. However, whether it be experiential or conceptual, I still believe the centre to be an important tool for you as an actor, for a number of reasons.

Before elaborating on these, I want to say that centre will be a slightly different experience for each person. I have located it somewhere between your belly button and the tail of your spine, but the exact location may vary from person to person. The reason for this is that it is, on one level, your centre of gravity, and the exact location of this varies from person to person because each of us has an habitual use, in terms of our alignment, that reflects the physical habits we carry around with us. When we go through the process of grounding and aligning as a starting point from which to work, we attempt to shed some or all of these habits. If we are successful in this shedding process, then the centre of gravity within the body is much the same for all of us.

## The Concept of Centre – A Physical Centre

However, I believe that each of us is inclined to hang on to some of our physical habits, even when we aim to shed them, and for this reason where we experience the centre of gravity is slightly different for each of us. And, indeed, if you have a sense of centre, you may feel that your centre is in one place today and that it has slightly shifted to another location within on another day for the simple reason that we, ourselves, are not exactly the same, psychologically, emotionally and physically, on a day-to-day basis. So if you were to experience your centre in one place today and feel that it is in a slightly different place tomorrow, that is normal and something to be accepted and embraced.

One of the reasons why centre is important to you, physically, is that it is not only your centre of gravity, which means that an awareness of centre helps you to ground and to balance, but that working from your centre enables you to harness and focus your energy and your effort. If you work from centre so that in your mind and body most of your effort is located here, then you are more likely to be able to keep other parts of you freer and more relaxed, and more expressive. Working from a physical centre can also result in your voice being more at ease and it is less likely that musculature within your vocal tract will constrict.

Centre may also be important to you as an actor for other reasons, psychophysically. I began in the introduction to this book by citing a range of evidence to support the crucial relationship between the mind (imagination) and the body. If we simply consider polyvagal theory, for instance, it becomes clear that the mind is wired into various organs and parts of the body through the polyvagal nerve. If we consider this idea more broadly, part of the function of your spine is to protect the spinal cortex – this is hard wiring that is channelled from the brain down into the body and the vital organs through the channel that is the spine. At every point along the journey of the brain into the body through the spinal cortex, where the discs occur between the vertebrae, 'wiring' from the spinal cortex moves out into various muscles and organs so that, in the end, every part of us has a relationship with the brain and is responsive to it, and controlled by it. In terms of our sense of centre, the fact is that, besides the brain, the other place where many of these 'wires' interconnect and meet up is the gut.

We know this is true because, colloquially, there are expressions in our language that acknowledge this: 'I have a gut feeling', for instance, and an American expression, 'I feel sick to my stomach', reflect this. Other expressions include 'My stomach turned over' and 'I have butterflies in my stomach'. All of these expressions acknowledge a central, physiological response through which we identify an emotional experience or reaction. The heart of our emotional life is actually located in and around this sense of centre. So, when we have a strong sense of this centre, when we 'think from centre' (in the words of Maggie Ross) or when we connect our imagination with the experience of a physical centre, we are automatically connecting with our inner emotional life, too.

Our centre is a place where we can be both physically, psychologically and emotionally centred. This enables us to focus our energy and effort more efficiently but it also helps us to connect with our inner emotional and physical life.

The Integrated Actor

## Emotion

I'd like to spend some time at this point discussing emotions and emotional experience as part of the processes of acting. By and large the Western world encourages us to repress or hold back our emotions and not fully express them. This is traditionally so in the UK. This is part of the way we are socialized as we grow and develop but, of course, there are all sorts of exceptions to this. Also, the degree to which emotions are expected to be contained and not expressed varies from culture to culture in the West.

Whatever the reasons for it and the conditions that may give rise to it, if we are not to express our feelings (usually because, within the situation in which we find ourselves, it is not considered appropriate to express them) how do we identify that we are experiencing them and then in what ways do we choose to hold them back or block them?

The experience of emotion is, largely, a psycho-physical experience but it is often through our physical responses, the physiological feedback we receive from our bodies, that we identify that we are experiencing an emotion. We may identify the onset of an emotion because our thoughts are provoking it – and this is an important awareness for you as an actor, in fact – and an emotional response may also be a physical impulse. However, it is likely that we know that we are upset, for example, because we suddenly sense that we are about to cry through the physiological information that we receive. Our tongue root may tighten, our throat may begin to clench or constrict, or we may even be holding our breath. These are the physical things we do in order NOT to express the emotion. Anger is another emotion that, in many contexts, we are not supposed to express. The stronger the emotion grows within us the more tense some parts of our bodies become in order to control the emotion or not express it. It is also possible, if we are able to change our thought processes, that we may be able to let this emotion go. I don't know about you, but I am frankly not good at doing this but, then, I have never really understood why we cannot express the way we are feeling at any given time. For whatever reason, certainly if I am angry, for instance, I find it difficult to let this go.

However, what I would like to assert here is that emotion itself is NOT tension and, therefore, becoming tense in different ways in an effort to find an emotion will not enable us to express an emotion as an actor. It is, in fact, difficult to identify what an emotion is: simply put, I would say that it is an inner psycho-physical response to a stimulus. This stimulus can sometimes come from our imagination or mind but is frequently the result of an external stimulus: an event in which we find ourselves, something we witness, something that is said or done to us. I think, though, that what you need to be clear about, as an actor, is that emotion is NOT tension, so replicating tensions in the body that you associate with not expressing an emotion will not necessarily help you to find a particular emotion or experience it.

**The result of all of this discussion is that, if your imagination is working and connected within you through the experience of becoming centred, you will not need to think about, or work for, an emotion and, I believe, it is not beneficial to us, as actors, to try to experience or work for a particular emotion. This just makes the actor tense. If emotion is to be useful to us as actors it must, as in life, arise within us**

unbidden. If, and when, emotion rises up within, then the actor must be physically free enough to be able to express it.

Many actors can become obsessed with trying to find a particular emotion within a character or a scene. There are so many other more useful things to focus the attention on as an actor – who you are, the circumstances you find yourself in, what you want, the other character or characters within the scene, how you try to get what you want, what might be stopping you from being able to get what you want, and so on. If you pay attention to all of these other elements within the scene and inhabit them physically and imaginatively, then you may find that emotional responses arise within you, unsolicited and unbidden. This, then, might be a component part of what could be deemed truthful in acting.

## Pragmatic reasons why we might experience centre

For those of you who may prefer a less esoteric and complex explanation as to why we may have a sense of a centre, let me remind you about what happens physiologically when the breath drops in, i.e. when we take a breath.

As mentioned previously, the act of breathing is a reflexive activity. The reflex is, principally, in the diaphragm – the dome-shaped muscle that lies below the ribs, the edges of which are connected to the bottom of the ribs all the way round. The breath dropping in is initiated by a movement in the centre of the diaphragm, which contracts downwards, thus creating a vacuum in the lungs which draws the breath inwards. As the diaphragm contracts downwards, in order for this muscle to work efficiently, there needs to be a small displacement in the organs below the diaphragm – these include your stomach and your intestines. It naturally follows then, if you allow this movement of the diaphragm to take place naturally, gently release the lower abdominal wall in order to facilitate it, you will feel a small movement – probably your intestines moving against each other – within your belly.

I'd like to say that all of these movements are, in fact, relatively small and subtle. The diaphragm is a very large muscles, for instance, but when it contracts downwards the movement is quite small. Similarly, the displacement of any organs below the diaphragm is also a small movement and, it follows, that it is not our objective when we release the lower abdominal muscles to distend the belly. I'll be encouraging you to explore your potential breath capacity in various ways later in this book, but I'd like to say now that you do not get very much more breath into your system by distending the outer wall of your belly further out. It is also questionable as to whether it is desirable to work for large amounts of breath. Furthermore, encouraging such a movement in the abdominal wall is unnatural. However, without a small release within the lower abdominal area, you will not have a deeper experience of breath dropping in, you will be unlikely to sense your centre (or your centre may seem to you much higher in the body than I have suggested that you might experience it) and it is also unlikely that your larynx will relax into the neutral position which is desirable if we wish to access a more relaxed and open sound.

The Integrated Actor

## Summary

So, this has been a lengthy discussion about things relating to centre. In the work I carry out, the notion of a physical/vocal centre is at the core of the actor's work and as you have just started to explore a sense of centre, it seems appropriate to share my belief that your ability to access and relate to your centre is a crucial element in your ability to harness your resources, physical and imaginative, in acting. Centring is also a practical, psychophysical tool in which we make a direct connection between imagination (mind) and body and our emotional experience.

# CHAPTER 9
# PITCH 1

As you explore grounding, alignment and the touch of sound, this naturally leads on to the question of pitch.

Every voice has an optimum pitch, this is a sound we make when we are optimally relaxed – there will be a balance of tension within the body (there must be if we are to be upright, to stand or to sit), but we will not be holding any unnecessary tension anywhere – the larynx will be in a neutral position which is where, under normal circumstances, it naturally moves in the moment after we swallow or when a low breath drops in, and the vocal folds (which actually make the sound) come together with a relative ease and economy. The note we make around the optimum pitch tends to be in the lower part of our range – it may be perhaps five notes up from our comfortable lowest note, though it may be a bit higher than this, or a bit lower.

What is important about this relatively easy and comfortable place in our vocal range is that it is the place where the voice works most efficiently and it is the core sound of our voice. In everyday speaking, most people begin a spoken thought around their optimum pitch, moving away from it as they become more fired up and/or more expressive, but returning to it when they finish what they have to say. This is an important part of your vocal range and your ability to use your voice healthily and over a period of time without compromising it in any way depends on your being able to access your optimum pitch and use it.

Later we will be exploring potential range and different resonant qualities, but it is important to say, at this stage, that the rest of your voice operates in relation to your understanding and experience of your optimum pitch and so it is important to explore where your optimum pitch may lie. Some people find that this lies above or below where they believe they are most comfortable. Whether you are comfortable with exploring your optimum pitch is dependent on many factors, not least your sense of your own identity, but also on general behaviour and habitual use. When we are, generally, relaxed, however, allowing the breath to drop in more deeply, and we make an unconscious sound, it is likely that, if we do not interfere in any way, a sound around our optimum pitch will result. The optimum pitch is a natural response to a relaxed physicality and is a response to our size and shape, the spaces within us that are available (particularly in the pharynx and the oral and nasal cavities) and to the length and thickness of the vocal folds which vibrate within the larynx to produce the sound. It is arguable that it may also be a response to cavities that lie within the chest or within the head, too, though there is, as yet, no concrete scientific evidence for this.

## The Integrated Actor

The question of identity is an important one, and a very current concern. It would seem at this time that identity is something we choose rather than something that we are given at birth or that is formed as we grow up. I would agree that we all probably hold a sense of who we are, and how we wish to be perceived in the world, in our minds, and we moderate our behaviour, physical and vocal, as a consequence.

It's not my purpose, in this book, to comment on the processes we may go through in order to establish our physical and vocal identity or to make judgements about this in any way, but I would like to ask you to consider a few things.

Firstly, it is helpful, in establishing a vocal identity, to know where your optimum pitch falls within your range, even if you choose not to make this a strong part of the way you choose to speak. It is also true to say that if you work habitually above your optimum pitch, or you choose to speak well below your optimum pitch, that your voice is likely to become tired more quickly – as stated already, the optimum pitch of your voice is a small range of notes around which your voice works most efficiently. As an actor, embracing your optimum pitch is, therefore, really useful, particularly if you intend to work in the theatre where you may be required to perform at least eight times a week and may perform in a long run or in a national or international tour. In these circumstances, your voice will need to hold up over a lengthy period of time.

Secondly, I think it is important to recognize that we should not be bound by stereotypes. By this I mean, for instance, what we consider to be a 'male' or 'female' sound. There are many instances in which women's voices can be quite low – my mother and my cousin, who were both designated female at birth and who identified as women, were frequently taken as male over the phone. There is also nothing to say that male voices should be heavy or full of bass notes. We are all different and acknowledging and accepting difference, in terms of the way we sound, seems to me to be healthy and the way forward.

Thirdly, we need to know that the way we sound to ourselves, and the way others hear our voice, manifests differently. We have probably all had the experience of hearing a recording of ourselves that was made when we did not know we were being recorded and of being horrified by what we heard. Our friends recognized the way we sounded on the recording yet it did not sound, to us, like us. Simply put, the sound we heard did not match with our own perception of the feedback we received from our voice within ourselves – principally within our own head – at the moment when we spoke. Perhaps we shouldn't be too concerned, then, about the way we sound, at least not in the first instance.

For these reasons, I think it is unwise when you first begin to work on your voice, to make too many judgements about it so that you can embrace all of the possibilities that lie within it, and within you, rather than starting by moulding your voice in some way in order to match your preconceptions or ambitions about yourself. Later you may wish to make choices for a whole range of reasons, personal or artistic, but as you begin this work, try to be open to all of the possibilities.

# Pitch 1

## Optimum pitch

First of all, don't make the mistake of thinking that your optimum pitch is just one note – it's a short range of notes, perhaps five (it can be less or slightly more) – that occur when your larynx is in a relaxed, neutral position within the vocal tract.

If you are familiar with the work of Josephine Estill and with Estill Voice Craft, you may recognize what I am referring to as optimum pitch as Speech Quality. Jo Estill's research and her lifetime's work resulted in observations about laryngeal function when making sound that enable us now to identify a whole range of vocal qualities – Speech Quality is one of them – all of which we are able to reproduce, if we take charge of the larynx and how it functions.

Within more traditional vocal practice, particularly with those voice practitioners who work with actors, the work of Jo Estill has been treated with some suspicion. However, what Estill Voice Craft provides us with is information concerning vocal function that we did not have access to before she conducted her research, and it needs to be embraced by anyone who works with the voice, not least because her research dispels many myths that have existed in voice work. I will not spend time here detailing the work of Jo Estill but there are a number of excellent books that describe her work, and which provide exercises – compulsory figures – that will open up the voice, extend the range and the expressivity of any voice. (*The Estill Voice Model: Theory and Translation.* Kimberly Steinhauer, Mary McDonald Klimek, et al., 11 May 2017.)

Returning to a consideration of optimum pitch and what it is, within Estill Voice Craft there are a number of elements that must be in place in terms of laryngeal function that produce what is called Speech Quality; however, the optimum pitch I refer to here is simply a small range of notes produced when we are at our most relaxed. It is likely that the larynx will be in a neutral position.

### Exercises to establish optimum pitch and explore centre

#### Stage 1

Return to the exercise in which you are grounded and aligned and then drop down through the spine to hang from the tail bone over your knees. As you drop quickly down through the spine, release the breath – as before, this should be a completely free release, with no sense of control. Sense that the breath is being pushed, naturally, from your centre. When you return to standing, grounding as you do so and building the spine, vertebra by vertebra, as you come up, continue to let breath drop in and out of you, keeping a sense of where your centre might be. Repeat the drop down through the spine quickly, releasing the breath freely as you do so. Continue to repeat this process several times then, without thinking too much about it, as you drop down through the spine without control, release a sound from your centre. It is quite likely that this sound will be around your optimum pitch.

### Stage 2

Repeat this a few times, noticing the sound you are producing, particularly the pitch, and when you return to standing try speaking something you know around that pitch.

This exercise is not guaranteed to identify your optimum pitch but it works for most people. It's very important that you do not predetermine the note you will make when you drop down through the spine – just let a sound happen and fall out from your centre. For some of you, the sound you make may seem quite low. If this is the case, accept that it is the sound you make when you relinquish any sense of control and when you imagine the sound falls out from your centre, and embrace it. If you then try to speak around that part of your vocal range, you should find that you feel relaxed and easy, even if the sound you are making seems unfamiliar to you. Remember that this is a place in your voice where the vocal folds work easily and with efficiency and economy.

### Alternative exercise

Another exercise – again, not always reliable – is to imagine that you are about to step off the pavement to cross the road and narrowly avoid being hit by a car – as you step back onto the pavement to avoid being hit, release a sound automatically, it might be on, 'Uh!' or, 'Oh!'. It is likely that the sound that results will be around your optimum pitch.

### Final exercise for optimum pitch

Finally – and this exercise may be more reliable for you – intone down a scale, one note at a time, until you reach your lowest, comfortable note. It is important that this is a 'true' note, i.e. not breathy or airy, or croaky, though it may be quiet. However, it needs to remain comfortable enough that it vibrates efficiently and is fully sounded. From this comfortable low note, if you intone back up your range one step at a time (i.e. a scale of notes) counting on pitch, when you have reached a count of four or five you should have arrived at your optimum pitch. Remember, there is a small range of notes that fall around your optimum pitch and that you should have arrived at your optimum pitch by a count of four, or five, or six. Try speaking a text that you know around that pitch. Don't try to hold your voice on one note, you can allow the natural rise and fall of your voice within the spoken cadence, but you should find that you feel comfortable there and that, as you speak, your voice returns to the note you started on fairly frequently: your voice will sometimes work below that note as you speak, and sometimes above that note, but you will start each sentence around that note and return close to that note when you finish speaking.

## Speech quality

This is one of the vocal qualities identified by Josephine Estill through the research that resulted in Estill Voice Craft. Speech Quality lies within the range of your optimum pitch and can only be made, comfortably, within this range of notes. Jo Estill named it Speech Quality because it is the place in the range, and the vocal quality, that the majority of people use when they speak. It is important to recognize that, in fact, not everyone accesses this quality when they speak. However, it is also important to recognize that we all have the potential to make this vocal quality and to use our voice in this way, if we choose to do so.

For an actor working particularly in the theatre, I would say that Speech Quality, which lies within the range of our optimum pitch, is an essential use of the voice that needs to be embraced because it places the least pressure upon our vocal use and it is likely, therefore, that our voice will hold up well with extended use.

Accessing speech quality is reliant upon our being able to make a glottal onset. This is a particular kind of onset – meaning the approach to making a sound – when the vocal folds come firmly together to hold the breath beneath them. Then when the sound is made there is a slight 'pop' at the start of the sound, or you may hear it is a sound that begins with a slightly 'hard edge' to it.

### Glottal onset exercise

#### Stage 1

Glottal onsets are easily made if we speak, on a comfortable pitch, two vowels in quick succession: 'Uh-uh', for instance, but any pairing of vowels will do, such as 'Oh-oh', 'Eh-oh', 'Ih-Oh'. (These are all short vowels as in the words NUT, NOT, NET, NIT.)

As you do this, aim to sense what is happening at vocal fold level, and listen to the sound in order to identify and recognize it. Then try speaking a text that you know bringing your vocal folds together in the same manner as you speak it – you should now have found and be able to sustain Speech Quality.

## Stage 2

You can experiment with the potential range of notes available in this quality by counting up a short scale from a comfortable low note on one, two, three and so on. You may get as far as five or six, at which point you will sense that your larynx and vocal folds may need to make an adjustment if you are to continue up your range comfortably. It is important to say that you do not want to force your Speech Quality sound upwards – that will place undue pressure on your voice and if you were to do this habitually, voice loss would probably be the result, eventually.

What do you notice about Speech Quality? It is fundamentally loud, without undue effort – one of the reasons that it might be useful to actors in a theatre space – the sound has a certain weight and it sounds naturally resonant.

## The glottal onset and the glottal stop

In my own actor training, which was many years ago, we were discouraged from using a glottal onset and equally discouraged from utilizing a glottal stop.

A glottal onset may be made when we begin to speak on a vowel – in conversational speech it might occur in a phrase, such as 'I met a friend ….,' a phrase that begins with an open vowel. A glottal stop is made when we end what we are saying by bringing the vocal folds firmly together to stop the sound at vocal fold level. In everyday speech we often substitute a glottal stop for a /t/ when a word might end with this consonant, as in the phrase, 'I don't like that.' We might substitute the /t/ at the end of 'don't' and the /t/ at the end of 'that' with a glottal stop.

I was taught that these kinds of sounds were to be avoided because they were potentially damaging to the voice, but I now know that glottal onsets and stops are natural sounds that need not be any more dangerous or damaging than any other sounds that we may make, and some accents of English – many in fact – now feature the glottal stop and glottal onsets strongly. However, I think it is important to bear in mind that, in order not to be unduly tiring for the vocal folds, glottal stops, ideally, should be light and not unduly pressurized by the breath as we make them.

## Stage 3

Try the glottal onset exercise above again, consciously making the glottal onsets more loud and more aggressive and then firmly, but quietly, and applying the breath to the vocal folds with less pressure. Feel the difference between a hard glottal onset and a lighter one. The lighter one is preferable for the simple reason that it is less tiring.

# Pitch 1

There are various kinds of onset that are possible when we approach the speaking of an open vowel as in phrases, such as 'I think I should …, ' 'Are you going to ……,' 'And then I thought that ….' All of these phrases begin with a vowel. We can utilize a glottal onset, a simultaneous onset or an aspirate onset. Essentially, each of these is defined by the way in which we are applying the breath to the vocal folds as we speak.

## Other kinds of onset

I don't want to spend a lot of time here, on the consideration of onsets, but will simply state that a simultaneous onset occurs when breath is moving between the vocal folds before and during the moment they come together to make a sound. However, when the vocal folds do come together in a simultaneous onset, they do so firmly. An aspirate onset is similar but the folds don't come together firmly, or in a sustained way, in order to produce the sound, and the resulting sound is breathy.

I think it is important to say that the aspirate onset is to be avoided in vocal use for any length of time because it is extremely tiring. To function well, the vocal folds need to be moist – they are kept moist by tiny glands, if we are sufficiently hydrated – and when air (the breath) is passed through and over the vocal folds constantly, this dries them out. Once the folds are dry the friction that results between them can lead to the folds becoming swollen and pre-nodular and the sound we make will be compromised. In the longer term, nodules on the folds may be produced and various forms of voice pathology can result.

I think it is interesting that in various forms of entertainment now there seems to be a preponderance of actors speaking with aspirate onset. I don't know whether this is something actors are beginning to prefer to use themselves or whether it is something directors are encouraging. We hear aspirate onsets being used frequently in voiceover work for advertising – presumably because the sound that results is deemed 'sexy' and therefore good for selling products. This offends me less than the filming of intimate scenes, for the large or small screen, in which actors appear to whisper to each other rather than actually speak. To my way of thinking this is completely unreal and I am not sure why it is deemed desirable in contemporary screen acting. I can honestly say that, in my own life, when I am in intimate situations I do not whisper to my partner when I want to communicate – but perhaps I am odd in that regard and people all over the world are constantly spending their time whispering their endearments. At any rate, in drama, these scenes that are constantly whispered result in the audience not being able to understand what is actually being said. Without resonance being present in the sound, microphones cannot pick up enough information when we whisper – or speak with aspirate onset – to render the words comprehensible to the watcher/listener.

One of my current students recently asked me, 'But don't you watch television with the subtitles turned on?' Apparently, that is the way they solve the issue of not being able to hear or understand what actors are saying. Personally, I prefer to watch the scene rather than read subtitles, otherwise I may miss visual information within the drama, and I think it is for the industry to address the issue of the audience being able to hear sounds but not make out what is actually being said.

I would only reinforce that, if you are speaking for any length of time, from the point of view of vocal health, aspirate onset is tiring and may result in poor vocal health. Arguably, if you are working for a microphone, doing voice-over work or working on a television or film soundstage, as you are not likely to be placing undue pressure on your voice, aspirate onset is not very dangerous. Your vocal folds may get dry but you will be able to hydrate within breaks in recording or after your work, and once the recording is finished there will be time for you to rest your voice, hydrate and to recover. This is not the case in the theatre where your voice may be used over extended periods, and for at least eight times a week and, anyway, words spoken utilizing aspirate onset within a theatre space, even with the aid of microphones, will not communicate to your audience.

Going back to my own training, we were always encouraged to employ a simultaneous onset and told that this was preferable, and some voice coaches today still believe that this kind of onset is ideal. I am not inclined to agree with this point of view – at least, not from the point of view of vocal health – although I would say that if we constantly use a glottal onset, it should be kept light in the best interests of maintaining healthy vocal folds and, also, perhaps, that constantly hearing glottal onsets in someone's speech can become tiring for the listener, especially if these are made in a way that is quite harsh and aggressive.

Also, it is important to remember that English is a language of connected speech, meaning that ordinarily in a spoken thought the string of words we speak connect each with another and are not separated. Meaning is then conveyed through where stress is placed on particular syllables. In connected speech, then, glottal onset will not occur frequently. However, I believe that the vast majority of us employ both glottal onsets and simultaneous onsets, naturally, in our speech, so as long as we are avoiding the constant use of aspirate onset, we will maintain our vocal health as well as a range of expressivity in the voice.

### 'Creak'

While we are discussing types of onset it is worth considering the quality known as 'creak', frequently referred to as 'vocal fry' in the United States. This is becoming a common phenomenon in everyday vocal use for a wide range of speakers, irrespective of gender or ethnicity, although it is arguably more strongly featured amongst younger speakers, though not uncommon in speakers of any age. (Denzel Washington, for example, constantly speaks utilizing 'creak' in his movies.)

'Creak' occurs when the vocal folds are unduly relaxed as they come together to make sound. It is easiest to produce the sound known as 'creak' very low in the vocal range, though some speakers who feature 'creak' habitually when they speak can produce it throughout their range. If you move several notes below your optimum pitch, you are quite likely to be able to produce this sound.

It's important to say that there is nothing unhealthy about 'creak'. It may be annoying to some listeners, and it is not a particularly expressive vocal quality or one that communicates well in a larger space, but it is not potentially damaging to employ it.

However, 'creak' occurs particularly when the speaker is not committed to what they are saying and, in fact, it occurs in younger speakers often because they wish to appear 'cool', unconcerned and unfazed by everything around them. In this sense, then, it is a very uncommitted way of speaking and, perhaps, this is not of great use to the actor, except, arguably, if they were to play a character who is a habitual 'creaker' – someone who goes through life being uninvested and unconcerned with the things going on around them.

To produce a sound without 'creak' being present, the glottal onset exercises above will help to solve the issue, as 'creak' is a sound that results when the vocal folds are not brought firmly together to produce a sound. It may also help to explore and to establish where your optimum pitch is as it is likely, if you notice that you are 'creaking' in a very low part of your vocal range, that if you raise the pitch of your voice slightly – by a semitone or a tone – that 'creak' will disappear, though this is not a foolproof solution.

## Some thoughts about technique – 'Don't want to show your technique.'

When I was studying to be an actor at the Bristol Old Vic Theatre School in the mid-1970s, there was an inspirational acting teacher – Rudi Shelley – who dedicated his lifetime to the education of actors. He is the one tutor from that period at BOVTS whom everyone who has trained there remembers and graduate actors, now famous, invariably have stories to share about working with Rudi. One of my memories of Rudi was his use of pithy sayings that summarized fundamental truths in relation to acting processes. One that has stayed with me is: 'Don't want to show your technique.'

The word 'technique' in relation to acting can seem to be a mysterious one. Certainly, when I was an acting student, it was a word that was bandied about as if everyone knew what it meant, though I must confess I hear very few teachers and students using the word today so, perhaps, I need not dwell on the use of it here. However, I would like to clarify my understanding of the use of the word 'technique' in actor training.

The work you have undertaken within this book so far is part of what is meant by the word 'technique'. Technique can be physical, for instance when you focus on training your body and your voice – speaking a longer thought on one breath, effortlessly and skilfully, for example, can be part of an actor's technique – or it can be internal and imaginative – focusing on what a character wants in a scene, usually called (in the UK) playing your objective, is one example of an actor's imaginative technique. I would argue that both kinds of technique, which are really elements within an actor's tool kit, are important and, within the work of this book, I am seeking ways in which the internal and imaginative are inter-connected with the physical so that, hopefully, we stop thinking of technique being a matter of either/or – internal, imaginative technique or technique that is concerned with physical skill – and begin to experience that the imagination and the

## The Integrated Actor

physical expression of what lies within our imagination is intrinsically linked. I would argue that physical technique, for the sake of it, is only of limited use to you as an actor and will almost certainly be visible to an audience.

If technique is internally stimulated and is a product of the stimuli provided by our imagination then, to paraphrase Rudi's words, indeed, we will not 'show' our technique. The exercise that follows is all about techniques that enable the actor to lift words from the page and make them their own.

# CHAPTER 10
# LANGUAGE AND TEXT 1

Having spent time exploring elements such as grounding, alignment, release, breath and the touch of sound, let's consider our relationship to words and, particularly for the actor, to the speaking of words written by someone else: words that are not your own but that must become your own if an audience is to believe you.

As an actor, the words given to you by the playwright represent thoughts. Frequently these are the thoughts of the character you play, but they may take other forms, such as narration, for instance. How can the words on the page, then, become thoughts?

This begs the question, what are thoughts? How do we know we are thinking? I often ask this question of my students, and it can result in quite a heated debate about what individuals do, or don't, believe they experience. Rather than argue, perhaps I can ask you to engage in a simple task.

### What are thoughts exercise

Sitting comfortably, can I ask you to cast your mind back to a time you remember when you were happy? Put yourself in that memory. What particular sensory elements do you recall? Take a few minutes to explore this.

The chances are that you saw where you were in your imagination. You may well have recalled visual details, and along with this there may have been remembered smells, sensations, textures, sounds and so on. Some of these may seem to you to be quite vivid – as if you are there.

Essentially, then, the majority of us think through our imagined, visual sense and, potentially, through our other senses, too. Some individuals, who may be neurodivergent, do not have an ability to conjure up visual images. (This is known as aphantasia.) However, I would like to suggest that even if you happen to be such an individual, when you try to involve yourself in the memory task above, your other senses will have seemed to you to be more alert and seemingly active. If this is the case, then trust that you have the ability to think through your senses and, for those of you for whom the ability to visualize is strong, be aware that your other four senses can be stimulated by your ability to visualize.

So, words on a page have to become thoughts before we can speak them, and an ability to allow someone else's words to trigger your ability to visualize is a key stage to the words becoming thoughts within you.

## The Integrated Actor

I would now like you to work on a text, *Colours* by Yevgeny Yevtushenko, a Russian poet. This can be found in Yevtushenko – Collected Poems, published by Penguin Classics. I will quote sections of the text here but ideally I would like you to get hold of the complete poem. If you do have a copy, please take your time to look it over now.

The poem begins:

When your face
appeared over my crumpled life
at first I understood
only the poverty of what I have.
Then its particular light
on woods, on rivers, on the sea,
became my beginning in the coloured world
in which I had not yet had my beginning.

And ends:

I am conscious that these minutes are short
and that the colours in my eyes will vanish
when your face sets.
> *Yevtushenko: Selected Poems*, Yevgeny Yevtushenko, Penguin Classics, 2008.

I have chosen this poem because it is expressed in a simple, direct way, in the first person, in easily accessible language, and about an experience that is easy for most of us to relate to.

Often the first thing we do when we read a text is to feel that we have to understand it and, if we are in a group setting, to discuss what it means. There is time enough, perhaps, to engage in this activity later, but can I suggest that you resist the need to do this for now. It's possible that you have understood it easily on your first reading – that is fine – but you may not, or you may have misunderstood it. For now none of these aspects of your reading the poem matter. As a first step to understanding and connecting with the text, you are going to speak it.

### Psycho-physical exercise – Imaging

Working with images has been covered in considerable detail by Kristin Linklater in her book *Freeing the Natural Voice* (Nick Hern Books, 2006) and by other voice practitioners. I have always found the original edition of her book particularly useful, which comes with cartoons within the text which illustrate imaginative and physical processes within

# Language and Text 1

the exercises. This is out of print, but you can still get hold of a copy if you search for one, and I would highly recommend it.

Working with images originates within the work of Konstantin Stanislavski, in fact, and other practitioners, such as Cicely Berry, also refer to it. As I think it is an essential part of lifting words from the page and making them your own, I will spend time on describing an exercise here, utilizing the text printed above.

## Imaging exercise

### Stage 1

I would like you to take a short section of the poem and to let your eyes and your mind linger on those words. You might, for instance, focus on the opening two lines, 'When your face/Appeared over my crumpled life … ' but do feel free to choose any short section within the poem – you need not start at the beginning. Let the words as you look at them suggest images to you – pictures that come into your mind. For instance, with these words, whose face do you see? When did they 'appear'? What in your life is crumpled and what does that look like or feel like? Also, remember that the images that come to you may be random – allow this to happen and don't censor yourself.

As you get the hang of it, you will be tempted to work your way through the whole of the text. Resist this impulse for now and stay focused on the two lines, the phrase that you have chosen. While you are allowing the pictures the words stimulate to come into your imagination, be aware that you are breathing – breath is falling in and out of you as your imagination works with the words. As the next breath drops in, imagine you drop the images that are conjured by the words into you with the breath so as the breath touches down inside you so, too, does the image. Then, when the breath falls out of you, the images you dropped in are released on the breath.

To begin with, this may be best explored using just one or two words – for instance, the words, 'your face'. Each time the breath drops in, re-see the image – it will naturally alter or change and as long as it is a version of 'your face' the changes don't matter: in fact, it is good for the image to change rather than trying to keep it exactly the same every time you drop the image into you with the breath.

### Stage 2

Then, having dropped an image in with the breath, touch off the words from the centre in a similar way to the way you touched off a sound in the earlier touch of sound exercise. As you do this, don't be afraid to commit to the speaking of the words. Very often when individuals explore this for the first time they mumble or whisper but you are trying to connect your imagination to your breath and to your voice, so when you speak, speak with a firm intention.

Now take another section of the text – just a few words or a phrase – and explore it in a similar way. As I mentioned above, you do not need to start at the beginning and work your way through the text – you can, of course, if you choose – but select phrases at random and take time to explore them, connecting image to breath to centre and then to sound.

Remember, too, that 'thinking' may not just be a sense of visualizing, and that you may find your other senses stimulated by the words. This is equally valuable to you. For instance, in the short section that is worded, 'on woods, on rivers, on the sea', you may visualize a wood, a river or a sea that you know or have experienced, but you may also find your other senses stimulated. If recalling standing in, or walking through, a wood that you know, do you find yourself hearing the sounds around you or underfoot? Do you have a sense of the air, or the breeze or wind, brushing over your skin? What temperature is it? What smells do you recall in this place?

Let me address another point – you may never have stood by, or sailed, upon a sea, for example, or indeed, have direct experience of something else within the poem. Can I suggest, if this is the case, that you can simply imagine it and allow your imagination to go where it wants to go.

Through this process I would like to suggest that words on the page are translated into thoughts, and that thoughts are made physical through the dropping-in process. Similarly, we may find our emotions stimulated by the images and the sensory responses we have to them. If this is the case, embrace this and allow it to happen but, at the moment, it is not necessary to focus on your emotional experience or on whether you are having emotional responses to your thought processes. As I have mentioned earlier in this book, if emotional responses spring up within us, they do so unbidden and it is best that we don't search or push for them.

I would like to say that, for now, it doesn't really matter how you visualize the images that come to you, or whether you have other senses within you that are stimulated by the words, but it is important that you explore how you may experience the words on the page within your imagination and your body, and by going through this process you begin to make the words your own.

### Stage 3

You might like to end this section of exercise, once you have randomly worked your way through most of the images in the text, to go back to the start of the text,

# Language and Text 1

> taking your time to speak it through, attempting to co-ordinate receiving images, dropping them into your centre with the breath, and speaking the text aloud. By giving yourself over to this process you may also find that its meaning starts to be revealed to you.

At this point, I don't want to spend time discussing what the text may mean – we can come back to the question of meaning later. I would like to move on by returning to floor work – the work in semi-supine – and exploring more in relation to alignment, body, breath and voice. Before leaving this work on imaging, however, can I suggest that you may be someone who will find it useful to draw the images on a sheet of paper. This may be particularly true if you have found this work difficult. You might find it useful to print out the poem and to cover it with the images the words suggest – perhaps placing them to the side of the line, or at the top or the bottom of the page, or indeed, using a different coloured pen or felt tip, across the words themselves. This may then help you to find the words within you and to speak them.

## Summary

One of the things that I think is important about the first time we pick up a text that we have to speak is NOT to try to first work out what it means. As an actor, you need to seek out ways to experience the words which make up the thoughts. The more you speak the text, allowing your imagination free rein and exploring the way that the language stimulates your senses, the more you will begin to discover the meaning that lies within it.

# CHAPTER 11
# WORKING IN SEMI-SUPINE – FLOOR WORK 2

This section will recap the work you have already undertaken in Floor Work 1 but will also lead you deeper into the work and, hopefully, clarify what is meant when we think of the spine lengthening in two directions, simultaneously. It should also provide you with a better understanding of the head/neck relationship which is so crucial in relation to the way the voice functions.

### Stage 1

Have two or three books ready on the ground to support your head, later, when you move down to work in semi-supine. As previously, take a moment to ground yourself in standing and to think through some of the key elements of alignment and release: the knees are released, not locked, and should remain released; as you bring your attention to the tail of your spine, sense that it wants to move in the direction of the floor; the rest of the spine is lengthening upwards away from the tail. You can remind yourself of the phrase, 'Let my neck be free to let my head move forwards and upwards'. The head leads the spine and assists in encouraging the sense of length through it. Take your attention to your breath and notice that it drops in and out of you naturally and easily.

From this starting point, allow your elbows to float up towards the ceiling, as you did earlier, and then let the wrists float upwards, and finally the hands and the fingers. This is a simple way of stretching the arms upwards without, as it were, stretching them because we want to avoid bringing unnecessary tension into the body as we prepare to move down to the floor to work in the semi-supine position.

Allow a deep breath to drop into you, then drop your head, hands and arms as you fall from the tail of the spine to hang over your knees. Do this in one swift, free movement allowing your breath to be released as you do. Notice that the breath is naturally pushed from the centre of your body.

Move into the semi-supine position on the floor. Rest the back of your head on the two or three books that you have already prepared for your use. Remember that your feet are hips-width apart and that the kneecaps want to float towards the ceiling while you keep the soles of your feet firmly in contact with the ground.

Remind yourself that the floor behind you is there to support your weight – give your weight to gravity and as you do so sense your back lengthening and widening across the floor. The more you are able to give your weight to gravity, the more you will have a sense of your back being able to lengthen and widen across it.

### Stage 2

Take your attention to the tail of your spine and imagine it lengthening in the direction of your heels. Think through the length of your spine and imagine it lengthening along the floor as the spaces between the vertebrae gently open up, each vertebra floating away from the one below it in your imagination. The neck spine lengthens, naturally, out of the top of the back spine. Take your attention to the occipital joint. This is the place where the top vertebra of the neck spine sits inside the space in the back of your skull. Imagine space all the way around this top vertebra: a cushion of air upon which your head is poised. Imagine your head wishes to move forwards and upwards off this cushion of air. (In this case, in semi-supine, upwards means in the direction of the wall behind you. You can direct yourself to think the words 'forwards and out' if this is easier to imagine when lying in semi-supine.)

Your shoulders are hanging off your spine, and also supported by the floor – let the weight of the shoulders fall back towards the floor: they may not be touching the floor but they wish to fall back in that direction. They also want to float in opposite directions away from each other – the left shoulder directly off to your left and the right shoulder directly off to the right. As you let them release and you imagine them moving off in opposite directions, away from each other, you will sense your back spreading and your upper chest opening up as it widens.

Your sacrum and your hips are also spreading as the sacrum widens across the floor.

Notice that your breastbone is naturally in quite a high position – when the spine is long and is releasing into length, this is where the breastbone, in the centre of your chest, naturally sits. As you take your attention to your breath, noticing that it falls out of you without any control, think of the bottom of your breastbone falling back towards your spine (or towards the floor, if this is easier) with the outbreath.

Remind yourself that, if the floor is supporting your weight, you do not need to hold on to musculature in the front of your body. As you tune in to the breath as it falls out of you, allowing the breastbone to fall as the breath falls out, let go also in the area of the solar plexus – let it soften – and think of allowing your belly to be softer and looser. When the breath drops in – and you can wait to find the moment that the breath needs to drop back in – focus on allowing the breath to release the lower abdominal area as it touches down inside you.

Work for a while on being focused on these two activities – sensing that the breastbone falls as the breath falls out of you (and this is a tiny movement, in fact) and that the belly releases as the breath falls back into the centre. Remember, too, that the low belly release is a relatively subtle movement – it's a release, a letting go in that area: it's not a forcing outward or a distension.

Focus also on allowing the breath to drop a little deeper within each time it drops in. You will find that this seems possible if you allow yourself to relax a little bit more deeply each time you sense the impulse for the breath to replace.

### Stage 3

Trying to maintain all you have achieved in terms of lengthening, widening and releasing in your body, you are now going to do some focused work on the lower spine. Try not to bring unnecessary tension back into your body when you undertake this work, though some muscles will have to work harder to execute what you are now going to do but try to keep the process as easy as possible.

You are going to raise your pelvis away from the floor in a kind of slow pelvic thrust, but you're going to do this in a very particular way. First of all, be aware that you are breathing and try not to hold your breath through the course of the exercise. Imagine an eye in the tail of your spine. As your spine rests on the floor, this imaginary eye is looking at the wall between your heels. You are going to push down through your feet and lift your pelvis away from the floor and as you do so you are going to rotate the eye in the tail of your spine to look up between your knees at the ceiling. Once your pelvis is as high as it can go – and the eye in the tail of your spine is looking directly up at the ceiling – hold the position and while you are holding your position be aware that you are still allowing breath to drop in and out and that your lower abdominal area is still flexible.

You are now slowly going to lower your back down to the floor. Stay in touch with your breath and keep your lower abdominal muscles flexible and responsive to your breath whilst you keep the eye in the tail of your spine looking up at the ceiling as you lower your back towards the floor. When your hip girdle is about four centimetres away from the floor, pause and imagine that your pelvis is like a hammock hanging off your knees and allow it to hang suspended a few centimetres from the floor. Then give it a gentle swing imagining that it is like a hammock swaying in the breeze: the eye in the tail of your spine is still looking at the ceiling and your breath is still dropping in and out as you gently swing your pelvis. Now lower your back to the floor, still maintaining the notion that the eye in the tail of your spine is trying to look up to the ceiling.

As you allow your back to rest once again on the floor you should find that your relationship through your lower back with the floor has changed. You should now have a strong sense of the tail of your spine wanting to lengthen downwards in the direction of your heels.

### Stage 4

Now take your attention to the top of your spine and, in particular, to your head and your neck. In preparation for the next sequence, slide your arms and hands across the floor so that you can make a cradle with your hands for the back of your head and allow your head to rest within the cradle of your hands. As you do this, attempt to keep your shoulders as relaxed and as free as possible and notice that your breath is still falling in and out of you. As you move into the next physical manoeuvre, consciously remain in touch with your breath – try not to hold it nor to tense the muscles in the abdominal areas. You won't need these muscles to help you with the next exercise but they may wish to 'help' you and one of your objectives is not to allow them to engage as part of the next movement.

You are going to roll your head forwards and upwards away from the floor so that your eyes can look directly ahead, between your knees, at the wall opposite to them. However, your objective is to use only your hands and arms to facilitate this movement of the head and neck – that is to say, in your mind, your neck is not doing any of the work: it is your hands and arms that are working. So, using your hands, lift your head away from the floor and slowly roll it forwards and upwards, allowing breath to fall in and out of you as you do this. You're going to bring your head right up so that the top of your skull is parallel to the ceiling above you and your eyes are able to look directly ahead of you to see the wall between your knees. As you do this, try to keep your elbows in an open position – they may want to fold in towards each other, but try to resist this if you can so that your upper chest remains wide and open. Hold this position with your head up for a few moments, noticing that the back of your neck now feels really long and, again, ensuring that you are still breathing naturally without gripping in your belly area. Then, maintaining the sense of length in the back of your neck, still using your hands and arms to support your head, slowly lower your head back towards the floor (or the books it was previously resting upon) and once your head is at rest again, gently take your hands out from behind your head and allow your arms to relax on the floor on either side of you.

You should have remained connected to your breath throughout these exercises: reconnect with it now, allowing the breath to drop out and in, and sensing the flexibility in your lower abdominal area in response to the breath. Take your attention again to your spine and allow the tail of your spine to lengthen down towards your heels as you also allow your neck spine to lengthen away from the tail, reminding yourself that your head wants to float forwards and upwards (or forwards and out) off your neck spine.

## Stage 6

Now allow your arms to lie directly to either side of you on the floor so that you have made a cross shape, as it were, with your body and arms. Use a minimum amount of effort to re-position your arms and enjoy the time in which you can, simply, rest against the floor, lengthening and widening through your back.

Lift your right hand and lower arm gently away from the floor – not far: perhaps three or four centimetres away from the floor. Thinking of the finger tips of your right hand leading the arm, extend your fingers and arm to the wall on your right-hand side. Think of this as an always flexible movement – you don't stretch the fingers and then hold the arm position, rather your fingers lead the arm as they extend away from the body and towards the wall on that side of you, and the fingers continue to extend throughout the movement. Imagine that the arm is gently releasing out of the shoulder socket as you do this. Then, slowly lower your hand and arm back down to the floor to rest there.

Repeat this in the fingers and hand on your left-hand side, lifting the hand and arm away from the floor a few centimetres and, allowing the fingers to lead the arm, extend them towards the wall on your left-hand side sensing the arm releasing or floating out from the shoulder socket. Again, then lower the hand and arm back down to the floor to rest there.

You are still maintaining a cross shape with your body and arms on the floor, but you may now feel somewhat different in your upper body with a greater sense of width across your upper back and upper chest, and perhaps your relationship with your shoulders has also adjusted. Notice whatever you notice.

## Stage 7

With your left arm extended out to your left, now slide your right hand and arm across the floor until your hand is resting on the floor above your head. Your arm will be gently curved as it rests here. Bring your knees and feet together. Now drop your knees to the floor on your left-hand side: your left knee should touch the floor and your right knee should stay in contact with your left knee. You will feel that the right-hand side of your body has opened up as you stretch through it. Try to keep your right shoulder in contact with the ground, and rest in this position for a couple of minutes aware that as breath falls in and out of you that there is now a good deal of space, and the potential for flexible movement, in your rib cage, through the right-hand side of your body. As you rest here and allow yourself to breathe, sense the rise and fall of your ribs on your right-hand side as breath drops in and out of you.

Roll your knees back towards the ceiling and your feet back in contact with the floor, and allow your right arm now to rest on the floor to the right-hand side of you in any position that you find comfortable. Prepare to repeat this exercise on your left-hand side. When you're ready, with your knees and feet together, slide your left hand and arm along the floor until your hand is resting on the floor above your head with a gentle curve through the rest of your arm. Now allow your knees to drop to your right-hand side until they touch the floor – the right knee touching the floor and the left knee resting against the right knee. Again, in an ideal world, attempt to keep your left shoulder against the ground, and notice how the left-hand side of your body has opened up and sense the potential for breath to fall in and out of the rib cage on your left-hand side.

> After a few minutes of resting in this position, roll your knees back up towards the ceiling and allow the soles of your feet to once again make contact with the floor. Slide your left arm down to your side and allow it to rest wherever you are comfortable on the floor and take your feet back into a neutral position, hips-width apart. Rest here, noticing whatever feels different to you in your body. I'd like to suggest to you that you may feel longer and wider through your back, that you have a stronger sense of the potential of your spine to lengthen in two directions – the tail downwards and the neck in the opposite direction, away from the tail. You may feel wider across your shoulder girdle, and you may notice, as the breath falls in and out of you, that your ribs seem to be responding, perhaps in subtle ways, to the breath as it falls in and out.

It is always useful to direct your thinking in relation to your body and its alignment. You can take your attention to any area that you think may need it, but remind yourself that a useful mantra is: 'Let my neck be free to let my head move forwards and upwards'.

> ### Stage 8
>
> I'd like you now to pay some more attention to your ribs. Again, without bringing any unnecessary tension into your shoulders, rest the backs of your hands (or you may prefer this to be the palms, it's up to you and what you find most comfortable) on the bottom of your rib cage on either side of you. It is important that your hands are resting towards the bottom of the ribs on either side rather than the middle – you have more flexibility at the bottom of the ribs at the side and the front because of the way your rib cage is constructed. Let the breath fall out of you and at the end of the outbreath, when you are empty, and before the next breath wants to drop in, give a small push with your hands to the bottom of the ribcage on either side of you. Then let go and allow the next breath to drop in. Repeat this action three or four times. Remember that you are only pushing with your hands when you are waiting for the next breath – you are not pushing as you breathe out, and you are definitely not still pushing when the breath wants to fall back in.
>
> Again, once you have completed this exercise, allow your arms to rest on either side of you where they feel most comfortable. For most of you this will be with your arms to either side of you with the palms facing the floor and the elbows slightly crooked. This will also maintain width and openness across the upper chest, the upper back and through the shoulders. However, we are each different from each other and some of you may not feel comfortable in this position, so don't force anything – just find a position for the arms that is comfortable for you.

Spend time again, now, lengthening and widening against the floor and through your spine, back and shoulders. Send the direction that the spine lengthens in two directions simultaneously and that the shoulders spread, each shoulder wanting to move in opposite directions away from the other shoulder. Be aware of your breath dropping in and out of you reminding yourself that, when you are relaxed, the breath falls out of you, like a soundless sigh of relief and without control, and that, if you wait, the breath will drop back in when you are ready for it.

As your spine continues to lengthen along the floor, be aware that each of your ribs is attached to your spine at the back so that, as it lengthens, there is a sense of your ribs, as it were, floating in space. And there is space between them. Imagine, also, that your ribs almost have a life of their own, that each rib is free to move, to respond to the breath dropping in, in its own way so that, rather than thinking of the rib cage you think of the ribs as individual bones each with a life of its own.

At this point you can touch off a sound or two from your centre, on 'Huh', or 'Hah', and then move into speaking a text that you know aiming to work from centre.

It's not really for me to tell you what you will sense at this point but, if you have been able to work through this sequence employing a minimum amount of effort, maintaining freedom in your neck so that the head is poised at the top of your neck-spine and not fixed, and if you are allowing your belly muscles to remain free and responsive to your breath as you speak, that you will both feel and sound different to yourself. You may find that your voice sounds more relaxed, or more open, and after this sequence of exercises, you may feel as if your voice is deeper or richer or has more resonance than usual. None of these possible phenomena are guaranteed, but this exercise is leading you to a place where you are more relaxed and at ease, and this should have a positive impact on both your breath and your voice.

In this sequence of exercises you have spent some time exploring the potential of movement within the ribs as well as in the lower abdominal area, largely in response to the breath as it drops in. If you have been successful at finding some flexibility within your rib cage, particularly towards the bottom of the ribs where the ribs have the potential to 'swing', you will probably find that the sound you make does have a richer resonant quality, even if the difference is only subtle.

## Speaking when standing

You might also want to try transferring yourself from the floor back into a standing position and then speaking your text in standing.

### Stage 1

Roll first to your left or your right to initiate bringing yourself off the floor, maintaining a semi-foetal position as you lie there. Spend some time on your side allowing breath to drop in and out and reminding yourself of your directions – for instance, in this position you should still be able to sense your tail bone wanting to lengthen in the direction of your heels and be able to maintain the sense that your neck spine wants to lengthen in the opposite direction, away from the tail. Your belly will still be relaxed and the lower abdominal muscles will still be responsive to breath when it drops in.

Then transfer yourself onto all fours: your feet remain around hips-width apart, your hands are on the floor directly under your shoulders and your hands and knees are supporting the weight of your torso. Your face should be parallel to the floor – some practitioners prefer to allow the head to hang off the spine in this position, and by all means try this, but as you are bringing yourself from the floor to standing, and in standing your neck will support your head, I prefer that the head is supported now in this transition stage. You should notice that, in this all-fours position, your belly is still loose and able to respond to breath as it drops in to you.

The final part of this floor-to-standing process is the trickiest. Essentially, I think the individual can find what seems to be the easiest and most comfortable way to come to standing, bearing in mind that you want to maintain as much of the freedom you experience on the floor as possible. However, I will recommend here a way that I think you can come from the all fours position into standing that you should find easy and that should assist you in maintaining length and width through the back, the low belly release, and the sense of alignment from feet, to knees, to hips, to spine, to neck spine to head.

### Stage 2

From the all-fours position, allow one knee to float forwards and upwards – it will probably come quite close to your chest as you do this – so that the sole of the foot of that leg makes contact with the floor. At the same time, allow your head to drop and to hang off your spine, dropping towards your knee, and monitor that you are still allowing the breath to drop in with a nice, easy low belly response. As you start to stand, try not to hold or inhibit the breath, i.e. remember that you do not need your abdominal muscles to assist you in standing.

From this position, with one foot in contact with the floor, you should find it easy to bring yourself to standing. Allow breath to fall in and out of you as you come to standing so that you do not hold the breath and lock the muscles in the abdominal area. As you bring both feet to make contact with the floor, remind yourself that your feet will be hips-width apart and that your knees will not be locked as you straighten your legs – legs will be straight but not locked. Allow your spine to uncurl, as you do when coming up out of a spinal roll, remembering that your head will be the last part of you to come up. If possible take time with this final moment, allowing your shoulders to hang off the spine and fall into place, and using a minimum amount of effort in the muscles in the back of the neck to bring the head up. As the head arrives atop the neck spine, you want to sense that it is poised not fixed or held at the base of the skull.

Once standing you can take a moment to remind yourself of grounding through the feet, and of the lengthening and widening process through the back and, hopefully, you have left the lower abdominal muscles free to respond when the breath drops in. This is the trickiest part of returning to standing as many of us hold the lower abdominal muscles taut thinking this helps us to stand but if you have taken care at each stage of the process of moving from lying to standing, reminding yourself to keep your abdominal muscles flexible in response to the breath dropping in, then you should find, once standing, that you have maintained some free, flexible movement in your abdominal wall. You may find that low belly release in standing does not feel as efficient as it did when you were working in semi-supine – for now, if you have maintained some flexible movement in this area, and if you still have a sense of breath touching down inside you, then you are beginning to maintain some healthy vocal use.

You can also think your directions – principally, 'Let my neck be free to allow my head to move forwards and upwards'. This direction is quite powerful and can facilitate many things: for instance, the head being allowed to move forwards and upwards encourages the spine to lengthen away from the tail; it encourages you not to fix your head at the base of the back of the skull, and enables the larynx to be freer and more flexible within the vocal tract; and because you are not allowing the weight of your head to sit back on the top of the spine, as the spine releases into length, the ribs, which are attached to the spine, also remain freer to move and to respond as you breathe or speak.

### Stage 3

Now speak the text. For now, allow time for the breath to drop in when it is needed, even if this slows your speaking of the text down. In this way you reprogramme your body, your breath and your voice. Explore the images that lie within and behind the words as you speak. Explore dropping the images into centre, and sense the sound touching off within you as you speak words and phrases. All of this is exploratory and you do not need to worry too much about the result, though it is good to stay aware and to notice what you notice.

# CHAPTER 12
# MORE ABOUT BREATH – BREATH CAPACITY

I have spent time in preceding sections of this book to describe the basic physiological process by which breath is initiated into the body, and some low belly release is a natural result of allowing the breath to drop in efficiently.

There are in fact a number of muscles groups besides the diaphragm that may be involved in the process of breathing. You have just explored how some other muscles groups – principally the intercostal muscles between the ribs – may be part of the act of allowing a breath to drop in. Some vocal practitioners emphasize conscious work on a range of other muscle groups in relation to breathing. However, whilst science does know which muscles groups are likely to be activated when a breath is taken, at the moment science does not know whether there is a more efficient way of coordinating this muscular activity. For this reason, I do not advocate paying attention to other muscles groups as part of the processes of breathing, with the exception of the intercostal muscles between the ribs as, in my experience, if we give ourselves over to the simple process described in the initial exercises introduced so far, breathing takes care of itself.

The first semi-supine sequence addresses alignment and release, and the physiological responses to breath dropping in and out of us. It introduces the notion of centre – a place where breath seems to touch down inside us and from which sound seems to touch off.

The second semi-supine sequence, as well as extending your understanding and experience of the notion of the back lengthening and widening, introduces you to some other elements in relation to breath and to sound.

We have not explored yet the length of spoken thoughts. The Yevtushenko poem consists of relatively short thoughts expressed in contemporary language – one of the reasons why I have chosen it – so the chances are that, when you spoke it, you didn't experience any fundamental issues in terms of whether you had the breath to say what you wanted to say.

Some vocal practitioners talk about ways of managing the breath, and I sometimes use this notion myself, but only in terms of thinking about the moment when we need to allow breath to drop in. Simply put, the breath should drop into us for a new thought and we shouldn't be speaking if we have not allowed a breath to drop in prior to speaking, so when speaking a text it is useful to know when the breath should drop in as the progression of the text, thought by thought, determines where each breath should be.

**Generally, if thoughts are short, as they are, often, in contemporary conversational speaking, a low breath that results in a small amount of low belly release will be**

enough breath to enable us to say what we need to say. Indeed, it is worth saying that, in everyday life, when we are at ease and relatively relaxed, perhaps just chatting with our friends or family, we automatically release in the lower abdominal area when we speak. The exercises so far have been encouraging you only to replicate natural, organic responses that you are already capable of, but by exploring and identifying them it is possible for you to take charge of them and harness them.

You should be careful, though, when approaching longer, more complex thoughts. It is tempting to assume that you will need to access greater resources of breath in order to sustain the speaking of longer thoughts. This may or may not be true, but assumptions should not be made and can be dangerous.

In general, if you have a lengthy thought to speak, you may need access to greater resources of breath and, if this is the case (and this depends, partly, on the length of the thought) then you will need access to a low belly release working in collaboration with some flexible rib swing. This is the physical capability that has been introduced in the last set of semi-supine exercises. For now, it is good just to be aware that a low belly release is part of an organic breath that provides you with a good amount of air for the speaking of relatively simple or short thoughts, but that if the belly releases and the ribs are also a part of a flexible movement around your centre, the speaking of longer thoughts may require this.

However, it is really not as simple or straightforward as this, and in terms of the speaking of shorter or longer thoughts, we will all find that we have a slightly different relationship to our breath and to the amount we need.

## Is breath managed – If so, do we need to manage it?

It is worth spending some time now to consider whether breath can be managed and, if it is, how it is possible to manage it.

Some practitioners maintain that breath is managed in a number of ways – sometimes by the lower abdominal muscles, sometimes by the descent of the rib cage, sometimes by other muscle groups within the torso, for instance. At the moment, the evidence for any of these is, at best, anecdotal. However, we do know from the research of Josephine Estill, that the vocal folds play a role in the management of breath, and that if the vocal folds are engaged in making sound efficiently this will affect how long the resources of your breath may last.

There will be exercises in this book later on to address any issues related to air flow – and I believe you will find that you can 'manage' air flow without very much conscious effort – but you certainly will not need to consciously work different muscle groups to achieve it.

**For now, be aware that if you favour an aspirate onset so that air is constantly moving through the vocal folds without being turned, efficiently, into sound, your breath will need to be replaced quite frequently. If, however, you are able to achieve**

a clear Speech Quality in which your vocal folds make gentle but firm contact just before and throughout the production of the sound, you will find that your breath resources will last longer.

For this reason, some people can take a seemingly small amount of breath and yet still speak a quite lengthy and complex thought without needing to replace air, simply because their vocal folds are utilizing the air really efficiently and turning it all into sound. Those who produce a breathy or an airy tone will find that their resources of air seem to run out quickly, and that they need to allow breath to drop in much more frequently than the person who is able to make a firmer, fully phonated sound.

Making light glottal onsets – the 'Ah-ah/Uh-uh' exercise previously described in this book – is one way in which to address the matter of bringing your vocal folds together efficiently to make sound within the easy, optimum pitch range. When exploring this exercise, focus on the nature of the contact between your vocal folds so that you can replicate this contact when you speak a phrase or a sentence. This should help you to address the matter of habitually accessing a breathy or airy sound.

**I'd like, at this stage, to reinforce that taking greater amounts of air does not, usually, help us to solve a problem. So, although I have introduced the idea that when the breath drops in, the belly is released a small amount and the ribs may also move flexibly in response to it, this is not because I think you will always need to have to access this flexible movement in your ribs. However, you do need to have access to it when you need it and, I would argue, that when you need movement in the lower part of your ribs, you should be able to access this spontaneously and without having to think about it. Your body needs to be ready to respond, in the moment, when you need it to.**

For this reason, it is useful to engage in regular mindful exercise, as outlined above, that helps you to coordinate thought, breath and body so that they are all available to you in the moment when you need them.

### An exercise for capacity – Box Breathing

The next exercise helps you to explore the potential space available to you within your body for air. I'd like to suggest that it is just an exercise designed to expand the space available within you and exercise a range of muscles potentially involved in assisting the act of breathing. I am not introducing the exercise here to encourage you to think that you need access to this kind of breath capacity all the time. You don't.

It is based on an exercise introduced by Kristin Linklater in the original edition of *Freeing the Natural Voice*, now out of print. The latest, revised edition does not include this exercise, which is one of the reasons why I am including it here as I think it is useful and would like to share it. I have also adapted it so the version of the exercise, below, is not identical to that described by Kristin Linklater but it is very much inspired by it.

# The Integrated Actor

### Breath and body potential exercise

Lying in the semi-supine, or fully supine position, imagine that your torso is a five-sided box. The floor of the box lies across the lowest part of your pelvis and, if you were standing, would be parallel to the floor. The front of the box runs from the pubic bone, at its lowest point, to the top of your breastbone, at its highest point. The back of the box runs from the tail bone up to the top of the back spine. The two sides of the box run from the bottom of your hip bones up into the armpits on either side of you. You'll notice that I am not asking you to imagine that the box has a top, a sixth side – I'd like you to imagine that the top is open – a box with the lid taken off it, if you like.

Now imagine that the floor and the four sides of the box are all elastic. When the breath drops in, imagine it falling to the floor of your box and that, as this is elastic, somewhat like a trampoline, as the breath arrives there, the trampoline floor responds. Then allow the breath to fall out of you without any control. You can stay with this exploration for some moments, exploring the relationship of the breath falling in with the floor of the box that is your body.

Then, when a new breath drops in, begin to explore what happens if you want to allow more breath to drop in, so that you will, gradually, begin to explore the elasticity in the front, the sides and the back of your box. You may find that a particular area – one side or another, or the back of the box – does not seem to be responding. If this is the case, take a little time to work with the breath to expand this less responsive area.

I would suggest, though, that every breath as it drops in should land in your imagination on the floor of your box and that it should move this elastic floor before the breath starts to stretch the other sides of the box. Always let the breath fall out of you, without control, prior to allowing the next breath to drop in – you are not aiming with this exercise to speak.

Some of you will find that you can allow quite a large amount of air to fall into your body in this way, and you may be surprised how far the body that is your 'box' can be expanded by the breath. If you find as you move closer to achieving capacity, that you start to feel unduly tense in your upper chest or in the throat area, let the breath fall out of you and relax because you are, essentially, overworking if you feel this kind of tension or pressure.

All I would say as a result of this exercise is that it is interesting to note how much potential capacity you have within you for breath. You are unlikely to need this kind of capacity very often as an actor, but it can be useful to know that you have the capability to access this should you ever need it.

## Summary and exercise

If you are someone who finds, when acting, that your breath seems to run out very quickly, the chances are that you are either: inclined to take too much air in the first place; or you are driving air so that the vocal folds find it difficult to resist the air passing through them in order to make a sound. It may also be that you are speaking the thought before you are ready.

If you suspect that you have an issue with air flow – that is in maintaining a gentle and consistent flow of air to the vocal folds – below is a simple exercise.

### Air-flow exercise

Take a good-sized glass (pint-sized), fill it with water, and then blow into the water through a straw. A straw with a thinner bore is more useful for this exercise. The objective is to keep the bubbles being produced in the water in a consistent and steady flow. You do not need a lot of air for this exercise – aim to keep your breath pressure even and sustained, working to the end of each breath, and then allowing the next breath to drop in. To be useful, you need to spend five to ten minutes on this exercise.

If you are finding this exercise difficult to achieve, perhaps try to start with a smaller amount of breath. It is sometimes tempting with exercises involving breath, to take a large amount of breath and this can make us feel as if we are working to our fullest capacity. The point of this exercise is to be able to sustain a gentle, steady and consistent stream of air, and you will probably find that taking a moderate amount of air will enable better focus on producing a steady, sustained stream.

It's useful to notice that when we consciously take in a large amount of air it simply wants to rush out of us – you should have experienced this at some point with the box breathing exercise above – and that it is difficult then to use the air efficiently. Longer spoken thoughts, then, do not necessarily require large amounts of breath. **Our aim, perhaps, is to enable the vocal folds to meet the air moving through them so efficiently that we do not necessarily need large resources of breath in order to speak a longer or more complex thought.**

# CHAPTER 13
# LANGUAGE AND TEXT 2 – PHRASING AND MEANING

I'd like now to return to the Yevtushenko poem and to explore some further work with this text. This work relates to the work on body and breath that you have just been exploring and it also brings you to consider a bigger question: when you speak a text, someone else's words, whom are you serving?

I believe very strongly that when an actor speaks a text – and I am thinking now about play-texts, the work of playwrights, and not just about the poetic texts that I will include in this book as things for you to practice – it is the actor's job, in the first instance, to serve the text. The phrase, serving the text, works on a number of levels. On one level, I would argue that a great deal of what you need in order to speak a text lies within the text itself: within the language selected by the writer, within the use of punctuation, the length of phrases and the way the words are laid out on the page. All of these are clues as to how the writer imagines the text might be understood, experienced and spoken.

In attempting to serve the text, the actor also aims to serve the writer. What did the writer intend when they wrote the monologue, the poem, the play? I'd like to suggest, then, that you can gain a great deal as an artist, whether actor, director or another creative member of the team, by attempting to give yourself over to the text itself, exploring the ways in which the text can be served.

**I'd also like to suggest that central to an actor's role within the theatre event is a sense of service: the actor serves the text, serves the other actors, the director, the space and the audience. The actor is not there to serve themselves.**

### Response to structure exercise

### Stage 1

I'd like you to speak the Yevtushenko text again giving due consideration to the way in which the thoughts are laid on the page. The first question is, does where each line ends on the page matter? I think we should assume that it does, that the writer has made a choice in laying the words on the page in this pattern. I think, as you speak it through, you will sense the natural cadence of each phrase by the way it is laid on the page.

Is there a way, then, to respond to the way these phrases are laid out as we speak them? Experiment with a number of choices. You might pause, momentarily, at the

> end of each line. You might run on, and not pause, from line to line as if simply speaking through the sentence that the phrase is a part of. You might do this and honour the line ending by emphasizing the final word of each line in some way – and there are different ways to do this that you can experiment with.
>
> Then take a look at the punctuation of the text and consider what this represents in relation to the way you might speak the text.

**At this point I would like to say that the things that are being offered in these pages are <u>tools and not rules</u>. I will come back to this phrase again when you are working on Shakespeare. There is never only one right way to do something but there are many wrong ways.**

In terms of the speaking of a text, I think punctuation is there as a useful signpost to the kinds of choices you might make and you will find that different writers may use punctuation in different ways. Generally, I think it is unwise to respond to punctuation within a text as if there is some rule about it. For instance, some people are taught that a comma represents a place in the text where you should take a breath. I think you *might* take a breath at a comma, and you might not, but it is not a rule and, as the point in the sentence where the comma comes is not the end of the thought, I would like to suggest that a comma is, ideally, not a point where a breath is taken.

If there are any 'rules' about punctuation I would say two things: that the writer has placed the punctuation within the thought to give you some idea as to how the thought develops – if you like, the way in which the thought 'thinks' when you speak it – and, secondly, that a full stop, or period, marks the end of a thought and, indeed, is a place where the next breath should drop in, because a new thought will follow. (It's also true that, at the end of a thought, very often we are at the end of the breath and, therefore, it is natural as we end one thought to allow a breath to drop in for the next.)

**I'd like to suggest, therefore, that there is a strong connection between breath and thought for an actor and, indeed, for ourselves when we speak in everyday life. When we finish one idea, when we come to the end of a spoken thought, as the new thought is formed a breath drops in so that we are able to speak it. So, in one way, a breath is a thought dropping in – or should be.**

> ### Stage 2
>
> Experiment, then, with the speaking of the Yevtushenko text exploring the ways in which you might respond to both the line endings in this poetic text and the punctuation. Responding to these elements in the text is a matter of finding the thought and allowing it to be realized as you speak it in a certain way. Again, there is no one 'right' way to respond to the information that the layout and the

punctuation provide, but you should find that these clues within the writing inform your thinking and the way in which you experience the thoughts as you speak them.

I would also suggest that when we speak someone else's words we want to engage the listener in such a way that they want to listen to us and that they receive and understand what we say. Part of whether the listener wants to listen is to do with whether they believe we are connected to what we say, and whether we are experiencing the thoughts as we say them. Another part of someone wanting to listen is connected to whether we speak with honesty and simplicity. So in attempting to honour some of the structures within a text, allow your responses when you speak to convey the thoughts simply and directly – don't over-embellish your speaking of the text as it is likely that this will not help you to communicate it.

## Meaning

If you have spoken the Yevtushenko text now a number of times it is likely that you will have come to understand it and that you will have forged a relationship with it. I think it is very important to recognize this and I think the work you have done so far is an excellent way to find a connection with a text and its meaning.

**Simply put, you are better to speak the text, exploring it from different points of view several times rather than simply sit pondering what you think it means. Meaning reveals itself the more you speak, and begin to experience, a text.**

It is possible, of course, that Yevtushenko's *Colours* can have different meanings. However, if we explore the language and the thought processes – the narrative within the poem – then we may come close to what the author may have intended.

First of all, I hope you have discovered that there is an over-arching image that frames the poem. It begins, 'When your face/Appeared over my crumpled life'. And ends with, 'When your face sets'. Also, when the face appeared, suddenly the world was filled with light and colour, as the poet goes on to explain. The overarching image, then, is of a sun that rises and sets. And the sun is, in fact, the face of a person who came into the speaker's life and changed it – and much of the poem is about the way in which the speaker has come to see and experience things differently, through the influence of this person.

The evidence within the text suggests that the poem is attempting to crystallize the experience of finding oneself in love for the first time and the fear we might have, in the midst of all of the happiness the other person brings into our life, that as suddenly as the revelation began, it might all be lost if, and when, this person leaves us.

It is possible to find other meanings within the text but, from the evidence within the thoughts, images and words of the text, I think other interpretations may be imposed rather than generally found within the text itself.

### The Integrated Actor

We could spend a long time working with this relatively simple text – for instance, could you explore why some of the lines are longer and some shorter? How does this awareness of the way the poem has been written affect our understanding and our speaking of it? Why does the phrase, 'of revelations', have a line all to itself, for instance? What is the impact of the short line, 'Fear hems me in', which is made up of one syllable words only? I could answer these questions for you but I would rather you speak the text and explore it, asking your own questions about it, rather than attempt to provide you with a series of answers which, after all, only convey to you what I find within the poem.

To summarize, then, working around a poetic text in this way aims to encourage you to really explore the language in a text so that you can be stimulated by it and connect to it, and to explore other structures within a text as a means of allowing the text itself to guide you towards its meaning. Everything on the page must be able to be turned into living thoughts within you if you are to be able to speak them.

# CHAPTER 14
# SEMI-SUPINE – FLOOR WORK 3 – WHISPERED 'AH'

We come now to a classic Alexander-related voice exercise, and it's one that I have found tremendously useful over the years.

Move down to the floor to work in the semi-supine position you will now be familiar with. I will not talk you through all of the detailed thinking that you need to do when working in semi-supine again here. If you need specific guidance, refresh yourself by revisiting *Floor Work 1* or *Floor Work 2*.

As a reminder I will suggest that, ideally, your head needs to be supported by a couple of books, and you need to spend time allowing the weight of your torso to be supported by the floor, lengthening and widening through the back before you take your attention to your breath. As your shoulders spread, remind yourself to let your neck be free to let your head move forward and upwards – or forward and out.

When focusing on breath work, it is important, simply, to turn your attention to your natural breath and notice it. Focus on the out-breath first – it falls out of you like a silent sigh of relief, without any control – and as it falls out of you, imagine a letting go or subtle release in your breastbone. Allow the breath to drop back in again when you sense the impulse to do so.

After you have given your attention to the letting go sensation of the out-breath for some time, begin to focus on what occurs when the breath drops in. On each new in-breath, allow yourself to relax a little bit more deeply within yourself each time, and explore the notion of the breath touching down inside you. When the breath falls out, where does it seem to touch-off within you?

Experiment with touching a sound off from centre on, 'Huh'. After you have touched off a sound, relax and let the breath touch down again. Allow the breath to fall in and out of you a few times before you touch off another sound.

### Whispered 'Ah' exercise

#### Stage 1

You are going to imagine that you are speaking the vowel, 'Ah'. Think that you are going to send this extended vowel to the ceiling above you – find a point there to which you can imagine you are sending the sound. You will make the shape of, 'Ah', with your mouth and your vocal tract but your speaking of it will be silent.

Don't think too hard about this – the muscles of your mouth, tongue and vocal tract essentially know what to do to formulate an, 'Ah', shape: just trust them. I like to call this a 'true whisper'. The 'Ah' is not in any way sounded, though as the air moves from your centre through your vocal tract and out between your teeth and your lips, you may hear the sound of the breath as it passes through.

There are a number of things to think about as you explore this exercise. Take your time – work to the end of the breath on each, 'Ah'. After you have made each, 'Ah', remember to allow the breath that follows to drop in and to touch down within you.

If you are letting your neck be free, thinking of it lengthening away from your tailbone, simultaneously sense that you feel more at ease in your jaw joint and that your lower jaw wants to float down and away from your upper jaw. When you think, 'Ah', and whisper it, just allow your lower jaw to fall down and away from the upper jaw. In fact, the natural function of your lower jaw is to want to do this.

Notice throughout your whispered, 'Ah', that you have a sense of a wide-open channel through your vocal tract and it is almost as if the 'Ah' sound begins in your centre and that it is shaped, from your centre to the front of your mouth, by the open channel that it moves through as you whisper it. Notice that your tongue is resting against the back of your bottom teeth and is fairly flat within your mouth.

Where does the energy of that whispered, 'Ah', begin inside you? What is the nature of the effort you need from centre that will carry this whispered sound to the ceiling? I'd like to suggest that this does not take a lot of effort but whatever effort you are sensing, you should feel that it is centred within you.

Remember that this whispered, 'Ah', should be more or less inaudible. If it becomes quite noisy, this suggests that the channel through which the breath is moving is partly closing or shutting down. If you are moving the air through the channel silently then you are executing the exercise perfectly. Make this your goal and don't be overly concerned with what is happening in the vocal tract or what I am calling the channel. If the whispered, 'Ah', is more or less silent it is enough, then, to sense the space that the breath is moving through.

### Stage 2

Then getting as close to the feeling of the whispered, 'Ah', as possible, thinking from your centre, allow a voiced, 'Ah', to come up through the space. Send this to the ceiling and be sure to commit to voicing the sound fully – this is not a sound that is half breath, half sound. If you are very close to the physical sensations you experienced when you whispered, 'Ah', sense the freedom of this voiced version as you send the sound away from you to the ceiling.

Alternate now between the whispered and the voiced, 'Ah'. Take time to do this. It's important to feel that complete openness within the vocal tract, or that sense of space, each time on the whispered, 'Ah'. Then, on the next out-breath, when you voice the, 'Ah', sound it should be as close, physically, to the sensations of whispered, 'Ah', as possible but be fully sounded.

If you are working to the end of your breath on each whispered or voiced, 'Ah', you should find that you need a very quick release in the musculature in the lower abdominal area at the end of the breath so that the next breath can drop in quickly and easily. If you don't feel the need for this quick release so that the next breath can drop in, it is possible that you are not working to the end of your breath. This quick release in the area of the transversus abdominus (lower belly area) is referred to as a recoil breath. Don't worry about it too much if you are not experiencing this at the moment, but it is a physiological response to the need for breath that it is possible to experience with this whispered, 'Ah', exercise.

### Stage 3

Move now to a text that you know – this could be the Yevtushenko poem or any speech from a play that you know. Keeping the thought of whispered, 'Ah' in your mind, take a few lines of your text – a few lines rather than barging your way through the whole text, so that you can focus on what you are experiencing – and, taking your time, whisper them through. As you mouth the words the breath is moving through the channel, and the channel remains open and free, as in the feeling of whispered, 'Ah'. Send the thoughts within the text away from you – perhaps to a point on the ceiling.

There are a number of aspects to focus on. First of all, you should feel yourself working from centre as the breath moves through your vocal tract and your mouth. Next, work to the end of each thought and then allow the breath to drop in and touch down at centre. Remind yourself that your neck should be free and your head moving forward and upwards (or out) off the spine. As you do this, also be reminded that your lower jaw wants to move down and away from your upper jaw – this free, flexible movement facilitates the shaping and articulation of the vowels in the text.

### Stage 4

You can work through the lines you have chosen as many times as you wish in order to facilitate a different focus each time you work the text through. When returning to the starting point you have chosen, remember that you should whisper the text through (and remember, your whisper is, more or less, inaudible) as if you are thinking and experiencing it for the first time – don't just use the words of the text as if they are simply part of an exercise: they should be living thoughts.

### Stage 5

You can also explore the notion that the shaping of the vowels and the articulation of the consonants help you to realise the meaning of the text – both for yourself and for anyone you might be speaking to, such as another character or the audience. Taste the alveolar consonants /t/, /d/, /n/, /l/ – how active can you make them – how active do they need to be? If you move through a velar consonant /k/, /g/ or possibly the 'ng' sound that can occur in 'singing' or at the end of 'thing', can you sense the springing apart of the area towards the back of your tongue and the soft palate? If you make a plosive consonant, such as /b/, /p/ or a bilabial continuant such as /m/ can you sense your lips doing the work rather than your jaw? How active do your lips need to be for each of these sounds to be realised? Do you notice that /m/ need not be a short consonant but can be sustained?

### Stage 6

Finally, go back to whispering through the text letting the thoughts drop in with the breath and getting as close to the feeling of whispered, 'Ah', as you can. Then speak the text, sending it away from you to the point on the ceiling you have chosen – if you were standing, this could be another person you are speaking to or your audience – feeling the freedom and ease of this.

If you have time, you may wish to transfer yourself to standing and repeat this process. If you do this, remember as you move into standing to maintain as much of the physical freedom, and the sense of lengthening and widening through the back, that you found on the floor. Allow your lower belly muscles to stay flexible and not to grip in the effort to stand and remember to allow breath to touch down to centre, before you repeat the whispered, 'Ah', exercise and the whispering of the text. You can focus on a point ahead of you on the wall and let this be the person to whom you imagine you are speaking or the audience.

### Summary – A pause in which to evaluate

You will probably be aware now that you are working, step by step, to a place of freedom and ease from which to access your breath and your voice so that you are working economically as well as expressively.

There's a good deal to coordinate. Thoughts that give rise to the words should be detailed and specific and should drop into centre with the breath. The breath is then touched off from centre into words. Words are muscular and active and communicate when the neck remains free and the lower jaw is flexible enough to help you both to articulate them and to express and release them. All of this should feel and appear entirely natural and easy.

The principal focus of the whispered, 'Ah', exercise is the freedom that you can experience in your vocal tract as you make sound and as you speak, so that there is no constriction present.

Constriction is something that can occur when muscles in the vocal tract want to assist in the production of sound. Sometimes this is just habitual – we've learnt it somewhere along our journey at an earlier stage and come to rely upon it. Sometimes it occurs, in the moment, with the expression of certain emotions. However, this constriction is a form of tension and, remember, that tension is not emotion – tension certainly doesn't help the actor to express an emotion.

Constriction can occur in two main ways. The commonest form is that the false vocal folds, which lie in the vocal tract above the true vocal folds, want to 'assist' the true vocal folds in making sounds. When this happens, the false vocal folds bear down upon the true vocal folds and, in doing this, the sound becomes compromised. When it is extreme, when the false vocal folds are trying to work hard, there is a resulting rasp in the sound that sounds as if it might be dangerous. And it is, in fact, dangerous to rely on this way of producing sound – it is very tiring for the vocal folds and is likely to result in pathology. Another form of constriction is when the middle constrictor, an area of muscles within the vocal tract which lies above the false vocal folds, narrows, decreasing the space in the vocal tract at this point. This can produce a somewhat strangulated sound and it is not uncommon to hear it in certain kinds of singers. It is, perhaps, less dangerous than the constriction that results from the involvement of the false vocal folds in making sound, but I would argue that it limits the range of expression available in the voice and unnecessary tension within the vocal tract is still potentially dangerous, so is probably best avoided.

The whispered, 'Ah', exercise, then, leads you away from constriction to a place of ease and freedom, but it can also help you in so many ways as an actor, allowing you space and time to investigate physical/vocal function as well as exploring language itself, and the thought processes that give rise to words which become spoken thoughts.

## Some thoughts about preparatory work in semi-supine

So far you have spent a considerable amount of time working in semi-supine but in life, and as an actor, you spend most of your time standing, sitting or moving. The work so far has been about identifying and marshalling your essential resources, imaginatively, physically and vocally and in working towards physical freedom so that you can free your imagination, free your breath and access your voice without blocks or unnecessary tensions. In part, the work has also been about relinquishing habits – ways of being that seem part of who you are but which can potentially get in your way.

I'll say again, as you move forward in the work, that the point of the work of the applied Alexander principles is not that every character you play will have this neutral physicality. Rather, the Alexander-related work takes you to a place of greater freedom and to a physicality that is neutral and open, free of your own habitual tensions, that provides you with a good starting point. And I would beg the question, why should we assume that the character we are going to play is not, in themselves, aligned and free?

Very often, when an actor approaches a physical characterization, they emphasize their own habits and mannerisms – heightening them – and then call it a character. This is probably something that happens unconsciously but this is not the most imaginative kind of acting, and relying on personal habits and mannerisms could lead to all kinds of other issues for the simple reason that working from unnecessary tension is tiring.

In a way, when you are able to be grounded, aligned and released you have already moved away from who you are – you have already entered into a kind of transformation – although I would also argue that, when you let go of habitual physical use that may not really be necessary or helpful, you become more yourself.

My argument here is that being grounded, aligned and centred is a very good place to start. It is also worth bearing in mind that the semi-supine work described in this book so far is a good way of practising mindfulness, and that letting go of tensions as you allow your spine to realign and your body to reintegrate when working on the floor, in particular, is a very good way of reducing stress, both physical and emotional. Allowing yourself to be in touch with a natural breath and exploring a tidal breath also helps you to let go of anxieties and can lead you to a place where you feel more peaceful and calmer.

There is also a discipline in this work. Some of you may find it difficult to focus on alignment and semi-supine work for any length of time. This work may make you feel impatient or restless, and you may have an impulse to be up and doing. There are a number of things to consider here. First, that it will be of value to you to try to focus on yourself and to let go of the need to be constantly doing something. Learning stillness and an ability to focus internally will be useful to you as an actor. Second, within the way the work is laid out in this book, I've introduced a simple version of the semi-supine work which need not take a lot of time – perhaps twenty minutes to half an hour – before taking you deeper into the work and providing semi-supine exercise that should take more time and attention, so you have an opportunity to start simply and then to develop your abilities to concentrate and focus within the work as you bring yourself to the lengthier exercises.

The semi-supine work outlined in sections 1, 2 and 3 should be regular and ongoing in terms of the work you might be undertaking on yourself. You need to know that working in semi-supine is only of any real use to you if you are able to give at least twenty minutes to it. When you work in semi-supine and your back is supported by the floor, your spine does, in fact, lengthen out because the discs between the vertebrae expand as they fill with fluid. This is a completely natural process that occurs when pressure is taken off the spine and it is worth working in semi-supine partly for this reason. This expansion that takes place within the discs takes time, however – at least twenty minutes – so don't short-change yourself by spending a few minutes on the floor before you then move on to undertake some other form of exercise.

For now, I would recommend at least half an hour in semi-supine two or three times a week, covering some concentrated physical/vocal work, following one of the sessions that has already been described here. However, not all the work that you can do should be in semi-supine and at this point it is worth exploring some other simple, physical exercise that will stimulate your breath and free up your access to it, and simultaneously release your voice.

# CHAPTER 15
# FREEING THE BODY TO FREE THE VOICE

It is important to recognize that there is a fundamental, organic relationship between your body, your breath and your voice: put in simpler terms, any movements you make will, potentially, stimulate and affect your experience of breath, and this, in turn, will affect vocal response. I believe that this should always be the case in the best interests of vocal health. So, for instance, if, within a play, your character had to run around the stage for some reason and then speak, it would be inappropriate to then try to 'control' your breathing in such a way that it should appear that you have not been running. A higher energy activity will stimulate your body's need for breath – the breathing reflex changes and responds more rapidly. (It would be a different matter if you had to be extremely active, physically, within a scene and then leave the scene to then come back on stage as if in another time and place in the following scene.)

The next short sequence of exercises explores this body/breath relationship.

## Swings

The swings that I describe here are derived from the work of Litz Pisk, a movement practitioner who worked extensively with the RSC and within the film industry in the 1960s and 1970s and swings are also included in the work of contemporary movement practitioners, such as Lorna Marshall. The swings described here represent a sequence that I have found particularly useful in relation to body, breath and voice, but there are many other kinds of swings, and if you find this work of particular interest, do investigate the work of other practitioners who utilize them.

You have already explored, in a simple way, the relationship between your body and breath when standing and grounding, then dropping down through the spine to hang over your knees to then return to standing. This work with spinal rolls from standing establishes your body's relationship with gravity and explores ways in which giving in to gravity affects your breath and your voice. The pendulum swing explores this relationship further.

### Pendulum swing

### Stage 1

Take a moment or two to ground yourself in standing. To begin the exercise, bring your feet and knees together and bend at the knees. Simultaneously, lean forwards through your spine so that your back is, more or less, parallel to the floor (flat), reaching your hands and arms straight forwards and lifting your head up.

Drop your hands, arms, head and torso towards the floor, being sure to allow your head to drop towards gravity as you do this. As your head drops down, your arms will swing back and up behind you, returning as your torso bounces on your knees and your arms, torso and your head will then return to their starting position.

It is important, once you commence the swing by dropping the weight of your head, neck, shoulders, arms and torso, that you allow momentum to take over – you are not in control of the swing, as momentum takes control of you. This is just a matter of allowing the weight of your upper body to give to gravity with your head, neck and spine being flexible and responsive as you swing. Apart from the preparatory moment, when your head is held up, your neck should remain completely free. There are two bounces in this swing, one as your arms swing back behind you and up and another as momentum brings your arms back to, roughly, where they started – your head and neck should be bounced by the swing and not held. As your spine, neck and head are swung forwards and up as they return, allow your head to go where it wants to go – it's not your objective to bring your head back up in the second part of the swing to its starting position.

One of the key elements is that as the weight of your upper torso drops down, you should sense breath being pushed naturally from your centre. Unless you are, for some reason, holding your breath, this will happen naturally, but it is good to notice. Another breath is released as your arms and spine swing on the return – there are two bounces in this swing and, therefore, two moments where breath is released. Notice, also, how immediately after the breath is released, it automatically falls back in.

This swing is quite simple, but the freedom in your upper body that is necessary can be difficult to achieve: it can be difficult to let go. Remember, your feet and your legs are working and support your upper body through this swing. With this in mind, it is very important that your knees remain bent throughout this process – if you start straightening your knees, you will find that your weight will come forwards and you will want to fall over.

This swing is about freeing your body in order to stimulate and free your breath. If you swing for, say, a minute or two, if you then allow the swinging to die down in its own time so that you end with the weight of your head, neck and spine hanging over your knees (the position you are in when you drop down through the spine from standing), and then return to standing through the spine in the usual way (not holding your breath but allowing breath to drop in and out as it naturally wants to do), you should find, once you are standing, that there is a greater sense of release in the abdominal and lower abdominal area as a result of swinging. As you ground yourself and think of aligning, stay aware of the breath and explore that sense of the breath touching down inside you and of allowing a flexible response in the lower abdominal area.

### Stage 2

When you are ready, repeat the pendulum swing, noticing again how the breath leaves your body and returns naturally as a result of the swing. Then, thinking from centre (or from deep within you if that is an easier concept) as you swing, let breath turn into sound. Again, there are two bounces within the swing – the bounce as you drop down and allow your arms to swing back and up, and the bounce when your arms, spine, head and neck return – so, allow two sounds to happen as a result of the bounces.

Remember that your head and neck should remain completely free throughout – it should seem to you as if the sound you are making has very little to do with the head or the neck – and the sound should be free and not controlled. If you aim for the 'Huh' sound that you have employed with the touch of sound exercise before, this should help. The sound should seem to happen without effort and may seem unpleasant to you, or it may seem as if this is not the way you usually sound – if that is the case, just embrace it: this is part of your voice and it is the kind of sound you make when your body is freer and when you are not, consciously, thinking about trying to control the sound in any way, and not looking for a particular result.

Let the swinging die down again. Stop sounding and allow your upper body, head and neck to hang over your knees – stay in touch with the breath and don't control it: allow your body to breathe. Come back to standing through the spine, uncurling through the vertebrae as you have done in previous exercises. Again, don't hold your breath at any point during the return to standing – come up through the spine and do not grip in the belly area. In standing, take a moment to think about how you are grounded, and remind yourself that your head is poised on the neck spine and not held – in your imagination, you could say to yourself, 'Let my neck be free to let my head move forwards and upwards.' Sense breath touching down within you and tune in to the small, low belly release that allows breath to touch down. Then speak some text that you know.

You should find, after investigating this pendulum swing in various ways, that your voice seems to be more relaxed or more easy and you may find, if you yourself are more relaxed in the lower belly and the neck areas that, perhaps, the pitch of your voice seems to have changed. If this is the case, notice all of the various physical elements that give rise to this shift within your voice: can you sustain these elements and take them into your work?

## Side swings

The pendulum swing, described above, and the side swing are similar exercises and produce very similar results in the sense that, if you are able to give your upper body completely over to the swing, this will free up both your body and your breath and connect you to your voice. The side swing has the added benefit of stimulating the bottom of the rib cage – you've explored potential movement here in semi-supine 3 – and it may be interesting after exploring the side swing to see if you sense greater awareness in the lower rib area.

### Stage 1

Prepare by finding the neutral grounded and aligned position. It's important with this swing that you allow your knees to bend or your weight will fall forwards as you start the swing. You may also find it useful to place your feet slightly wider than a neutral stance – normally the feet would be hips-width apart, but you may find slightly wider is helpful.

Turning your upper body either to the left or the right, reach your hands and arms out to that side in preparation for the swing. You are then going to drop your head, shoulders and arms towards the floor, releasing to the tail of your spine as you do this. The momentum stimulated by this action will then swing your spine, head and arms up to the other side, and as you give all of the weight of your body to gravity in the swing, you will find yourself then swinging back to the side you turned to in order to start the swing. Allow gravity and the natural momentum of the swing to swing your upper body, head and arms from side to side – allow your breath to be released from centre as you drop through each time.

As with the previous swing, throughout, your neck needs to be completely free and flexible once the swing has begun and your neck should respond to the momentum of the swing throughout. Similarly, you should sense that your spine, arms and shoulders are also flexible and responsive. Once you drop your head and all of your spine towards the floor as you begin the swing, there is no sense of control in your upper body. Once again, your feet and your legs, which bend at the knee, are there to support your weight as you swing through and from side to side, but there is a sense of letting go and of being as free as possible in your torso, neck, head and arms.

After a few swings from side to side, allow the swinging to die down naturally so that you are hanging from the tail of your spine over, or between, your knees. At this point, in preparation for your return to standing, adjust your feet so that they are back below your hips and roll up through the spine to a standing position. Remember that you think down through the soles of your feet and that the tail of your spine moves in the direction of the floor as you uncurl, vertebra by vertebra,

> through the spine. The neck will uncurl towards the end of this sequence and your head will float forwards and upwards to sit in a poised position on the neck spine. Throughout this process, stay aware that your breath is dropping in and out of you and that you are not gripping in the belly, but leaving it flexible and available, as you come to standing. Also, don't want to control your breath as you come back to standing, just let it drop in and out as it will.

Once standing, you may notice that as well as an efficient low belly release, you have flexible movement around your centre, i.e. in the bottom of your ribcage and/or in your waist area, and possibly in your lower back, too. If this is the case, it's useful just to notice that this movement around the centre can always be available to you, if it is needed, and that this is part of a fuller experience of breath. As mentioned earlier, at this stage, it is not necessary to think too much about when we might need access to this amount of breath and it's dangerous to make assumptions about the amount of breath we might need for a particular vocal activity. However, it is good to be aware that we may need access to this kind of breath at some point and that, if we are relaxed and at ease within the lower back area, and if the bottom of the ribcage is available to us, then we will be able to access the breath we need, when we need it, spontaneously and easily.

As in the previous pendulum swing, the exercise can now be repeated so that once you are swinging efficiently and freely, you can allow a sound to touch off from your centre as you drop through in the swing. Start the swing in exactly the same way and focus, first, on the quality of your swing, then on the breath as it is naturally released from the centre of your body, and then allow sound to happen, thinking of it falling out from the centre. When connecting with sound during these exercises, it is always desirable that the sound, as it were, just happens and that you don't anticipate exactly what kind or quality of sound will be the result. You are getting in touch with the natural sound you make when your upper body, head and neck are as free as possible and when you do not apply judgement to, or have any expectations of, your voice.

It is important when engaged in these swings that, when you allow a sound to happen, you do not allow it to be a breathy sound. There needs to be a clear intention within you either to make sound or just to release breath – the two activities need to be clear in your mind and in your body so that you do not end up with a breathy sound.

Once the swinging has died down and you have come back to standing from the hanging position, through the soles of your feet and your spine, and your head is once again floating, or poised, at the top of your neck spine, speak some text that you know, thinking from centre and allowing your lower abdominal muscles to be free to respond when breath drops in.

And again, a reminder that if and when you use text as part of a vocal exercise, it is important that you are thinking the thoughts, as if for the first time, and that your imagination is working with the words and the thoughts as you speak.

## The Integrated Actor

### Gathering water

This exercise is an excellent way to experience the co-ordination possible between your body and the experience of breathing. It comes from the Eastern practice of Qigong (pronounced 'Chi-gung').

> Starting from a grounded and aligned position in standing, imagine there is a body of water immediately before you. You are going to imagine that it is possible to bend forwards, pick up the water with both arms and then, raising your arms above your head, pour the water over your body, and then lower your arms once again to your sides in order to, once again, 'gather' the water. You are free to imagine this body of water at a height that suits you, depending on your flexibility and the range of movement available to you. So, the water can be at waist height, as if in a barrel, or it can be a pool of water at your feet, or some container that is at the level of your shins.
>
> When you bend forwards, aim to keep your spine in alignment as you bring your hands and arms forwards to collect the imaginary water. As you raise your arms up to the side of your head, imagine the water pouring over your head and body as you lower your arms back to your side. Repeat this exercise, slowly and in a controlled way, several times.
>
> You should find, as you continue to gather and pour the water, that your breathing rhythm becomes a natural part of the exercise and that your lower abdominal muscles naturally release. As a result, when you return to standing alignment, you should find you have accessed a centred breath with a natural low belly release.

# CHAPTER 16
# SUPPORT

I'd like to spend some time now considering what we might mean by support.

A word that has recently come into the vocabulary of voice practitioners is the word 'embodiment'. I'm not sure yet if anyone has attempted to define what might be meant by the word 'embodied' when used in relation to voice work, but I believe that this is linked to the concept of 'support' which has been around for a long time in the world of voice practice.

I think that traditional concepts of 'support' and what it may mean are not particularly useful – and perhaps this is why the word 'embodiment' may now be becoming popular, as a means of redefining the kinds of physical engagement that can occur within us when we speak, as well as linking physical engagement with a sense of ownership: **when an actor speaks, it should sound as if they own what they say, that it comes from them, that it matters to them and that they really mean it. To embody spoken thoughts, then, means to connect the mind and imagination to the body – you have been exploring this in the exercises that precede this section – so that the actor is physically engaged in the act of communicating and the sound is 'embodied'.**

Perhaps this all seems self-evident. Don't actors do this anyway? I would argue that many do, but that if our relationship with language is a purely intellectual one (which is how we are educated to relate to language) and if in the process of rehearsing a play, perhaps in a shorter time than is desirable, the actor has to cram lines, it can end up that, at least for some of the time, the actor will sound as if they are just saying lines and not fully engaged in meaningful communication with their fellow actors and that they do not really mean what they are saying. No audience wishes to witness this.

Let us deal with the notion of support. Traditionally, support is often located to a particular group of muscles – the transversus abdominus in the lower abdominal region, or the general area of the belly itself. It has been observed in clinical settings that when a sound is touched off from centre, there is a tiny movement in the transversus abdominus that appears to be connected to the onset of the sound. I would maintain that it is desirable both to sense this and to facilitate it. However, what this should never become is a pumping activity with the belly moving forcefully and repeatedly under the breath or the sound – this is not support but overwork and it will simply result in the speaker or singer driving air. That is to say that the forceful movement of the belly pushes upwards to the diaphragm which, in turn, over-activates the air, so that the breath is driven too forcefully against the vocal folds. In order to make sound, the vocal folds need to be able to come together to resist the breath, and if air is coming at them with some force, it is difficult for the folds to resist the air so that they have to work much harder in order to resist the breath force. In this way, long-term wear and tear to the vocal folds can occur. This, simply, has to be avoided.

Any engagement in the lower belly area, then, in relation to making a sound, needs to be quite subtle as well as sustained during the speaking of longer thoughts. It is also advantageous to experiment with how much air you need in order to speak a thought. Generally, it may be less than you expect, and it is unwise to think of breath as part of your support system. **Breath is not support, and taking more air, generally, does not solve an issue related to support** – as we have already seen, taking more air is more likely to create a problem at vocal fold level.

However, I also believe that there are other groups of muscles in the body that can provide support in order that the voice can function optimally, healthily and expressively in order for the actor to sound physically engaged with what they say. **My definition of support is this: it is a gentle engagement of musculature within the body that stabilizes the body in such a way that the larynx is able to move freely and flexibly within the vocal tract.**

As you have observed before, in previous exercises, the free and flexible movement of the larynx is crucial to vocal health and being able to achieve a range of expression within the voice, and support within the body is able to facilitate this. I admit that this definition may seem a bit general and mysterious, but, in fact, it is my experience that groups of muscles in different locations within the body have the potential to work together to provide support. It may be healthier to approach the idea of support in this way rather than trying to locate support within a particular muscle group. This would then suggest that the notion of 'embodiment' may be a better imaginative approach than simply thinking about notions of 'support'.

Muscle groups that may be accessed to form your support system can include the musculature of the pelvic floor, muscles in the lower back (the latissimus dorsi), the transversus abdominus in the lower belly area, and the sternocleidomastoid muscles on either side of the neck can also support the production of sound. Some exercises to help you identify these different muscle groups and the way they may be involved in supporting the sound now follow but, again, I would like to suggest that you do not want to locate your sense of support in only one area – the exercises that follow will focus, place by place, on the activation of particular muscles or muscle groups in relation to sound but, ideally, when you speak, you are aiming to sense that support is provided by these muscle groups working together. This, in itself, is tricky because as I have stated earlier in my definition of support, **efficient support is a gentle engagement of muscle** so when you are trying to monitor the ways in which musculature in your body may support your voice, the physical feedback you are looking for is subtle and not in any way violent or extreme.

## Support awareness exercises

### Exercise 1 Transversus abdominus

Let's start with the transversus abdominus. This area, or the more general area of the belly, has traditionally been associated with providing support for the voice. I have encountered professional actors and other voice users who, somewhere along the way, have gained the impression that if you make these muscles rigid under the breath and the voice or, worse, that if you pump these muscles as you speak, these activities provide the support your voice may need in order to work for a larger space. Both of these activities will only result in driving air and will make it more difficult for your vocal folds to do the work they need to do in order to make sustained sound when you speak or sing.

Before we explore what may be meant when we refer to support in this area, I would like to reinforce how crucial it is that when the breath drops in, when breath replaces at the end of a spoken or sung thought, the muscles in the lower abdominal area must release to allow the breath to drop in. In fact, I would say that releasing in the lower abdominal area in the moment that the breath is needed actively facilitates the breath to drop in. All of the exercises earlier in this book are paving the way for this to be able to happen, spontaneously, and this low belly release is part of an organic, reflexive breath. If you are able to allow this to happen, then, in fact, you are likely to be able to access the kind of support your voice needs.

### Exploring support

#### Stage 1

With this in mind, speak firmly on a repeated voiced consonant. I suggest:

/v/ /v/ /v/ /v/ /v/, or

/z/ /z/ /z/ /z/ /z/

When you try this, you are fully voicing, but you are not necessarily being unduly loud. It's also useful to think of sending the sound away from you – perhaps to a point on the wall opposite to you. Take your time, too, with each sound and don't rush – you can allow a little breath to drop in after each consonant. (Don't worry too much about this as this is likely to happen anyway. For the moment, I am not asking you to sustain several sounds on one breath.) Be aware that in efficiently making these sounds, there should be no wasted air – all the air is turned into vibrations at the place of articulation.

If you place the fingertips of one hand in the middle of the area where your transversus abdominus is located – this is, essentially, just above your groin in the lower belly area – you should notice as you make each of these consonants that there is a tiny muscular sensation or pulse in the muscle here. It is the gentle engagement of this muscle as you make sound that can provide you with one kind of support for your voice.

### Stage 2

If you now take your attention to a wall, or to a point on the floor, some distance that is further away from you, and send a sustained /v/ consonant away from you and to that point, working to the end of each breath, you should sense a sustained, gentle engagement from the transversus abdominus area. Remember, this sense of engagement is quite subtle: it is hard to describe, but it is not a feeling of gripping in this area. It is more a sense of a subtle pulse, a subtle engagement of this muscle. You may also find that if you allow the contact between the inside edge of your bottom lip and your top teeth which forms the /v/ sound to be really firm, it helps to increase your sense of support in the lower abdominal area, so **it is good to be aware that the muscularity of articulate speaking can also stimulate a sense of support elsewhere in the body for the voice.**

I would also like to suggest that if you are able to touch off sound from centre, as in the earlier exercises, you are likely to involve the transversus abdominus in the activity of gentle support quite spontaneously. Again, we talk of the 'touch of sound', so this is not a violent activity but, nonetheless, if we are able to allow the lower belly area to release as the breath drops in and if we are able to sense the sound touching off from somewhere in our centre when it is made, then it is likely that the gentle support that can be given by the transversus abdominus will be activated automatically.

### Stage 3

Now try speaking a thought from a text that you know. Remember that this needs to be living thought as you speak it – it's not just gobbledygook that you are using for the sake of an exercise. Sense it touching off within you as you start to speak the first sound of the thought, and sense the tiny pulse within the transversus abdominus as you touch the thought off. Do you sense a gentle, sustained engagement here to the end of the spoken thought? Can you sense the low belly release as the breath drops in immediately after you finish speaking? Is it possible to repeat this spoken thought or move on to the next thought in the text, touching off the thought as you speak and sensing the gentle engagement in your transversus abdominus?

## Exercise 2 Latissimus dorsi

The latissimus dorsi are a band of muscles that lie across the back of your ribcage in your lower back. They can be responsive to the breath as it drops in and out of you, and they can also provide some support for sound when it is made. If you are familiar with the work of Josephine Estill then you will be used to thinking of these muscles as having the potential to provide 'anchoring' at certain places within a song, and within your range, when you sing. I don't want to spend time discussing anchoring here, but do want to acknowledge its value in high-energy vocal activity at particular places in the range. Developing now a sense of how these muscles might provide a gentle support for the voice may help you access anchoring, when it may be needed, later.

### Latissimus dorsi

### Stage 1

From a neutral, grounded and aligned position, drop your head onto your chest and initiate a roll down through the spine until you are hanging over your knees, having released to the root of your spine, and with your head and neck hanging off your spine and your arms hanging from your shoulders towards the floor. (You could, if you wished, repeat the dropping down and building up through the spine exercise in which you tie the physical activity to breath falling out of you as you drop down through the spine, and breath dropping into you as you come back to standing, as a precursor to the next exercise.)

As you hang, allow yourself to connect with your breath and focus on the notion that the breath can seem to come into you at the base of your spine. Patsy Rodenburg has a brilliant image to stimulate this which is to imagine that you have nostrils at the base of the spine so that you can sense breath moving into you in this area, so do use this imagery if it helps. Key to this exercise is your sense that when the breath falls out of you, it falls out from your lower back. You can imagine it travelling from your lower back, down your spine and into your head and out of your nose or mouth.

As the breath replaces – allow it to do this in its own time as your body knows when it is ready for the next breath – sense the lower back expanding as the breath comes in and you may also feel a sense of lifting that starts in the lower spine as you allow the breath to come into you. Sense each outbreath falling out from your lower back.

Next, imagine that, rather than just allowing the breath to fall out of the lower back, the lower back ribs can kick the breath off. You might find, to begin with, that it helps to exaggerate this sense of kicking off a sound from the lower back ribs. However, as we are working towards something that is more natural and organic, once you have sensed the breath kicking off the lower back ribs, aim to make this sense of kicking off as subtle as you can.

## Stage 2

Now imagine that you're kicking off a sound from the lower back – releasing a long 'Ah' vowel through your range may be useful, but it could be any vowel you choose – and allow this to fall out of you. Let the breath replace when it needs to, keeping your focus on some expansion in the lower back area as the breath replaces, and then touch the sound off from your lower back ribs again, gliding through a range of notes from higher to lower on a vowel. Throughout this simple process, remember that your head, neck and shoulders hang off your spine – they should not seem to be involved at all in assisting to make the sound.

You will possibly notice as you hang and repeat this exercise that although you are thinking in your lower back, your lower belly may also seem to be involved. It should release every time the breath drops in and you may sense the gentle involvement of the transversus abdominus when you touch the sound off from the lower back area. It is all natural and healthy if you sense these muscles also working collaboratively with the latissimus dorsi in your lower back.

Keep allowing breath to drop in, touching off a long sustained vowel from your lower back and allowing it to fall out of you as you return to standing.

As you have done before, come up through the spine vertebra by vertebra and remember to allow your neck to uncurl as it aligns with your head floating up on the top of your neck spine so that it is poised and not held or fixed.

Keep repeating the long vowel in your own time in a neutral, grounded, standing position and notice whether you can still sense some expansion in the lower back when the breath drops in and a sense of the muscles here being gently involved when the sound is made. Keep touching the vowel sounds off from your lower back area to assist in this.

## Stage 3

Then, again, try speaking a couple of lines of a text that you know, dropping the thought in with the breath, but imagining that you can sense the spoken thought touching off from the lower back area. Again, you may find that you can sense some connection or involvement with the transversus abdominus as well as a gentle engagement in your latissimus dorsi muscles in your lower back as you speak.

### Adaptation of Exercise 2

You may find it more comfortable, and some of you may find it more effective, to explore a version of this exercise in a seated position.

### Latissimus dorsi exercise – sitting

Taking a chair, sit astride the chair facing the back of it. You need to be reasonably comfortable, but it will be useful to seat your bottom as close to the edge of seat of the chair as possible. Now put your arms across the back of the chair and rest your forehead on your hands, curving your spine to achieve this.

This should result in your having a stronger awareness of your back ribs and a sense of the potential for the movement in your lower back as the breath drops in. You then proceed through the sequence outlined above in this seated position rather than in the standing position. As you move into touching off sounds from your lower back ribs, you can bring yourself up into a sitting position – your head floating forwards and upwards off your neck spine – finding a comfortable way to remain seated on the chair.

### Alternative pair work exercise

You could also explore this exercise with a partner. One of you sits and rests their head on their hands while the other places the palms of their hands on either side of the spine in the area of the lower back, the fingers spanning the outer sides of the bottom of the rib cage while the thumbs of both hands remain close to either side of the spine. The person sitting may find the contact of their partners' hands across the lower back and the outside of the ribs helpful in knowing where to imagine the breath and the movement, whilst the person placing their hands on their partner may find it illuminating to sense in their hands the potential movements that can take place in this area when breath drops in and when sound is touched off.

If you experiment with the partner work, you should make sure that you try the exercise from both perspectives, i.e. being the seated partner and also the partner who makes physical contact with the back and lower ribs with their hands.

If it is appropriate to do so, you could also then try a version of the partner exercise in a standing position, seeing if you can both maintain the flexibility and the sense of engagement in your lower back area as you sound and as you speak.

### Exercise 3 The pelvic floor

It is often difficult to know whether musculature within your pelvic floor is involved in supporting sound as you make it, and there may be very little evidence to support the notion that it can be involved. However, I find that simple exercises for the muscles of the pelvic floor that provide an awareness of it, and an ability to imagine that the pelvic floor can be involved in the experience of sounds and speech, is of some value both in terms of the sound that results and in terms of the way in which your body can support your voice.

Some people can have quite a strong sense of their pelvic floor while others have little or no awareness of it, and I suspect that many individuals make no imaginative or sensory connection between their pelvic floor and their voice. I hope, though, that you are open to exploring the idea. (You explored this in a general way, earlier on, when you experimented with the 'box breathing' exercise.)

### Pelvic floor exercise

#### Stage 1

Imagine your pelvic floor. The pelvic floor is a combination of muscles, ligaments and tissue that lies within the lower part of your pelvis. If you trace lines in your imagination from your tailbone to the bottom of your hips at either side, and then from the bottom of your hips to your pubic bone at the front, you should be able to visualize a large diamond shape that connects these four points together. Then imagine that this diamond shape, located imaginatively in your pelvic area, is made up of some kind of elastic material – a thin sheet of spandex, or some kind of elasticated trampoline.

#### Stage 2

Stand with your feet wider than the usual neutral stance – you may find it useful to allow your feet to turn out slightly. Bend your knees and imagine the tail of your spine moving directly downwards towards the floor, and once you have lowered your tail of spine as far as you feel it is comfortable to do so, hold that position. (If you have ever taken a ballet class, this is, loosely speaking, similar to a plié in second position.)

Keep your focus with the tail of your spine and imagine a paintbrush or some kind of writing device extending out of your tail with the tip touching the floor. Now, remaining grounded throughout, by rotating the paintbrush attached to your tail, paint an imaginary infinity sign on the floor. Make the loops of your infinity sign nice and wide and be as efficient at drawing the sign to the front, sides and back of you as possible.

As you work with your tailbone, you will find that you articulate your pelvis in different ways to accomplish this task, but it is helpful to keep your focus with the tailbone and with the floor below you in order to achieve really specific movements. You might also notice that you are better at 'painting' some lines of the infinity symbol than others. Really concentrate, then, on making all of the loops within the sign, both forwards, sideways and backwards, because as you do this, you are, in fact, exercising your pelvic floor.

While you are involved in this exercise, also ensure that you allow breath to come and go in a natural way and keep breathing – don't hold your breath, because it is counterproductive to do so. If you allow breath to drop in and out as you engage with this exercise, you are also making a physical connection between the musculature of the pelvic floor and the breath itself.

### Stage 3

After working the tail of your spine and your pelvic floor for one to two minutes, bring yourself back to a neutral, grounded stance. You should find that you now have a deeper experience of the breath dropping in, and that you have maintained the sense of a low belly release when the breath drops in.

Now, imagine the breath has the potential to drop down to the pelvic floor and that, as it lands there, the pelvic floor responds, elastically, to the breath as it arrives – one image for the pelvic floor is that it is a bit like a trampoline floor that gives as the breath lands on it. Then experiment with touching a sound off as if from somewhere on the pelvic floor – you can start with 'Huh' and then move to 'Ha-ah-ah', (a long, sustained sound) which you might feel more useful for this exercise. Try speaking some text that you know as if touching each thought off from the pelvic floor and as if each thought as you speak it remains connected throughout to the pelvic floor.

If you are thinking from the pelvic floor, this is almost certainly going to be a deeper place within you than you have previously felt your centre to be. (This may not be so in every case – I just mention that it is likely.) If you sense you have been successful in connecting sound to the pelvic floor, it is also possible that you may feel a number of things:

that this helps you to feel more deeply relaxed;
that this is a more efficient way of making sound;
that your voice sounds deeper and/or richer;
that the sound seems to resonate (i.e. vibrate) more within the body.

These are just some of the things that actors have said to me after exploring this pelvic floor exercise, and you may feel that there are other positive phenomena that you experience.

Some of you may feel that the sound you produce after this exercise seems to you unnaturally low, or that it seems dark or, to some degree, muffled. These perceptions can be easily resolved by thinking of sending the sound away from you as it leaves you.

### Final exercise for support

In an attempt to combine all of your experience in relation to support – what it might be and how you have experienced it – sitting or standing in a grounded and neutral position, imagine that the musculature of the lower back, the pelvic floor and the transversus abdominus can collaborate together providing a gentle engagement within your body as you speak. Aim to speak a section of text that you are already familiar with, ensuring that you are also speaking living thoughts.

You will probably find it helpful if, when the breath drops in, you think of it brushing across your pelvic floor, releasing the lower belly, and opening up the lower back, and you might find it useful to imagine breath can enter you through the tail of the spine or through the pubic bone at the front.

In this way, the support muscles may all be activated as the breath falls in so that, when you speak, if you are thinking either from centre or from your pelvic floor, you will sense these muscle groups gently collaborating as you speak. You may also find it useful to imagine that the sounds you make come up from the soles of your feet, through your legs and gather at your centre – this thought alone can activate in subtle ways muscles of the support system, and this is another way of imagining how being grounded through the feet can help you.

For now, you may feel that one or more of these areas is somewhat inactive, or you might not be able to sense that the muscles in a particular area are gently engaging. Some of you may find you have a strong sense of support in the lower back or in the transversus abdominus but not in the pelvic floor, for instance. For now, this is something you can note but you can still draw upon the sense of support that you do feel when you need it and, in time, if you keep exercising and thinking about your physical/vocal use, you will find more of your body becoming available to engage, gently, in the act of speaking.

### Summary of support

Support is a gentle engagement of a range of muscle groups when you speak, sing, chant or shout that stabilizes the body so that your larynx and, indeed, your voice are able to work freely and flexibly.

When your voice is embodied in this way, it makes other people (if you are an actor, your audience) want to listen to you. It is difficult to explain why this is, but support assists a voice to sound more confident and assertive and it contributes to what some would describe as an 'authentic' sound. By this I mean that your voice seems to belong to you, to come from you and to reveal something of who you are. Support also contributes to your ability to communicate in a larger space, such as a theatre, a concert hall or a lecture theatre.

You will notice that I frequently describe the sensations you may feel as 'subtle' or 'gentle'. I hope this is not confusing. I say this because, for some of you, when you release your lower belly for the first time, or when you touch off sound from the area of the latissimus dorsi, for example, the experience may seem quite profound to you and, consequently, it may not feel as if what happened was 'subtle' or 'gentle' at all but, again, in time as you practise and continue to explore all of the physical experiences that arise from the various exercises, your experience will begin to feel more familiar to you. The key thing is not to overwork – if an exercise is making you feel unduly tense or held, or if there is a sense of pumping or pushing connected to the breath or to sound, then it is likely you are overworking. Conversely, you should sense muscles that have been activated by these exercises working for you. It can be a difficult balance to strike.

If in doubt, check that you are grounded through the feet and the tail of your spine, that your knees are easy and not locked, that you experience a small amount of low belly release when the breath drops in, and that your head is poised and not fixed at the occipital joint.

You may also find it useful to move into the semi-supine position to work for the simple reason that you can find greater ease and relaxation through the body when working against the floor, and it is usually easier to experience the low belly release that occurs when a breath drops in, in semi-supine work, too.

# CHAPTER 17
# RESONANCE

The sound we make when speaking or singing is produced by the vocal folds, which lie within the larynx. The vocal folds themselves are very small – around the size of a five-pence piece – so if it were simply a matter of the sound we hear being the result of the vocal folds meeting and vibrating as the air passes through them, the sound that results would be very quiet and somewhat difficult to hear.

Resonance is the result of vibrations that amplify the original note and, like so much else connected with the production of human sound, the subject of resonance is still hotly debated as the scientific evidence for some aspects of resonance, traditionally referred to within voice practice, is still being researched.

Essentially, resonance adds volume, or perhaps the word 'body' is a better concept, to the sound we make. This helps the voice to communicate in larger spaces, though resonance alone does not solve all of the actor's issues if they can be heard in a larger space, but not understood. (And the use of microphones, which is becoming quite common in theatre events now, also does not solve all problems to do with audibility.) Rather than enter into a discussion now about why this may be the case, let's return to the matter of resonance itself.

Resonance, that is to say, vibrations that amplify the original note made at vocal fold level, is produced by any chamber that the note passes through. The easiest way to understand what resonance is is to consider that if you have ever stood within a cave, and then voiced a sound, you will have heard the sound bouncing back to you from the various rocky surfaces within that cave. The sound seems to come back to you both fuller and louder than you remember making it. This is as a result of the acoustic properties of the cave itself – sound waves produced by your voice bounce around the space, reflected by the rocky surfaces all around you, and it is this acoustic process that then amplifies the original note. (A similar kind of experience can also be had in many bathrooms.)

Given that the larynx is suspended within the vocal tract, as the vibrations of the note travel from the vocal folds upwards through the pharynx, the chamber of the pharynx is able to resonate, to add additional vibrations, to the note. The oral cavity is also a principal resonator. The space in the oral cavity runs from the back to the front of the mouth – from the top of the pharynx to the teeth and lips at the front – so this space, too, can add resonance to the original note. How much other resonating spaces may be involved in assisting in the production of sound is then up for debate.

The work I do is largely based on experiential learning. In relation to resonance, the speaker experiences the sensations in the head, face and body that occur when sound is made and this, then, becomes a means of exploring and understanding resonance. My own experience, both as a voice user and as a teacher, is that when the vibrations of sound are focused on in different parts of the body, beneficial changes within the sound that is being made can result. This seems to occur as a result of focusing on developing the resonant potential within the voice user, and as long as the user is not pushing, straining or otherwise overworking in order to explore different kinds of resonance, it appears to be beneficial to encourage speakers and singers to explore this potential.

Traditionally, in voice training we speak of 'true' and 'sympathetic' resonance. Concepts of 'true' resonance relate to the idea that, if sound is produced by the vibration of the vocal folds as they come together to resist the passage of the air, only the spaces above the vocal folds can truly resonate the sound, because the air which carries the sound travels upwards, directly through these areas. These spaces, then, include the pharynx, oral cavity (which includes the back of the mouth), the nasal cavity and the sinuses. The involvement or role of some of these spaces can be hotly debated as some vocal scientists suggest that, as some of the sinus cavities are tiny, they cannot possibly add much, in terms of resonance, to the quality of the sound made at vocal fold level.

'Sympathetic' resonance is a term used to describe vibrations in various areas of the body that seem to be produced in response to the sound being made at vocal fold level but which cannot be considered to be 'true' resonance because the air that produces the sound does not move through them, nor can the sound travel into or through those areas of the body.

'Chest' resonance is a good example of so-called 'sympathetic' resonance. The belief being that since the vocal folds lie above the chest cavity and the sound is not made until the folds resist the air trying to pass through them, that any vibrations produced by the vocal folds must then travel upwards through the vocal tract and into the oral and nasal cavities and the head. This would seem logical. Perhaps, then, the vibrations that may be experienced in the chest area are the result of vibrations being conducted through the bones of the chest themselves, particularly if the speaker or singer is relaxed so that muscular tension is not blocking potential vibrations, rather than the sound actually resonating within the chest cavity itself.

My personal bias is that vibrations experienced in the chest or in the back area may, indeed, be 'true' resonance. The vocal folds lie within the larynx which is suspended within the vocal tract. There is space below the vocal folds within the pharynx as well as above them. The air that meets the vocal folds as they come together to produce the sound is initiated below the vocal folds and, assisted by the diaphragm, travels up from the lungs and, as the vocal folds vibrate, I believe that the air both below and above the vocal folds can be vibrated by the sound the folds produce. The air may be travelling in one direction – that is, upwards and outwards – but the vibrations themselves may vibrate the air both above and below the folds, and these vibrations will multiply and travel through the air into whatever cavities that the sounds can find. It seems to me naïve to think that the vibrations of sound can only travel in the direction that the breath is travelling.

Research is being conducted into this area but, as far as I am aware, findings so far are not conclusive. Whether you buy into the theory I am proposing or not, it is nonetheless observable that when a sound is made vibrations can be experienced in many areas of the body – whether these are 'true' or 'sympathetic' vibrations is, perhaps, not important if we find that by focusing on the potential of vibrations within the body the sound being made can be enhanced in some way.

If you are an advocate of Estill Voice Craft, then it is likely that you will not be unduly concerned with the phenomenon of resonance as within the practice of Estill work focus is place on laryngeal and vocal fold function so that what has been traditionally referred to as 'chest' resonance is the product of thick vocal folds meeting to resist the air within a neutral larynx, and some kinds of 'head' resonance are the result of a tilting of the thyroid cartilage within the structure of the larynx so that the vocal folds lengthen and are thinned, and thus produce the lyrical sound in singing or speaking that has formerly been associated with 'head' resonance.

I have undergone a range of courses in Estill Voice Craft, so I am persuaded by all of Josephine Estill's findings with regard to vocal function and I think the information that has been gained through Josephine Estill's lifetime of research is invaluable and has greatly added to our understanding of vocal function and of the ways in which a variety of sounds can be produced. However, I also believe that there may be many ways for the performer to approach physical/vocal development and that different individuals may benefit from one approach, others from another and, indeed, that many of us will be aided to develop through a multiplicity of approaches.

Acting is, fundamentally, a physical process. The actor needs to harness, and work through, all of their senses, and through their sensory experience. For actors, then, I think approaches that emphasize their physiological experience are helpful simply because this kind of work brings actors into their bodies and enables them, later, to embody the character they may have to play and the imagined world of the play they may have to inhabit. For this reason, I have found experiencing what appears to be resonance in different areas of the body – the vibrations that result from making sounds – can be tremendously useful and can help to unlock or develop resonant potential within the voice.

### Exploring 'chest' resonance

Place the palm of one hand on your breast bone in the centre of your chest, and place the back of the other hand on the centre of your back, ideally immediately behind the hand on the chest. Placing your hand on your upper back can be somewhat uncomfortable, depending on the flexibility of the musculature and joints of your arm, but do what you can manage.

On a low note, on the vowel 'Ah', touch off a sound. Make sure the note is comfortably low and, without pushing or overworking, make a full sound. Then, gently, allow your lips to meet – they are just meeting and not pressing – so that you are humming around the initial low note. Breathe whenever you find it necessary, but ensure that there is low belly release as breath touches down within you.

> You should find that your hands can sense quite a lot of vibration where they are resting, in the centre of your chest and back. You may find there seem to be more vibrations in one place than another. Explore how much you are able to relax as the breath drops in – can you allow a bit more low belly release in the transversus abdominus area, for example, or can you imagine breath dropping down to your pelvic floor? – and as you let go, more and more, deep within you, can you imagine that you can send the vibrations to those areas that seem to be resonating less?

Generally, most of you will find that you can sense some vibrations in the chest area when you are humming on a lowish note, though one or two individuals may find even this problematic. This simple exercise necessitates some deep relaxation within which will enable the vibrations of the sound to travel, and the key to this is allowing the breath to drop, as it were, to the pelvic floor, allowing the muscles from your naval to your pubic bone at the front to let go in order for the breath to drop in. When muscles are tense, tight or held, the potential vibration of sound in the body is inhibited, so relaxation is a key element in exploring resonance.

> ### Exploring oral resonance
>
> #### Stage 1
>
> Now allow your attention to move to the lower half of your face. Using the fingertips of both hands, find the jaw joint – the place, just below your earlobes, where the lower jaw is connected to the upper jaw on either side – and, utilizing tiny circular movements in your fingertips, gently massage the muscles around the jaw joint.

(When preparing to undertake articulation exercises, traditionally, work is first focused on the jaw joint which then leads to the teacher asking you to stroke your lower jaw down and away from your upper jaw. First of all, I am not going to ask you to do that now, as our focus is on the potential vibrations of sound, but more to the point, this is not an exercise I will ever encourage you to undertake. The amount of space between the teeth and within the mouth that is possible and desirable varies from person to person and is dependent on our individual physiognomy – some sounds require more space within the mouth, other sounds less – what is key in your experience at the moment is being able to relax the musculature at the jaw joint that enables you to allow your lower jaw to relax away from your upper jaw.)

### Stage 2

As you are massaging the muscles around the jaw joint, take care not to tighten in the back of your neck. Remind yourself of the mantra, 'Let my neck be free to allow my head to move forwards and upwards', which will help you to keep your neck aligned and remind you not to fix your head. Then allow your lower jaw to begin to float down and away from your upper jaw. You are not looking for a large movement of the lower jaw, but when we are at ease in the jaw and the face, the lower jaw does, naturally, want to move down and away from the upper jaw, and a small space between the lips and the teeth is the result.

This natural space between the lips and the teeth is an important component for voice work and is also important for you as an actor. In life, when we are listening and engaged with what is being said to us – when we are genuinely interested in discourse – as we relax at the jaw joint, we naturally allow the mouth to open. It's almost as if we want to ingest what is being said to us. When we are children, we do this automatically and instinctively and, somewhere along the way as we are growing up, we are taught – perhaps by family, perhaps by a teacher or perhaps through being bullied by other children – that our mouths should be closed if we are not speaking. It used to be said, for instance, that a partly open mouth when listening looked 'stupid' or (in the North of England) 'gormless' and so most of us learn to keep our mouths closed. Learning to allow the lower face to be more at ease, then, and to allow that small space between the lips and front teeth when we are more relaxed is useful: it's part of the process of listening; it can assist with breathing; and this also means that we are ready if we need or want to speak.

### Stage 3

So, you have massaged the jaw joint and, hopefully, the lower jaw has moved slightly away from the upper jaw as it has relaxed. Gently massage the muscles in the cheeks and around the mouth, both above and below, and even the lips themselves. Then allow your hands to relax and the arms to hang in the usual way as you touch off a sound, on a comfortable note, on the neutral vowel ('Huh'). As you sustain this sound, gently allow your lips to touch as you try to keep the space between your front teeth so that the sound turns into a hum. Breathe when you need to and continue to touch off neutral vowels, turning them into a hum by gently allowing the lips to touch. With one or two finger tips, notice the vibrations of the sound are moving onto your lips – and you may also sense some vibrations happening in your teeth. The more relaxed you are in your face, the more you will

# The Integrated Actor

> sense these vibrations taking place. You can also change pitch on each new hum, if you wish – stay within a small range of notes around the middle of your vocal range, although you should find that any note will vibrate on your lips, whether lower or higher.

All of this vibration is a result of the resonance produced in the oral cavity which enhances the note made at vocal fold level.

> ### Exploring nasal and sinus resonance
>
> Now move your finger tips to the area on your face above the nasal sinuses. These are small channels that lie on either side of your nose. They can be tricky to find, but they are just below your eyes on either side. They are not very long, so if you massage here with your fingertips with an inward-outward movement of the fingers, starting gently, but then increasing the pressure (and you can apply quite a lot of pressure here), this will help to stimulate your awareness of this area. When you are ready, move to a slightly higher pitch (high mid-range) and touch off a neutral vowel, and as you sustain it, keeping your lips slightly apart if you can, bring your tongue tip up to your alveolar ridge to make a loose /n/ sound so that you end up with a string of sounds 'nuh-nuh-nuh-nuh-nuh', keeping the sounds made slowly and fairly loosely. You should be able to sense the vibrations arriving on the alveolar ridge, in the upper teeth, and in the nasal cavity and the sinuses. You may even sense some vibrations in the roof of your mouth (hard palate). Again, you can touch your lips and the area above your sinuses (just below your eyes on either side of your nose) with your fingertips to feel the vibrations here.

Simple though this exercise is, there's quite a lot that can go awry. If you have a cold or may have some form of allergic rhinitis, you may find this exercise will move the mucous in your nasal cavity and sinuses around – have a handkerchief nearby, though this exercise is possibly best avoided if you have a cold. When you make the /n/ sound, ensure that the back of your tongue is relaxed so that the consonant sound is just being made by the contact between the tongue tip and does not involve pressure in the root of the tongue, which should remain at ease. If you are pushing from the back of the tongue to enable the tongue tip to make the /n/ sound, you are overworking, and you will find the amount of resonance in this part of your face significantly reduced.

If the exercise is not working very well for you when you attempt an /n/ sound, then go back to humming on an /m/ sound as this sound can also vibrate in the sinus and nasal areas as well as in the oral cavity.

## Head sinuses

There are very small spaces within the skull, just above and between the eyebrows and within the top and front of the skull itself. It is a matter of debate as to whether these spaces significantly enhance the original note and whether they can contribute to the vibrations of sound, though it is my belief that they can and they do. Put simply, when a note is made by the vocal folds as they come together to vibrate the air, the note itself consists of a complex series of harmonics, some of which are the result of the sound passing into or through various spaces, such as the pharynx, the mouth and nasal cavities, and these harmonics enhance the original sound. If sound is able to move through the bones of the face and skull, then it may receive additional acoustic enhancement from within the sinus spaces of the head.

The shape and size of the spaces that the sound moves through – principally the pharynx, oral and nasal spaces – all contribute, through the resonance they supply, to the sound of the speaker/singer. Arguably, the chest cavity and the sinuses in the head can provide additional harmonics.

> ### Exploring head sinus resonance
>
> Tap gently and rapidly with the fingertips of both hands across your brow – this is the area immediately above your eyebrows. While you are rapidly tapping, make light and easy sounds on a fairly high note in your range – you can move into a falsetto sound if you wish – on 'me-me-me-me-me', 'nee-nee-nee-nee-nee', 'ninny-ninny-ninny-ninny-ninny'.
>
> You can vary the pitch, but be working towards the top of your range, keeping your head poised and neck long. You should sense the vibrations of sound moving into this area.

## Balance of resonance

When we are able to involve many of these spaces in resonating the sounds we make, then we achieve what I would call a balance of resonance. By this I mean that when we involve the whole of the voice, the sound we produce involves both upper and lower resonance and that, ideally, this resonance is balanced in such a way that neither upper nor lower resonance predominates. For instance, there are voices that could be said to 'boom' that seem the product of large amounts of lower resonance and, possibly, are also the result of a habitually lowered larynx. These kinds of voices can sound very impressive and can certainly, easily, fill a large space. Such a voice though tends to lack the clarity, or the brightness, that can be provided by involving the upper resonators – the mouth, the nasal cavity and the sinuses – and whilst a booming voice will carry well, the words spoken are often difficult to make out for the listener.

### The Integrated Actor

It may seem obvious to mention, at this point, that the main articulators for the sounds of English are in the mouth, and there are consonant sounds, in particular, that are made at the front of the mouth: /b/,/p/,/t/,/d/,/n/,/l/. (Not all the consonants of English are made here, of course, but a good many that are used in everyday speech frequently are.) It therefore follows that as sound is produced, it must meet these articulators on the way out and be shaped by them if the listener is to clearly understand the speaker. A voice that is predominantly 'bassy' then, that relies on pharyngeal and chest resonance, becomes difficult to understand when working in a larger space, hence the need for 'balance' in the use of resonators.

There are also voices that, through habitual muscular use, predominantly resonate in the mouth and face – voices that rely more on oral, nasal and sinus resonance. These carry very well in larger spaces, and the speech of these voice users is often easy to understand. Many listeners will describe such voices as 'clear' and 'bright'. When speaking, these kinds of voices can sound oddly disconnected from the speaker's feelings and, indeed, from their bodies and, from an acting perspective, audiences can find this difficult to relate to. It's a generalization, but one with some truth at the heart of it, that when a speaker's voice sounds relaxed, embodied and connected to their emotional life, the listener tends to feel more comfortable and consider the speaker more trustworthy or believable.

Balanced resonance, then, is about more than just the qualities of the sound the actor makes. When a voice is well balanced, it has a warmth as well as an expressivity that makes the listener feel comfortable and convinces them that the speaker is connected to their feelings and is, somehow, trustworthy. These are tremendously useful assets for an actor.

### Summary

In an ideal world, then, a voice that combines so-called chest and head resonance within its resonant mix is one that will communicate well, both in terms of the sound itself which can potentially move into and inhabit a space easily, and in terms of the thoughts and feelings that the speaker intends to express and communicate.

The balance of resonance from speaker to speaker (or singer to singer) will vary and is dependent on physiognomy, for instance the length of the vocal folds, the size and shape of the various cavities within the torso, the pharynx and the head, and habitual muscular use within the muscles of the vocal tract and postures in the tongue which, in turn, may be at least partly influenced by the accent in which the individual usually speaks.

*An exercise to encourage a balance of resonance*

This exercise is best explored with a partner, although there are adaptations of this exercise that you can do on your own if this is preferred.

### Stage 1

One partner should lie face down on the floor: the head can rest on the arms which are folded beneath it. It is best if the face is facing the floor with the forehead resting on the hands or arms, but if this is uncomfortable for you, the head can be turned so that you are facing to the left or the right. (If turning the head to one side is preferred, aim to keep the neck long – turn from the head and not the chin.) The person who is lying face-down should have their legs apart and their feet either in parallel – the ideal position – or, if this is uncomfortable, the feet can be turned out: it's a matter of finding a position that is comfortable for you as part of the way in which this exercise works is that you should be as relaxed as possible bearing in mind that muscular ease and relaxation will facilitate the vibrations of sound.

Before anything else occurs, the person lying on the ground should get in touch with an easy and natural breath. As breath drops in, some release in the muscles in the lower belly should be experienced – you may feel your lower back rise away from the floor, or the tail of the spine seem to lengthen in the direction of your heels, or you may feel your lower belly gently moving against the floor, as your breath drops in. You might also experience some movement in the bottom of your ribs or back ribs. Enjoy exploring this relationship between your body and the floor as breath drops in and out of you. (It might be helpful for your partner to place the palms of their hands gently on the lower back ribs, to encourage breath to move them.)

Once you are comfortable and ready, touch off a hum on a comfortable low note. Let breath replace, as required, but continue humming sustained notes to the end of each breath. You may notice some vibrations shared between your chest and the floor and possibly even between your hips or shoulders and the floor, but for the purposes of this exercise, focus your attention on the area of your back.

### Stage 2

Throughout the exercises that follow, aim to maintain a sense of ease in the tongue when you are humming. The tip of the tongue should be resting against the back of the bottom teeth and the tongue should not be unduly tense – for instance, the sides of the tongue should also be resting against the lower teeth on either side of your mouth: if there is any tension or holding in the tongue, this may not be the case.

As the exercise proceeds, you will be engaged with sustaining a constant, easy and loose hum, imagining the potential of the vibrations of the hum to travel to different parts of your body. It is not a rule, but you may find it easier to imagine the potential for this if you close your eyes, but by all means, keep your eyes open if you prefer. It is whatever you are most comfortable with and find easiest in order to facilitate the exercise.

### Stage 3

Once the humming is established, your partner, with relaxed wrists and hands, can commence patting the centre of your upper back, between your shoulder blades, with alternate hand taps. The partner humming can now focus the vibrations of the sound they are making to the place where your partner's hands are tapping or patting. For those of you tapping, it is important that your wrists and fingers are relaxed – you are not trying to cause discomfort to your partner: the tapping of your hands is meant to help them relax muscles in the area where you are working and also to help to provide a focus to which they can send the vibrations of their sound.

Partners who are tapping, you will probably sense when the vibrations begin to meet the area where your hands are working – gradually begin to spread the tapping outwards on either side of the centre of the upper back, eventually including the shoulders on both sides. Keep moving your hands across the upper back and include the shoulder blades as well as the shoulders, and also include the area across the centre of the back, below the shoulder blades.

The one who is humming and the one who is working with their hands should both find that they can sense that the vibrations seem, eventually, to fill the area of the upper back.

### Stage 4

The partner who is tapping with their hands should now move their hands, constantly tapping with relaxed wrists and fingers, to the area of the lower back. There are some major organs underneath this area, so be sensitive and, perhaps, ease off the effort of the tapping so that you are still working here with your hands but without using too much pressure.

The humming partner should now try to focus their attention on the area where the hands are working, in the lower back, and imagine that the sound can travel down into this area. The more you are able to relax deeply within – particularly in the area of the lower belly muscles (transversus abdominus) – the more likely you are to start to feel vibrations being able to move into this lower back area.

> As you are patting, gradually move your hands from side to side across the lower back and, also, include the area of the lower back ribs, working on the left and the right-hand sides of the lower ribcage.

Those of you who are humming may find it difficult to imagine sound in your lower back or may find it difficult to sense vibrations here. If you keep relaxing deeply in the lower abdominal area when the breath drops in and focus your imagination on the lower back area, gradually you will begin to feel that there is the potential to vibrate sound here.

> **Stage 5**
>
> Eventually, the partner who is tapping or patting should move their hands anywhere and everywhere up and down, and across, the back – keeping their taps quick and light by ensuring that wrists and fingers remain relaxed at all times. The hummer should imagine that vibrations can travel anywhere and everywhere within the area of the back of their body.
> The partner who is tapping should now relax and remove their hands from their partner while they continue to hum, allowing breath to drop in whenever necessary, imagining and sensing the potential for the vibrations of sound to travel throughout the area of your back. After, perhaps, a minute of vibrating sounds on your own, relax on the sound and continue to allow breath to drop in and drop out of you, maintaining that sense of low belly release.
>
> **Stage 6**
>
> The partner lying down should now roll onto their back so that they are looking up at the ceiling. There are several things you can do at this point to ensure that you are comfortable as you lie on the floor. Some of you may wish to draw your knees up, keeping the soles of the feet in contact with the floor, so that you are in the familiar semi-supine position and can sense strong contact between your back and the floor. Some of you may wish to place your hands behind the base of your skull to support your head and make a cradle for it. Some of you may do both, or simply prefer to lie with your legs down and your arms relaxing somewhere by your sides: aim to find a position that is the most comfortable for you.
> When you are ready, once again touch off breath into sound on a neutral vowel, gently bringing your lips together to turn the sound into a hum whilst you keep your jaw joint easy and a sense that the lower jaw wants to move down and away from the upper jaw, even though you are gently bringing the lips together.

> Before your partner starts to work on you with their hands again, imagine the sensations of being able to send the vibrations of the sound you are making into your lower and upper back and share them between your back and the floor. You may also be able to sense the area of the floor beneath you and around you vibrating in sympathy with the sound, particularly if you are lying on a wooden floor.
>
> The partner who has been tapping or patting should now place their hands in the area of the centre of the upper chest, immediately below the clavicle, and start to tap gently here. The one who is humming should focus the potential of the vibrations of the sound into this area, as their partner taps. Gradually, the tapping hands can move across the area of the upper chest, eventually including both shoulders. Those of you who are humming should imagine that sounds can travel wherever the hands are working in your upper chest/shoulder area.
>
> The hands can be moved down to the side ribs – probably the ribs opposite to where you are kneeling by your partner are the easiest to tap first. Again, the one who is humming should imagine the potential for vibrations here. Spend some time working on this side, and then move around your partner's body to tap the ribs on the other side. Eventually, the partner who is tapping should tap ribs, upper chest and shoulders. Moving their hands around these areas of the upper body, while the one who is humming should be attempting to send the vibrations of the sound they are making into any and all of these areas simultaneously. Those of you who are humming, remember that the more you are able to allow yourself to relax deeply so that the incoming breath can drop in, the more likely you are to be able to experience the sense of the sound being vibrated within the upper torso.

This work can obviously feel very personal to both participants. I will talk more about this in a moment. It is essential that the person tapping is sensitive to where they place their hands and in the way they move their hands, and thoughtful about the nature of the contact that is made with the body of their partner. I have been very specific in the instructions above as to where hands should be placed, for instance – touching the breasts is to be avoided, for obvious reasons, and tapping or patting around the stomach area or the buttocks is also not desirable – working with your hands here is not likely to produce any kind of a result, in terms of resonance, and many individuals will find someone touching the abdominal area uncomfortable.

It is probably desirable to initiate a conversation between partners as to the kind of contact they may feel comfortable with and what each person will consent to. Simple as they are, these kinds of exercises require a maturity of approach that then means that the exercises can be of benefit to both partners who will be able to work together with a sense of mutual trust.

### Stage 7

To complete the sequence, the partners who have been tapping should now move their hands to their partner's forehead and, using only their fingertips, should lightly tap across the brow – this is a bit like creating the sensation of raindrops falling on this part of the head. The humming partner should now imagine the potential for sound to travel here as they hum. The fingertips can then work across the forehead and up into the front of the skull, and into the part of the skull just above the ears on either side.

The fingertips can then be moved to the bones of the upper face around the eyes – it is perhaps wisest to avoid the eyelids themselves if your partner has their eyes closed – and below the eyes to the cheekbones. Then the fingertips can lightly tap around the bones of the jaw on either side, and the area above and below the lips, and on the chin. Eventually, the fingertips can be tapping, sensitively, all around the face and the front, and even the top, of the skull.

### Stage 8

Finally, the partner who is tapping should alternate working with fingertips on the head and face area, and then with relaxed wrists and hands on the areas of the upper chest, shoulders and side ribs, moving their hands quite rapidly from one area to another whilst the humming partner should imagine the vibrations of the sound they are making being able to travel anywhere and everywhere that their partner's hands are working, also remembering the potential for sound to vibrate between the lower and upper back and the floor.

The partner who has been tapping and patting should now remove their hands from their partner whilst they continue to hum, imagining the vibrations being able to exist in all the areas that their partner has stimulated simultaneously. From time to time, release the hum into a small vowel and then gently allow the lips to re-touch. You may notice how, as the sound is released on a vowel, you lose the sense of vibration within the body or the face, but the sensations will return when the lips are touching. Keep reminding yourself, as you hum, that vibrations can live in your lower back area, as well as in your head and face, and remember that the more you are able to relax to achieve a low belly release when the breath drops in, the more likely you are to sense vibrations within your body as you make the sound.

Trying not to bring back any undue tension within your body, now transfer your body from the semi-supine position on the floor to standing. Really take your time with this, taking time in each position to continue to hum and to explore the potential for vibrations in our body, head and face as you do so. As with previous exercises, you should find it easiest as you transfer yourself to standing to roll onto your left or right side first, rolling into a semi-foetal position. Then bring yourself onto your hands and knees with a flat back, supporting your head so that your face is parallel to the floor and, from here, into standing. Once standing, ensure you feel grounded through the soles of your feet and tail of your spine, that your knees are easy and not locked, that you are still accessing that sense of low belly release, and that allowing your head to float forwards and upwards as you allow your neck to be free assists your spine in releasing into length. Throughout this process, you are allowing the breath to drop in and touching the breath off into a hum or into little vowels.

Once standing and aligned, maintaining the freedom in your neck and the poise of your head, speak a text that you know – remember that once you start to speak you are owning the thoughts and meaning the words you speak, not simply intoning words for the sake of an exercise – and as you work your way through speaking the thoughts within the text, notice if anything has shifted within the way you sound or within the way you may feel physically engaged when you are speaking.

## Some thoughts about working with partners

Some individuals can feel uncomfortable with the nature of the physical contact that the resonance exercises, described above, require. For a variety of reasons, there has been a social shift in the nature of the personal contact some of us can allow or feel comfortable with. I would always advocate for the kind of physical contact and exchange required by the exercises above – particularly for those who are, or intend to become, actors. Physical contact is a necessary part of the work. However, acting by its very nature does require the actor to be at ease and relaxed, so any kind of activity that renders the actor uncomfortable or makes them tense is counterproductive, so if anyone is uncomfortable with any aspect of the partner work described above, then they should not be required to participate in it.

I would like to say, though, that touch is a very human kind of contact and a natural part of everyday human experience. We can communicate through touch, and it is traditionally acknowledged in a wide range of cultures that touch, itself, can be healing. If you are open to partner work, you should be aware of this and conscious that when you place your hands on someone else, you should do so with awareness and sensitivity. You should also recognize that whilst touch is, essentially, an intimate kind of gesture, there are professional boundaries that must be respected. I think if everyone involved in this kind of work is responsible and aware, then the environment in which we work will feel safe. I accept, of course, that there is also a huge element of trust involved here, but would simply say that acting, and the work of the actor, is all about trust, at the most fundamental level.

As indicated above, I think a conversation around the theme of consent would be advisable, inculcate a sense of trust, and would be helpful to everyone involved.

## Adaptation of the resonance exercise

If you are interested to know how the above resonance work can be adapted so that it is not reliant on working with a partner, here is a brief description of the kind of adaptations possible if you wish to undertake this kind of work on your own.

### Stage 1

If you are working on the floor, either laying on your front or on your back – wooden flooring is the best surface. As you start to hum, focus on sending the sound to different areas within your body and on sending vibrations from that area into the floor. So, for instance, if you are lying on your back, imagine that you are allowing the vibrations of sound to travel into your sacrum and lower back – working in semi-supine will probably facilitate this – and imagine vibrations travelling out of the bones of your lower back into the floor. Imagine you can make the floor beneath you vibrate.

If you are facing the floor, explore the potential to share vibrations between your hip bones, your chest, your face and the floor. You can focus on these areas individually at first and then see if you can imagine the vibrations of sound travelling to all those areas simultaneously.

### Stage 2

You can also conduct these exercises with your back against a wall. To do this, your feet will be a small distance away from the wall and your knees slightly bent; you should not place the back of your head against the wall as this will take your neck out of its natural alignment.

In standing (or lying), you can stimulate an awareness of the potential vibrations of sound by gently tapping or patting with your hands (wrists relaxed) on your breastbone and across the bones in your upper chest. You can use relaxed (soft) fists to do this, or your palms – whatever you feel most comfortable with. Whilst you are patting or tapping with your hands, hum and send the vibrations to the area where your hands are working, occasionally releasing little vowels as you allow your lips to slightly part before returning to a hum by gently allowing the lips to make contact with each other again. You will probably find comfortable, lower notes useful for experiencing these vibrations.

### Stage 3

Taking your attention to your face, placing a couple of fingertips of each hand on either side of your nose, gently massage the skin and muscles above your nasal sinuses – ideally, the musculature here should feel quite loose as your fingertips work around that area. While you are conducting this massage work, your tongue is relaxed within your mouth – the tip and the front edge of the tongue resting against the back of the bottom teeth. You can spread the fingertip massage out to include the cheeks and the musculature around the lips, and the skin and muscles covering the jaw. You can start humming, on a comfortable mid-register pitch, while you are massaging, or wait until you have completed the massage. When you hum, remember that there is a sense that the lower jaw wants to float down and away from the upper jaw, even though your lips will be lightly touching. If you moisten your lips, this may increase the sense of vibrations that arrive there as you hum. While you are humming, wrinkle the bridge of your nose – as if you are moving imaginary spectacles up the bridge of your nose. This will affect your lips, too, but continue to hum as you articulate these groups of muscles. You will probably find the sound moving to these areas naturally and feel as if the vibrations of the sound increase as you exercise.

You can also take the fingertips of your hands to your brow, forehead and the top of your skull, tapping with your fingertips to create a feeling of raindrops pattering on those areas. Again, hum while you are doing this, imagining the vibrations travelling to your brow, forehead and skull – to those areas where your fingertips are pattering. Spend time with your fingertips in each area before you then try to allow the sound to travel to all of those areas simultaneously. You should always feel comfortable as you make the sound – easy at the jaw joint with the tongue relaxed within your mouth – and there should be no sense of pushing. When you are working on your head, you may find it useful to move up in pitch in order to increase the sense of vibrations here, but if you do decide to raise your pitch, remain comfortable and at ease as you make the sound, and don't lift the chin or shorten the neck.

As in the partnership version of this exercise, once you have worked all of the areas of potential resonance within your body and your face, speak a text that you know, noticing if anything has shifted or feels different within your body or your voice.

## Quick resonance checks

Later, when you are already in touch with your body and your voice, if the focus of your work is on the interpretation of text or on some other aspect of acting, but you are using your voice, there are some quick ways to stimulate resonant potential in your voice.

### Exercise for body resonance

Place the palm of one hand in the centre of your chest and the back of your other hand immediately behind it (or as close as you can get) on your back. Speak and think of sending the vibrations of the sound to both of your hands simultaneously, i.e. to your chest and to your upper back.

### Exercise for face and head resonance

Place the palms of both hands, slightly cupped, on either side of your face – covering your eyes, with fingertips resting just above your eyebrows and the heel of each hand resting just below your bottom lip and/or on your chin. Hum, or speak, and imagine sending all the vibrations of the sound to your hands.

With all of the above, simple exercises, whenever the breath drops in, it is a low breath with a small amount of low belly release.

### Exercise for lower resonance

The next exercise is helpful if you are experiencing difficulty accessing what is sometimes referred to as 'lower resonance', i.e. vibrations in relation to the sound being made that seem to take place in the chest, ribs and back.

#### Stage 1

Starting from a grounded and aligned position, with feet under hips and knees (as always easy), allow your head to tip back on the top two vertebrae of your neck spine. This is quite a tricky manoeuvre as some individuals will allow their neck to collapse as they let the head fall back – this is counterproductive as it will result in the vocal tract being compromised, apart from the fact that it is not a healthy position for your neck to assume. Essentially, then, the neck is supported, with the exception of the top two vertebrae of the neck spine and, as the head tips back, allow the jaw to fall open.

You should now feel as if you have an open space – rather like a wide tube, a chimney or a stove-pipe – that starts as a space between your teeth, includes the oral cavity, the pharyngeal cavity, down into your chest cavity. With your head in this position, first of all, breathe through this channel. Imagine that this wide-open tube goes right down into your centre. As you allow the cooler air outside you to travel down into your centre, sense it painting the sides of this wide-open space as the air travels down and, as the air travels back out when it falls out of you, imagine that the tube remains completely open as the air, warmed by your body, travels through the channel, out through your mouth and the space between your teeth.

## Stage 2

Maintaining this position, on an outbreath, touch off a low, warm sound from centre on 'Ah-ah-ah' and allow it to travel up and out through 'the tube' in the same kind of way that you allowed the breath to travel through when it made its way out of your body: feel as if 'the tube' remains completely open throughout its length whilst sound is being made.

As you sustain the sound – allowing breath to drop in and replace whenever it needs to – gradually realign the head and neck whilst you are making sound. Your aim is to maintain the sense of width and openness within the 'stove-pipe' through which the sound is travelling, but as you bring your head back to the balanced and poised position it normally assumes, you will feel the 'tube' or 'stove-pipe' changing shape: it remains open, but it changes shape.

As a result of this exercise, you should find that you are making a well-resonated, full sound that falls out from the centre of you and seems to involve your body as you make it. When your head is falling back, as you allow the top two vertebrae of your neck to facilitate that adjustment, and as you make a full, low, 'Ah' sound, you should find it easy to sense your chest and upper back vibrating. As you bring your head slowly back to the upright, poised position on the top of the neck, keeping the channel for sound open, you may sense that the sound seems to move forward, travelling freely through the space within the vocal tract and out through your mouth.

## Stage 3

Maintaining a sense of openness in the vocal tract, now speak some text that you know. You will, hopefully, find that you are making a fairly full, more embodied sound as you speak that also feels as if it is moving forward.

If it seems to you that the sound is, in some way, swallowed or that it remains centred in the area of your chest or pharynx, you may have created some tension in your tongue or tongue root while you were exercising. Try shaking the tongue loose, and massaging the tongue root, then drop your head onto your chest – really allow the head to fall and the neck to be completely released – and speak long, 'Hee' sounds on a comfortable low note. You should have some awareness of this sound arriving in the front of your mouth and even stimulating vibrations on your teeth as you make it. Keep repeating the 'Hee' sound as you bring your head back to the poised, aligned position and, again, move into speaking the words that you know. You will, hopefully, now have a voice that is well-resonated and find that you are speaking with a good degree of clarity.

## Resonance and accent – full, free, forward

My former colleague, Sally Grace, an inspirational voice teacher and acting coach, always used to say that the voice should be full, free and forward, and I still think that these three concepts can offer some useful stimuli when we think about the voice as a communicative tool. The words are, perhaps, self-explanatory and many of the exercises explored thus far in this book focus on what we might mean by 'full' – the vocal folds meeting firmly and being vibrated by the breath efficiently whilst a balance of resonance is achieved – and what we might mean by 'free' which is a vocal response to physical freedom in the body and an ability to work with the voice without constricting or accessing unnecessary tension.

I'd like to spend some time considering what Sally might have meant when she used the word 'forward' in relation to the sound we can produce. This is, perhaps, quite an old-fashioned concept and it comes out of a time when it was generally believed that a voice that could communicate well was 'placed'. Placement is not, I think, a helpful concept in relation to vocal use today as it essentially comes from a time when there was an expectation that clear speaking relied on the speaker accessing the accent that has been known variously as Received Pronunciation (RP), Standard English and, more recently, as Southern Standard British. The resonant placement of this accent is, essentially, 'forward', that is to say, there is a sense that, whilst some chest resonance may be present, the sounds of this accent resonate mainly in the oral cavity, and in the nasal and sinus cavities, all in the front of the body and face. These qualities of resonance carry very well in a larger space, such as a theatre auditorium, and so for many years it was felt that this was a model that needed to be embraced.

In the early years of my life, I recall that every voice user on the BBC, whether an announcer, continuity person, presenter, children's entertainer or actor, spoke in the accent of RP. I also recall in 1960, when *Coronation Street* hit the small screen in homes across the UK, how shocking it was to hear characters who spoke entirely in Mancunian (and sometimes Lancastrian) accents. I was born and grew up in Lancashire, so it should not have been shocking to me since I was surrounded by people speaking in a whole range of Northern accents of English. Nonetheless, I still found it shocking because I had been groomed to consider that the appropriate accent for broadcast was RP.

We now expect to hear every accent of English represented in our entertainment, in theatre, film and television, as in our daily lives. Different accents of English favour a wide range of set-ups in terms of where the accent may sit, physically, within the speaker and where the balance of resonance within the voice may be focused. This has long been acknowledged by those who work with accents and, if you wish to understand more about how to access a range of accents in English, the books of Jan Haydn Rowles and Edda Sharpe will offer you detailed and specific insights into this.

I would not today advocate for a move towards embracing RP as a necessary accent, although for an actor, it is, arguably, still a useful accent for those plays that may need it. However, few contemporary dramas are written for speakers of this accent, and almost every drama we see on television now is located in a particular region of the UK and features the accents from that particular area.

However, I would like to suggest this – that whatever accent of English an actor is working in within a film, television or stage drama, we should be able, essentially, to understand them when they speak. This means, then, that there may need to be some adjustments in terms of physical/vocal use within an accent in order to communicate within the accent more efficiently.

Each accent of English has its own balance of resonance and I would suggest that if we address that balance, maintaining the essential resonant qualities inherent in the accent but also ensuring that there is a degree of oral and head resonance also added to the mix, that the sound the speaker makes will travel into the space, or to the microphone, more effectively.

Most conservatoire-based acting programmes now include many hours of work on ways of acquiring different accents of English which attests to the demand now for actors to be able to work in a range of accents. Interestingly, though, it is frequently the case that if a specific accent is required for a particular character, or the location of a drama, a director will choose an actor who is a native speaker of that accent. The exception to this is when an actor is engaged because they are well known and already have a following – they are not a native speaker of the required accent, but they will work with an accent coach to acquire it – so it is arguable that today an acting student doesn't need to spend so many hours of training on accent skills. The likelihood is that, for most actors, these skills will not be called upon, but fluency and the ability to communicate clearly in your own native accent will be a definite advantage.

When working in your own accent, be aware that your accent has a particular resonant placement which is a part of the characteristics that define your accent and give it its particular character. You should not in any way aim to lose the natural character of your accent, but you may find, if you undertake the resonance exercises described above, that you achieve a different balance of resonance as a result of the work, and this may help your voice to communicate more effectively within a larger space. Perhaps the best way of thinking about this work is that it does not require you to take anything away from your intrinsic vocal identity, but that exercising may add something to it.

# CHAPTER 18
# RANGE, PITCH AND STRESS

Pitch and variety of pitches are important elements within spoken English. Pitch helps the speaker to communicate a number of things – principally, the sense of what is being said and the kind of emotions that we wish to express.

We have already looked much earlier in this book at the notion of 'optimum pitch' – the place in your voice where your vocal folds can produce sound with a minimum amount of effort and the place in your range where your voice sits most comfortably. Whilst this small range of optimal notes should be at the centre of our vocal usage, if we were to allow ourselves – and some people do – to speak only around these three or four notes in our range, our voice would sound somewhat inexpressive and, potentially, boring. Arguably, we would not be communicating very well.

One of the main uses of pitch in everyday speech is for stress or emphasis. A discussion about this aspect of pitch might more properly sit within a section on language, which I deal with later in this book, but it is worth touching on the fact here that one of the key ways in which we communicate in spoken English is through stress – English is a language of connected speech and it is through stressing particular syllables that sense is, principally, conveyed – and one of the ways in which stress is given to a syllable is through placing the syllable on a different pitch.

There are other ways in which syllabic stress can be conveyed, such as vowel length (i.e. extending the vowel in the syllable) and vocal weight, and you might find it useful at this point to experiment with the ways sense and feeling can be conveyed in a simple sentence. Take the sentences below.

> Will you be going tonight? See you there.
> I don't feel well, and I'd rather not go.
>
> If you speak these simply and economically, you will place stress on the words 'going' and 'there', and then 'well' and 'go'. There is no particularly right or wrong way to stress these syllables (which are also words), but the likelihood is that you will slightly change your pitch when you arrive on these two words and, probably, give them a little bit more vocal weight.

When I am working with actors on text, especially in the early stages of exploring something, I am very keen on the actor finding the simplest and most economical way to communicate the spoken thought. This will give us the simple sense of the words we speak – if you like, help us communicate the fact of what we have to say. This is

### The Integrated Actor

particularly useful if we do not really know the context in which we are speaking or our relationship with the other character or characters to whom we speak.

> You can now try speaking the sentences above and vary where you place the emphasis. I would suggest that you don't get too self-conscious about this and, consciously, manipulate your voice – this kind of work simply leads you, as an actor, to become external, always something to be avoided – but that you imagine the different contexts in which you might need to say this thought.

For instance, you might emphasize the word 'Will', in the first sentence, or 'feel' in the second sentence in a certain context. In another context, you might equally emphasize the two words, 'not go'. (You can try emphasizing 'not' and not emphasizing 'go' – I think you'll find this doesn't actually communicate very much. Actors often like to make the choice to emphasize the negative and, in fact, this rarely makes sense. This is for the simple reason that it is the verb – in this case 'go' – that conveys the sense of the thought, so if we undervalue the verb, the spoken thought does not work.)

The key thing with this exercise is to try a range of different emphases within the thought and to notice how you communicate these changes or nuances, vocally, within the spoken thought. One of your choices will have been pitch.

### Range

In an expressive voice, the speaker usually accesses a fairly wide range of notes, though this is dependent on the nature of the context in which they are speaking: if you are extremely excited or in a highly emotional state, then it is likely that you will access notes that you do not normally visit in casual, everyday speaking.

Opening up your range really needs to be part of the natural, expressive way in which you speak. By this I mean that you probably can't be too self-conscious about the range of notes you access when you speak because this will communicate to the listener as artificial or, essentially, untruthful because your attention is on the way you sound and not upon what you say or what you wish to communicate.

The optimum pitch should always be at the centre of your voice – remember that we usually start a spoken thought around our optimum pitch, move away from it during the course of what we have to say and then, as we come to the end of what we wish to communicate, we usually return to it. However, in some dramatic texts, characters can be in a heightened emotional state for extended periods. This is often true in a classical play – a play by William Shakespeare or any of his contemporaries, for instance, or a Greek tragedy – but can also be true in a highly charged contemporary drama. When we become excited, we rarely stay centred around our optimum pitch, so in sustained, highly charged or emotional work, it is very important that the actor can access their voice with both freedom and the appropriate physical support that highly charged acting demands.

Exercises to access a range of notes in your voice or to sustain vocal freedom when we are distressed or excited are, essentially, technical. I do not think, when you are acting, that you should ever have a self-conscious awareness of employing your technique. This will seem to the audience artificial or simply technical and will get in the way of their ability to believe in you or the situation you are meant to inhabit. However, if you undertake some technical exercise when working on your body and your voice on a regular basis, then musculature will be primed to respond, healthily and expressively, when you inhabit a scene that necessitates intense and sustained emotional work requiring an extended use of vocal expression.

### Simple exercise to begin to access range

First of all, if you find any of the exercises described below problematic, you will probably find that if you revisit the exercises on resonance, these will help you to open up your range.

#### Exercise to start to access range

#### Stage 1

Take a monologue – it may be helpful if it is something that you are already working on but which you don't yet know by heart, but a monologue you already know can also be useful material – and, after some physical and vocal preparation, begin to speak it in a relaxed and comfortable way. Whenever you start a new thought, allow the thought to drop in with the breath in the usual way, but speak each new thought by starting on a different note.

This is a somewhat technical way of approaching the speaking of a monologue, and, as I say above, you will not think of doing this, consciously, when you are acting it. However, in life, when we speak a new thought we do, usually, access a new or different note in our voice, so whilst this exercise may feel to you somewhat external, it is, in fact, awakening you to something that should be happening organically.

#### Stage 2

Work through the entire speech in this way, even if you are uncomfortable with this as a process, and then go back and speak the speech again, not consciously aiming to play with pitch and range, and see if anything has shifted in it as a result of the exercise. You may find this difficult – to speak the speech spontaneously and yet be simultaneously aware of what is happening within your voice, and if this is the case, by all means record yourself and then play the recording back. You should find that some possibilities have opened up within your speaking of the speech as a result of the previous rather technical exercise.

### Simple exercises to extend range

One of the best exercises, both to extend your range and to warm up your voice, is the siren. If you are familiar with the work of Estill Voice Craft and the research of Josephine Estill, then you will already know this exercise.

### Extending range

#### Stage 1

Say the word 'sing' and notice the place where your tongue meets your soft palate on the 'ng' consonant at the end of this word. Using as little breath pressure as possible and without wishing to make the siren in any way loud, begin to exercise on 'ng' around your optimum pitch. You are making a sustained sound, a bit like a hum, but with your soft palate and tongue touching instead of your lips. As you make the sustained 'ng' sound move up and down in your range – just a small range of notes to begin with, and then, gradually, widen the range of notes that your voice is moving through. The breath pressure must always remain light – you can in fact perform a siren with very little air, and it is useful to practice it this way – and you are not attempting to be loud in any way. Eventually, as you siren through a wider and wider range of notes, you should find that you are exercising through a very good range, from high to low.

#### Stage 2

You can also start your siren, lightly, on the highest note you can imagine (and a falsetto note is absolutely fine) and then, gently and slowly glide down through your range on the 'ng' sound until you arrive at the very lowest note you can make. As you do this, your voice will move through a number of different qualities, and you may find that you go through several 'breaks' in the sound. To begin with, this is absolutely fine – accept the breaks and notice where they are – but you can then use the sirening exercise to smooth out those areas in your vocal range where the breaks seem to occur. Everyone will have at least one break which usually occurs between what we used to call the 'head' and the 'chest' voices, but some people will experience more than one break.

To exercise muscularly in order to smooth out these 'breaks', as you are sirening and you know you are approaching the place in your voice where the break is likely to occur, ease off the breath pressure as you approach and move more slowly through the siren around the break. If you practice this, giving it due attention, time and care, you should find that you can move through the 'break' without there being a discernible 'clunk' or tonal shift.

In terms of developing access to your range, it is useful to exercise with a siren gliding from your highest note to your lowest note, and also from the lowest note to the highest. Just be aware that at either end of the scale, you do not want to force, push or use undue amounts of air pressure to make the note work. The efficiency of your siren is, essentially, produced by essential muscular activity and not by taking more air or increasing breath pressure, so always maintain a gentle air pressure and don't attempt to solve what you perceive to be a vocal issue by taking more air: this will not help and may create more problems for you.

## Chanting

For sustained vocal activity when working with an extended range, a chanting exercise can be helpful.

### Chanting exercise

### Stage 1

Taking a text that you know that perhaps requires a heightened emotional life or a level of intensity or excitement, chant the first line (or the first thought) on one note. Start this on a comfortable note, extending the vowels and not worrying too much about the consonants – produce a long, sustained stream of sound, which is the first thought, chanting on one note. Then take the next thought, choose another note and chant the next thought on the new note. With each new thought, choose a different note to start the thought on. At this stage, don't worry too much about the consonants; let them be quite loose so that you can keep as relaxed as possible.

## The Integrated Actor

When working higher in your range, maintain the relationship between your head and your neck, i.e. keep length in your neck and do not allow your chin to lift. Higher notes require your larynx to rise within the vocal tract – when you lift your chin as you approach a high note, you compromise the free, flexible movement of the larynx within the vocal tract and make it more difficult for it to rise. At the same time, there is some shutting down within the pharyngeal resonator and, potentially, at the back of the oral cavity, and this, too, will restrict the sound.

### Stage 2

For this exercise, your aim is to maintain the fullness of resonance as you move up and down within your range, so avoid moving into falsetto at the top of your range. As you chant a thought on one note, feel as if you are 'throwing the sound away'. When moving to a higher note, if you start to feel uncomfortable at any point, pause and restart on a slightly lower note. Similarly, if, when working on a low note, the sound is 'gravelly' and, again, feels uncomfortable in any way, you have gone to a note where your voice is not yet comfortable so pause, and then restart on a slightly higher note.

Over time, as you continue to exercise regularly, you will find that it is possible to extend both the lower and upper ends of your vocal range. As you move higher in your range, you will probably need to engage your support system in order to maintain freedom within your vocal tract – and freedom in the sound itself. As you move lower in the range, you may need to relax more deeply as the breath drops in, so that you can access some of the lowest notes possible within your vocal range.

### Stage 3

Once you have exercised with chanting fairly thoroughly, return to speaking the text. Remember that when you speak a text, you are never just reciting it – you are aiming to speak living thoughts, so that your imagination and inner emotional life should be engaged as you speak the thoughts within the text. You may wish to record this, or you may be able to be aware, in the moment, as to whether anything within your voice has changed. Hopefully, you may find that you are accessing a wider range of notes and that your voice is full and may be more expressive.

# CHAPTER 19
# THE CHANNEL FOR SOUND

What I am calling the channel for sound is, essentially, the area immediately above the vocal folds in the vocal tract – the pharynx – and the back and front of the oral cavity. When wishing to produce a full, free sound, essentially the channel for sound needs to be an open space. This is a rather big generalization – in fact, the pharynx and the space in the oral cavity change shape as you speak and as you move up and down within your vocal range but, essentially, when we speak or sing vowel sounds, some space within the vocal tract is necessary.

When we speak or sing I do not believe that it is particularly useful to be overly aware of the space that is being created, but I do think it is important to sense whether the space through which the sound is travelling is free. For this reason, it can be useful to exercise particular vowel shapes and appreciate the nature of the space when more open vowels (e.g. 'AH' as in SPA) are being made and when more close vowels are being made (e.g. 'EE' as in FREE). However, I do not want to focus on vowel shapes at this point in your journey through this book but I would like to focus on sensing when the vocal tract is free or open.

There are a number of aspects to be aware of in relation to the freedom of the sound:

Constriction/Retraction
Tongue Root Tension
The Soft Palate

## Constriction

Constriction can manifest in a number of different ways, but the most usual sort of constriction occurs when the false vocal folds attempt to assist the true vocal folds to make sound. In order for a sound to be made freely, the true vocal folds come together lightly but firmly while the breath moves through them in an even and sustained way. The movement of the breath through the vocal folds makes them vibrate and this vocal fold activity produces the sound we hear. In some voice users, the false vocal folds – two muscular flaps that sit just above the vocal folds in the vocal tract (and which are not, in fact, vocal folds at all) – bear down upon the true vocal folds, as if to assist them. This results in a sound that is 'squeezed' or compromised in some other way and, in more extreme cases, the sound can be rasping or can just cut out. Constriction is one of the main contributors to voice loss and to the development of pathological vocal conditions, such as nodules, so it is clearly something to be avoided.

### The Integrated Actor

The whispered 'Ah', exercise that you encountered earlier in this book, is a very good way of avoiding constriction. However, you may find it helpful to define what constriction is in your own practice so that you may then know if you are avoiding it, so here is an exercise that helps you know what is constriction and what is retraction, i.e. when the false vocal folds are lifted out of the way so that constriction at vocal fold level is avoided.

#### Exercise to help you identify constriction and retraction

##### Constriction

Take the /x/ consonant at the end of the Scottish word for 'lake', loch. Many native English speakers pronounce this as 'lock' but if you are of Scottish heritage you will be aware that this is an approximation and that the /x/ sound that is at the end of the word 'loch' is a velar fricative not a plosive – a voiceless sound made between the soft palate and the back of the tongue as air moves between them. Make this sound, bringing the soft palate and the back of the tongue firmly together, but being sure that you can allow air to pass through the place of articulation. If you exaggerate this consonant, you are approximating a form of constriction.

##### Retraction

Now allow the soft palate and the back of the tongue to move apart from each other and imagine the space between soft palate and tongue is being replicated within the vocal tract, allowing the air to pass through the space in your vocal tract and at the back of your mouth as you do this. You should find the passage of the air is now completely silent, and this is the state of being retracted. This is a simple way of identifying for yourself what retraction feels like.

It might also be useful to say that when you undertake the whispered 'Ah' exercise described earlier in this book that is another way of experiencing a feeling of retraction.

### The tongue

We will spend more time considering the tongue and its importance when we consider aspects of speech a bit later in this book.

The tongue is one of the main muscles involved in the production of sound – it is one of the chief organs of articulation, in fact – and if the tongue is unduly tense then this can compromise the quality of the sound that is made and can contribute to the possibility of constriction.

It is quite useful for a speaker or singer to know when their tongue is at its most relaxed. In more traditional kinds of voice work, it is maintained that when the vowel sound 'AH' as made (as in the word SPA in a Southern Standard British accent) that the back of the tongue is low in the mouth, the tongue is flat and the edge of the tongue rests against the back of the bottom teeth, and that the whole of the tongue is relaxed. However, if Southern Standard British is not your native accent, this may not at all be the case. When we go to make a sound on a neutral vowel, around our optimum pitch, we should find that the tongue is relaxed and fairly low in the mouth, the front edge resting at the back of the bottom teeth. In an ideal world this is where the tongue rests at its most relaxed. For the neutral vowel, however, the tongue is not flat.

Partly dependent on the vowel sound that is being made, and partly in response to rising and falling pitches that we may speak or sing, the back of the tongue will not be stationary, nor will it lie in the lower position that you have just been exploring when you made a neutral vowel. However, in an ideal world, the back of the tongue remains free whatever vowel and whatever pitch is being made.

When I was in training, many years ago, there was an emphasis on the need to keep the back of the tongue in a low position at all times. Quite simply, this is counterproductive and not at all helpful, as the back of the tongue needs to be allowed to rise and fall in response to the desired vowel shape and the pitch of the voice, too. (I think the mistaken theory was that by creating space at the back of the mouth you accessed the maximum amount of resonance possible within the vocal tract.) If you speak or sing on 'EE' for instance and attempt to keep the back of the tongue in a low position the vowel is distorted and a good deal of tongue-root tension is produced which can only lead to vocal strain and, in the longer term, pathology. Whatever position the back of the tongue needs to take up in the mouth, it needs to remain free rather than held, fixed or unduly tense.

I was also told, at another stage in my own vocal development, that some speakers or singers are more relaxed, more free, on the vowel AH whilst others are more free on the vowel EE. Apart from my own personal experience, as a voice user and as a teacher, I don't have any evidence as to whether this is a fact. However, this did come as something of a revelation to me as I subsequently found that singing on an EE vowel was, personally, much easier than on an AH vowel, and I had previously always considered that AH was the most open, and therefore, the freest sound.

I think that what I can assert is that each of us is different and that for each of us some vowels will be easier to exercise around than others. I don't think there is any rule about which vowels, and it is more complex than simply saying some prefer AH and some prefer EE. However, if working on range, and resonance throughout the range, I have found the AW vowel (as in THOUGHT in a Southern Standard British accent) to be really useful, if it is produced with some degree of lip rounding when it is formed. Lip rounding is not a feature of this vowel in all accents of English, but for the purpose of vocal exercise, some degree of trumpeting in the lips when making AW is helpful. If the front edge of the tongue is resting against the back of the bottom teeth as AW is made, and if some degree of lip rounding or trumpeting of the lips is present, the soft palate will automatically lift, and this creates a good deal of space at the top of the vocal tract, in the back of the mouth, so that the sound achieves quite a full resonant quality.

> ### Simple vowel exercise
>
> As an experiment, try exercising on the vowels AH, EE and AW, exploring a short, sung scale (perhaps five notes). Don't worry if you don't think of yourself as a singer or if you may have difficulty pitching – just experiment, sensing which of these vowels is easier for you, or feels freer.

## The soft palate

If you touch the roof of your mouth with the tip of your tongue and then run the tip of your tongue along the hard palate as far back as you can comfortably go, you will sense where the hard palate ends and the soft palate begins. Also, if you open your mouth and look in a hand mirror towards the back of the oral cavity, you should be able to see the end of the soft palate, the velum, hanging down (see Figure 2 on page 160).

This is a muscle, and the whole soft palate/velum area is capable of independent movement when we speak or sing. Generally, if the soft palate is lifted, space is created for any vowel that is being made – and vowels depend on their being some space within the vocal tract – and the soft palate is also used when making certain consonant sounds such as /g/, /k/, /ng/ /x/. As the consonant sounds require the velum to touch the back of the tongue, it naturally follows that there has to be a great deal of flexibility in the velum and the soft palate whenever we speak or sing words as the soft palate will need to lift for vowel sounds and lower to touch the back of the tongue for certain consonants.

In terms of resonance when we speak, the soft palate is an important muscle, then. When making sound, if the soft palate is lifted, the sound moves through the pharynx into the oral cavity – we produce resonance in the pharynx and the mouth. If the soft palate is partially lowered, then the vibrations of sound pass into both the nasal cavity and the oral cavity simultaneously and if the soft palate is very low, almost all of the sound we make moves into the nasal cavity and the sinuses.

Traditionally, in voice training, it has been considered desirable for the soft palate to be relatively lifted when a speaker moves through any vowel but there are a number of very successful and highly regarded actors whose soft palates are not so flexible and whose voices feature a good degree of nasal resonance when they speak. There are also a number of accents of British English that feature significant degrees of nasal resonance – even some speakers of Southern British Standard can speak with a marked degree of nasality – so it is perhaps not useful to make 'rules' as to what is desirable in terms of balance of resonance within a speaking voice.

However, what I think we can say is that to be a flexible and versatile performer we need to have a degree of choice. There will be accents of English, and characters we might play, who will need a good degree of flexibility and lift within the soft palate, and other accents and characters for whom the soft palate may be less active. Below are some exercises, then, to maintain (or increase) the flexibility of the soft palate.

## Simple soft palate exercise

### Stage 1

Say the word, 'Sing', and sense the place where the velum touches the area towards the back of the tongue. Then say the word, 'Song'. You are likely to find that when saying, 'Sing', the velum touches an area on the tongue somewhat further forward than when you say, 'Song'.

Thinking of the place of articulation being the position of the 'ng' in 'Sing', articulate a /g/ consonant. Experiment with this, making it softer or harder. You can also experiment with making /g/ in the position of the 'ng' consonant at the end of 'Song' too. You should find that this kind of /g/ sounds somewhat swallowed, and you might feel that this is close to the /g/ sound you normally make – this depends largely on your accent and the region in which you have grown up. For the sake of the exercise, practise making the /g/ sound in the more forward, 'Sing' position, enjoying the brightness and colour of the sound.

### Stage 2

Now practise a stream of /g/ sounds: guh, guh, guh, guh, guh,guh, guh, guh, guh, guh. Invent different rhythms for this stream of consonants, adding more /g/ sounds if you want to. Sense that contact between your velum and the back of your tongue, play with that contact sometimes making it firmer, sometimes softer, but end with a string of /g/ sounds that is light but firm.

When playing with this consonant, be aware that the front edge of your tongue is resting against the back of your bottom teeth – it doesn't pull back and away from them. If you allow the tongue to pull away from the back of the teeth, there may be tongue root tension and you may be depressing the larynx or affecting the available space in your vocal tract which is one of your main resonators. Also, relax your jaw so that there is a small amount of space between your lips – we looked at this earlier as the place where your jaw and face naturally relax to – and then ensure that the repeated /g/ sounds are being made by the tongue and the velum and that they do not involve movements of the jaw. You can experiment with the degree to which your mouth is open with this exercise as it is likely if the space between your lips is very small that your lower jaw will move when you attempt to articulate a strong of /g/ sounds. Find a degree of relaxed jaw opening that enables you to make this strong of /g/ sounds so that the jaw remains free and the articulators, tongue and velum, do the work. This is a simple exercise but it is useful and encourages agility in your velum and soft palate.

# The Integrated Actor

## Soft palate exercise using /k/

The /k/ consonant is essentially made in the same place as /g/ – towards the back of the tongue as it makes contact with the velum.

This sequence of exercises is adapted from an exercise developed by Kristin Linklater which appears in her book, *Freeing the Natural Voice*. I have adapted and adjusted elements within it so that this version is different. If you are familiar with Kristin Linklater's version as you explore this version you will, hopefully, find some value in the adjustments I have made.

### Stage 1

Breathe in, slowly, on a whispered /k/ consonant. As the breath drops in, sense the springing apart of the velum, soft palate and the rear of the tongue as you move from the /k/ into a feeling of space. If it helps, you can think of allowing the breath to drop in on a whispered, 'Kah', so that you can really begin to sense the potential for space between the soft palate and the tongue as these muscles spring apart. When you have taken as much air in as you feel comfortable to do, you can just relax completely as you allow the breath to fall out.

### Stage 2

If you are taking time to do this slowly, focus your attention on the space between the back of the tongue and the soft palate, sensing the velum lift, and try to increase the degree of lifting and stretching in the velum and soft palate area during the time in which the breath drops in. As in the previous exercise, do not allow your tongue to pull away from resting at the back of the bottom teeth. This is partly an exercise to appreciate how much space it is possible to create towards the back of the oral cavity when the soft palate lifts and stretches away from the rear of the tongue and if you allow the front edge of your tongue to pull back from the lower teeth, you will simply make the space in the mouth smaller.

You may wish to look in a hand mirror at the back of the oral space while you are exploring this exercise, noticing the nature of the movement in your velum and soft palate and in the back of your tongue. You may find, as the soft palate lifts away from the back of the tongue that the back of the tongue also tends to lower and move away from the soft palate. Try not to allow this movement to occur, as the root of your tongue is attached to the hyoid bone at the top of your larynx and when the back of the tongue is pushed downwards, this also lowers the larynx and can push it into an artificially low position. (You may recall from discussions earlier in this book that the larynx should be allowed to remain free and flexible during speaking and singing so anything that encourages you to hold the larynx in a low position can be counterproductive.) Focus, then, on the velum and the soft palate stretching away from the back of the tongue and try to leave the back of the tongue as relaxed as possible.

### Stage 3

As you continue to explore this exercise, sense that your soft palate can stretch not just upwards inside your head but that it can also expand to the left and the right in the back of your mouth. In an ideal world, you do not only want to get the central area of the soft palate to stretch upwards but all of the surfaces of the soft palate, towards the rear of the mouth, to stretch, so there is a vertical and a lateral stretch that can take place simultaneously.

Some of you may find, as you execute this exercise, that stretching the space towards the back of your mouth open makes you want to gag, and some of you may find that this exercise makes you tear up – or, indeed, both things may start to occur. There is a simple reason for this: if your soft palate tends to be somewhat inactive, your body remembers those times in your life when the soft palate might naturally lift. When we vomit, the vocal tract stretches open to allow for as much space as possible and the soft palate automatically lifts as part of this action, also, when we really need to release sorrowful or painful emotions a similar action in the soft palate occurs so that we can wail, keen or cry. Obviously, in attempting this exercise, it is not the objective to throw up or to cry, but if you have this gag response, you should find as you exercise that, gradually, this passes and, in fact, in the years I have been teaching this exercise I have never known a student to actually vomit as a result of it. If this soft palate exercise makes you tear up, I think this is natural and something to be embraced – it may result in your feeling a little vulnerable, but this will not do you any harm when you are in a safe and supportive environment.

### Stage 4

Instead of relaxing as you allow the air to fall out of you, you keep the soft palate stretched and lifted, and you allow the breath to travel out of you, imagining you are saying 'Aah'. (In other words, ultimately, you whisper, 'Kah', on the in-breath and, 'Ah', on the outbreath, so there is no initial consonant on the outgoing breath.)

Some individuals find this really difficult to achieve but stay with the exercise until you can manage this final stage. Once you are able to allow the passage of breath out of you whilst your soft palate is lifted and stretched, try adding sound and voicing an 'Ah' sound, letting the sound fall out from deep within you. It is likely that this will sound strange to you. The sound may seem very 'dark', for instance – it's just an exercise and the objective is not for you to sound like this, ultimately, but it is useful both to know that you have this kind of space available to you and that your soft palate has this degree of elasticity and flexibility within it

### Stage 5

In the final stage of this exercise sequence, you can also try calling, 'Hey', as if to someone a distance away from you, imagining the potential space towards the back of your mouth as you do this. You should find that the resulting sound is full and free and has the colour of 'Hey', which is naturally bright and feels forward, but that you have managed to recall some of that sense of space from the previous exercise in the space towards the back of the mouth.

### Stage 6

Try chanting a text that you know, maintaining as much of a sense of space towards the back of your mouth as you can, and then speak it. Start on a comfortable note and chant the spoken thought on that note, stringing all of the sounds in the thought together in a stream of sound, extending the vowel sounds as you chant, and not worrying too much about the consonants. Then, follow this with speaking the same thought and notice if anything feels or sounds different to you. As a result of the work you have undertaken, you should sense that your vocal tract is more open, or that your voice feels freer in some way, or you may find that the sound of your voice seems fuller to you or more resonant.

If you have to rise to the challenge of extreme vocal demands, perhaps in a Shakespeare play or one of the Greek tragedies – one of Henry V's big speeches, such as 'Once more unto the breach dear friends', or one of Constance's speeches in *King John* – these soft palate exercises are a very good preparation for attempting to speak and release those texts.

# CHAPTER 20
# LANGUAGE AND TEXT 3

### Learning to speak

As a child, the process of learning to speak is not scientific. Essentially, we learn to speak through a combination of playing with sounds and imitating the sounds our parents make to us, and so learning to speak is experimental and experiential. It is not an accident that the first words we say are often, either, a version of 'mum-mum-mum' or 'da-da-da' and I would argue that 'mum-mum-mum' is easier to approximate than 'da-da-da' for the simple reason that with the articulation of the word 'Mum' or 'Mam' the actions of the lips that make the consonant sound can be clearly witnessed by the curious baby – two lips pressing together and then separating. What the tongue tip is doing when the parent says 'da-da-da' is partially hidden and so more difficult to replicate.

Some sounds of English are much more difficult to articulate for the simple reason that the articulation of them really cannot be seen. For instance, versions of /r/ are particularly difficult. Not only can consonant /r/ not be seen, it is also quite difficult to describe how it is made. So, if a child is struggling to articulate this consonant, it can be immensely frustrating as it is very unlikely that the parent or teacher they are imitating can explain to them what they need to do in order to articulate the sound successfully. In a way, it is amazing that most of us manage to pronounce this consonant eventually. It is also not surprising that some speakers approximate it and, in preference, find ways to substitute this consonant with another sound. The articulation of /r/ in words such as 'round' and 'risky' is tricky, and if the consonant appears in the middle of a word, such as 'rarified' or 'verification', it is even more difficult to get the tongue to articulate it.

We learn first, then, from our parents and then from our wider social circle, extended family, friends, and school mates as well as from the media. For instance, I grew up in Lancashire – my mother had quite a strong Lancashire accent and my father, who was from Yorkshire, had a milder Yorkshire accent. However, the children's television programmes I watched were all presented in the RP of the day, or BBC English as it sometimes used to be called. This was in the 1950s, and I appreciate that we now live in a very different time, but I grew up believing that the people around me, who all spoke in Lancashire accents and using colloquial phraseology, were speaking 'poorly' and my role model for speaking was the dominant accent I heard from the BBC. My parents reinforced this concept and, around me, tried to reduce their own accents in the hope that I might acquire what they thought of as 'good speech' or 'no accent'. It is not at all surprising that my own accent, then, was a strange mish-mash of Lancashire sounds and approximated RP sounds. Mind you, the other children around me were quite happy to

## The Integrated Actor

speak in their own Lancashire accents so it is puzzling, in a way, as to why I should have been so overly aware of the way in which I spoke. I can only observe that I was very much aware of the way people around me spoke and the way I thought I ought to speak. My teachers at school certainly spoke RP, or a version of it, too, so I think it is natural that I should have thought that the everyday, colloquial, accented speech around me was not necessarily the way that I should speak.

I share these insights because I want to be honest about my own bias, which I think was inculcated in me – even when I got to drama school and was told that regional accents were to be embraced, all of the role models who taught us were RP speakers. I would call that a very mixed message. However, the fact is that nearly all of us have a bias about the way we speak, conscious or unconscious, and perhaps it is useful to be aware of this.

The world we live in now – and I would stress that what I am about to say is principally true in the UK and not necessarily in other English-speaking countries – values all accents equally. I could argue that this is, in fact, notional as many individuals have a bias as to what is 'good speech' or 'educated speech', but it is certainly a much more inclusive spirit, in terms of language and the way we speak, than the one I grew up in.

### The actor speaks

So, today a great deal of weight is placed on an actor being able to work in their own accent and, also, on the need for speaking to sound 'natural' in order that the audience believe in the authenticity of what is being said. I have placed the word natural in quotation marks because if the actor is working in a theatre space, even a moderately sized one and certainly in a large one, they cannot simply transfer to the stage the way in which they speak in everyday life. This is equally true even if the actors are wearing microphones – increasingly the case in live theatre performances today.

At the same time, a good deal of contemporary drama now features a wide range of diverse communities, to reflect accurately the world we live in today and in order to speak to the needs of those communities, and this means that plays contain many accent demands. If a play, or a character in a play, requires a specific accent of English, it is becoming frequently more likely that an actor whose indigenous accent is that required by the character, or the play, will be cast. However, this is not always the case. For the actor, then, there is a need for a developed muscularity to be available to them whether working in their own accent or in an accent not native to them.

In live theatre performances it is necessary to understand that when the actor speaks, it takes time for the words being spoken by them to reach the ears of the audience – it takes time for sound to travel through space. This has implications for the actor. For instance, very rapid speaking poses problems for the audience unless the actor is sufficiently agile and muscular and, in a more general sense, it is more difficult for the audience to understand what the actor is saying if consonantal features of the accent the actor is speaking are not sufficiently muscular or are absent.

I would argue that this can be true, to a certain extent, for the actor working on film where any number of microphones may be strategically placed around and on the actor in order to capture the words being spoken. If necessary consonants are not present in the actor's speech, some words will be lost even when recorded by state-of-the-art microphones. This is frequently the case in filmed work when actors employ very quiet, sometimes overly aspirate, speaking. Microphones invariably pick up a voice when resonance is present, but struggle to some degree if sound is devoiced or if dialogue is spoken with breathy tone, or whispered.

Essentially, it is important to understand that a consonant, unlike a number of vowels sounds in English, is a short acoustic event and is, therefore, more difficult to hear. This is particularly true for the voiceless consonants, such as /p/, /t/, /k/ and also /s/ and /f/. Voiced consonants, such as /b/, /d/, /g/, /m/, /n/, /z/, /v/, are much easier to hear, especially when they are properly muscular and well vibrated, but they do need to be fully present, that is to say appropriately muscular, when working for a theatre space.

Final voiced consonants become particularly significant in live theatre performance – if they cannot be heard, very often the word spoken cannot be understood, or the audience think they hear a different word. Take the word 'sword', for instance. If the final /d/ is not really sounded, the audience will hear the word 'sore', which has a completely different meaning, and the word 'board' becomes 'bore', and so on. Some of you reading this will want to argue that mistakes in understanding on the part of the audience will happen fairly infrequently because they will understand the word that is meant simply because of the context within which it is spoken, but I'm afraid that this is often not the case. I think it is true to say that if the audience miss one or two words in a spoken thought, they may well spend time trying to work out what was actually said and in the time it takes for them to do that they then miss some of the phrases that follow.

In a world in which there is a great deal of emphasis placed on sounding 'natural' and 'authentic', clarity of speaking is a very finely judged skill and I believe a certain degree of experimentation needs to take place within each speaker in order for them to be appropriately muscular and clear for an audience and not to appear to sound unduly technical or, worse, artificial.

In the section, above, I may seem to be contradicting what I have said about there not being a better way to speak. However, if a character speaks in a particular accent of English, then it is important that the features within that accent are embodied. In order to be clearly understood by a theatre audience, it may then be necessary for some of those accent features to be heightened or more strongly featured. For instance, in an accent where certain consonants are substituted within the accent or where a glottal stop may be substituted for a /t/ sound, it is necessary to make a feature of these sounds so that they can be clearly heard by an audience. This has to be very finely judged by the actor, otherwise what seems to be a 'cod' version of the accent can result (think of Audrey Hepburn playing Eliza Doolittle in the film of *My Fair Lady* or Dick Van Dyke in *Mary Poppins*).

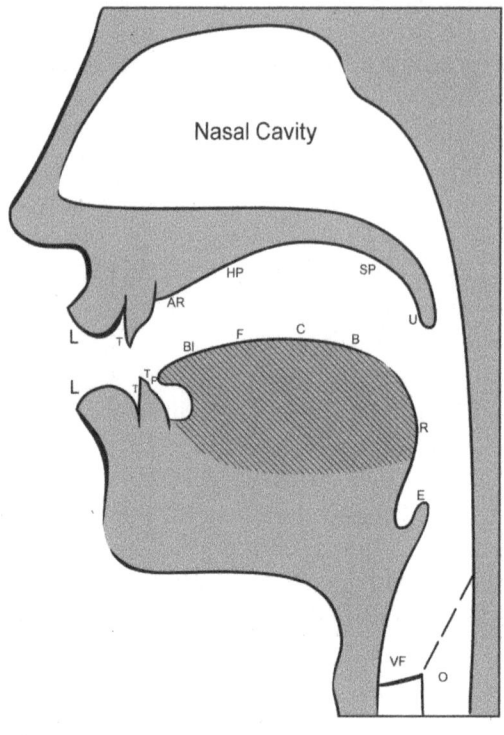

**Figure 2** Organs of Speech
This diagram shows all of the articulators involved in the formation of speech sounds.

To be clear, the tract called the oesophagus has no role in the production of sound. This is the passageway that carries food and fluids to the stomach. Note that when we ingest water, it bypasses the vocal folds, situated in the larynx, as it travels down the oesophagus.

There are some facts about consonants that it is useful to be aware of and to embrace. For instance, some consonants can be more significant than others because they have the potential to last longer when spoken. The consonants /m/, /n/ and the sound at the end of the word 'sing' or 'long' can all have length and, if the speaker gives them length, this makes these sounds easier to hear in a theatre space. This is equally true for /s/ and its voiced equivalent /z/. The consonant /s/ is a very difficult sound to hear in a theatre space if it is short, so finding acting reasons to emphasize this sound by lengthening it – that is to say, finding an acting reason to allow the /s/ sound to be more expressive – can be really useful. This would not be true on film, where, unless there was a very good justification for lengthening the sound in the acting choice, this would probably sound extremely unnatural.

The consonant /f/, which often occurs at the start of a word, can also be lengthened, and this can be extremely expressive – certain expletives spring to mind! (And this is something we might well choose to do in life when we have a strong need to convey our feelings.)

## Jaw

The organs of articulation for the English language are essentially within the mouth and include: the lips, the tongue tip, the blade, and the back of the tongue, the teeth, the alveolar ridge and the soft palate. (It is possible to make some consonant sounds within the vocal tract – glottal clicks, for instance – but these do not usually feature within spoken English, so my focus within this section will be on English vowels and consonants.)

Figure 2 on page 160 details the vocal tract and all of the main articulators for the consonant sounds of English. The tongue, one of the key articulators, moves independently of the jaw, or it should do, although some speakers attempt to assist the tongue as certain consonant sounds are articulated by supporting it with movement of the lower jaw. This is best avoided if possible as it will essentially lead to tension within the jaw as well as a tendency to overwork and, potentially, a lack of clarity.

Much has been made, in the history of voice work, of jaw tension. In my experience, if a voice coach identifies that a speaker evidences tension within the jaw, this usually makes the speaker self-conscious and leads to increased jaw tension, so it is better to work the musculature of the jaw without drawing attention to whether or not there is tension present there.

The degree to which the speaker may open their jaw varies from person to person, and it is important to be clear about this. When I was in training, we were led to believe that the vowel AH required an opening of two fingers' width at the front of the mouth. However, the degree of jaw opening for any version of this vowel is entirely dependent on the physiognomy of the individual speaker – some jaws are smaller and some larger, some oral cavities are naturally more spacious and some less spacious, so it is important not to insist on a particular degree of jaw opening for any vowel sound.

## Freeing the jaw

There are any number of exercises that have been designed to free up the jaw. Massaging the jaw joint and then stroking the lower jaw down with the heels of the hands is an exercise that many voice users are familiar with. I do not advocate for this exercise as I think it can often lead to increased jaw tension – the very thing that it is meant to release. If it is executed specifically and carefully, then I believe it can be useful, but I would like to propose an alternative exercise here.

### Stage 1

Placing your fingertips on the facial muscles over and around the jaw joint, perform small rotational massaging movements around this area. This is very similar to the start of the 'stroking the jaw down' exercise, but I would recommend that the circular movements of the massage are small and that you move the fingertips forwards, up, around, back and down and then return and repeat. This is simply because you want to encourage the jaw to move downwards, ultimately, but you are <u>not</u> going to use your fingertips to stroke the jaw downward other than employing these small, circular, massaging strokes to the musculature. Spend time gently massaging these muscles around the jaw joint. The objective, as with all massage, is to increase the circulation of the blood flow to these muscles. This can take time, so give this procedure at least a couple of minutes – in cold weather, or in a cold room, you may feel you need longer before these muscles, literally, begin to feel warm.

### Stage 2

While you are executing this simple sequence, consciously allow the lower jaw to start to relax and to move away from the upper jaw, slightly. You are aiming for a small space between the front teeth and the lips – we looked at this much earlier in this book when focusing on relaxing the muscles of the face and exploring the neutral vowel.

### Stage 3

Once you sense that the muscles around the jaw joint are sufficiently warm, take your fingertips and hands away from the jaw and allow them to relax wherever you feel comfortable – by your sides, or in your lap, depending on whether you are sitting or standing. There should, by now, be a small amount of space between your front teeth and lips. (This is the position to which your lower jaw and face naturally relax if you can allow them to do so.)

Employing very tiny movements, working around the neutral position of the jaw and mouth, articulate the lower jaw slightly to one side. Do not push the lower jaw forward to any degree when you do this – it is simply a small movement of the lower jaw to the side. Then allow the lower jaw to return to the neutral position. Now move the lower jaw a small amount to the other side, again being careful not to tense the jaw forwards as you articulate it. Now gently articulate the lower jaw to the left and the right, repeatedly. When I describe this as a small movement, you are moving your jaw, perhaps half a centimetre to one side and then the other side. This articulation of the lower jaw from side to side should also not be effortful in any way and the musculature controlling the movement of the jaw should remain very close to feeling completely relaxed.

If you execute this exercise for around two minutes – which is actually quite a long time – you should then find you feel ready to speak and, if you then speak a text you already know, you should experience a sense that the jaw movement, and articulation generally, is freer and easier.

It's important to execute this exercise with minimal movements of the lower jaw, as described above, because you are working the jaw in opposition to its natural movement, which is downwards and not from side to side. However, if this exercise is executed in a disciplined way, you will not be at risk of damage. The exercise is working the musculature around the jaw joint, stimulating these muscles so that they will be more inclined both to work and release when you then aim to drop the jaw.

## The sounds of speech

It used to be that books dealing with voice and speech would devote chapters to clear descriptions of how consonants should be made and how vowels should be formed. However, given that there are many varied accents of English in the UK and Ireland alone, as well as other multiple accents of English globally, it does not feel appropriate to spend time here to describe ideally formed consonants and vowels which may represent the speech of only a limited number of speakers within the UK.

I think it may be useful to discuss some general aspects of the way sounds may be formed, however.

The previous section offered an exercise to free the jaw – free and flexible movement of the lower jaw is crucial to being able to both release the voice and in order to speak with muscularity and clarity. There are two key aspects to this. If the jaw is tight so that the speaker speaks through a degree of clenching in the jaw, then this affects the potential resonance of the sound – the oral cavity is one of the main resonators in producing sound. An undue amount of tension in the jaw is also likely to affect the tongue, the main muscle of articulation, so that its freedom of movement may be compromised. Also, if tongue root tension occurs as a result of jaw tension, which is likely, this will then affect the free, flexible movement of the larynx within the vocal tract – essential in order to access an expressive range of notes. (Remember that the larynx is attached to the tongue root via the hyoid bone.) None of these things necessarily mean that your voice will not function, but that its function may be compromised to some degree. I also advocate that unnecessary tension anywhere within the system – the tongue, the vocal tract, the torso, the back, the belly, the knees – will in some way inhibit the voice and render it less expressive.

I believe there is a powerful connection between the musculature in the back of the neck and the lower jaw. It is likely to be more difficult to speak with a free jaw if the lengthening process that should take place in the muscles of the neck is compromised, i.e. if we habitually shorten the neck. (For instance, if we go through life with a lifted chin, and many individuals do, the neck muscles are significantly shortened and the jaw frequently becomes less flexible.) It is useful when conducting work focused on speech to remind yourself of the mantra, 'Let my neck be free to let my head move forwards and upwards'. The process of freeing the neck also aids in the free movement of the jaw.

It is also important for the tongue to have the potential to work independently from the jaw. It sometimes occurs that, for one reason or another, a speaker has difficulty to articulate a particular consonant sound – an initial consonant /n/ as in the word, 'Never', is one example, or an /l/ consonant at the start of the word 'Like' could be problematic. The consonant /n/ is a good example because it requires a certain degree of pressure between the tongue tip and the place of articulation (usually the alveolar ridge). This pressure can be difficult to create for some speakers – for instance, if the phrenum that attaches the underneath of the front of the tongue to the floor of the mouth is particularly short or tight. Where this occurs, it is likely that the speaker will move the lower jaw up as they articulate the /n/ consonant in order to assist the tongue. This then may create tension that could inhibit the voice in some way, as described above. In my experience, the phrenum needs to be exceptionally tight for someone's speech to be severely compromised. If this is the case, surgery – a very simple procedure in which the phrenum is cut – is an option but, very often, regular exercise for the tongue tip, over time, will gradually render the phrenum more flexible.

I could give multiple examples of ways in which the articulation of the tongue for certain consonants sounds can be compromised by unnecessary movement (or 'assistance') from the jaw. However, I think the point is clearly made that, ideally, we would like the tongue to work independently of the jaw and to be appropriately muscular and flexible.

### Some articulation exercises

In my own training as an actor, we spent quite a lot of time undertaking a range of articulation exercises using the figure of eight – a sequence of vowel sounds that were repeated in combination with particular consonants.

### Figure of 8 Exercise

AH AY EE AY AH AW OO AW AH.

### Stage 1

If you place an /m/ consonant before each vowel sound, and then speak the sequence, this is quite a simple way of checking that there is some free movement and flexibility in your jaw. The degree of jaw opening should vary through the sequence depending on whether the vowel is more open, more close, or rounded. AH is the most open vowel, EE and OO are the most close.

OH (which is not in the sequence above), AW, and OO are, generally, lip rounded vowels. However, whilst this was a generally accepted fact in my own training in the 1970s, this is not necessarily the case for some contemporary speakers of English. The vowel OO, for instance, is frequently less rounded, or not rounded at all, in the speech of some contemporary speakers.

### Stage 2

Try this vowel sequence (the figure of eight) placing a particular consonant before each vowel: /n/ /l/ /t/ and /d/ are useful consonants to play with in that you should be able to articulate them within the sequence without tightening the jaw or having to compromise the degree of jaw opening or the shaping of the vowel in order to articulate the consonant.

### Stage 3

It is also useful practice to work through this vowel sequence placing consonants after the vowels, making simple nonsense words, as in: DAHD DAYD DEED DAYD DAHD DAWD DOOD DAWD DAHD. Then apply these articulatory processes to words ending in /d/ such as: READ, CLOSED, AGREED, EXPLODE, and so on. You may be surprised to find that in your own, everyday speech, you are not always inclined to make the final consonant sound in some of these words but I would argue that for work in a theatre space, these final consonants need to be present and audible.

I think that actors need to have access to a range of choices within their speech in order to be flexible and to be able to inhabit a range of different accents which they may be called upon to acquire.

### Consonant clusters

Consonant clusters are challenging for many of us and occur naturally in the kind of speech we find in Elizabethan and Jacobean plays: in a phrase such as 'Lik'st though this', for instance, or, 'Thou canst not say.' These are relatively simple consonant clusters.

The standard text book for student actors was once J Clifford Turner's *Voice and Speech in the Theatre*, reissued and edited by Jane Boston in 2007 and published by Methuen Drama. There is a section for consonant cluster exercises contained here and the same exercises are more or less duplicated in Cicely Berry's *Voice and the Actor* (reprinted 2000, Virgin Books), so it is not my intention to, once again, replicate them here.

## The Integrated Actor

> **Stage 5**
>
> For those of you who may want to experiment with consonant clusters, by adding consonants before and after the vowels in the figure of eight exercise described above, useful consonant cluster exercises can be created, as in DAHDST, and so on, or DAHDTHDZ, to offer a couple of examples.

Simple as they are, I have always found these to be great fun and they are a really great way to improve agility, flexibility, and muscularity in your speech as well as a very good way to prepare to speak classical text.

## Accent

I do not wish to spend a great deal of time within this book discussing the subject of accent – there are so many very good books that offer a range of approaches to accent work available. However, I would like to share a few thoughts for further discussion.

I think it is important to say that, for an actor today, unless an accent (or indeed another language) can be accessed as if the speaker is a native speaker of that accent or language, then it is no use to the actor. If any aspect of an accent is approximated in performance or if there are inconsistencies within the speaking of the accent, then this is offensive to an audience member who may happen to speak, habitually, with that accent. Also, quite simply, approximated accent work is not, and cannot be, authentic.

With this in mind, I would like to spend a moment to address the topic of Received Pronunciation (usually referred to, simply, as RP). This is sometimes referred to as Standard English, which to my way of thinking is not an accent – it is a grammatically correct form of English, that does not include dialectical words or phrases, that we are taught in schools for the purposes of formal communication, and this grammatically correct form can be spoken <u>in any accent</u> of English.

Geoff Lindsey in his book *English after RP* (Palgrave MacMillan, 2019) argues that the RP accent has now evolved to a point where the term Received Pronunciation is no longer applicable. He prefers the term Standard Southern British which, clearly, locates this accent within the south of England. (When I was at drama school in the 1970s, I was introduced to a term which we called Southern British Standard – essentially, the same term used by Geoff Lindsey – and told that this was the correct term to use to refer to the accent of RP. This was shared with us by Greta Colson, Head of Voice at the New College of Speech and Drama, and J. C. Wells, who taught us phonetics, and who has written the foreward for Geoff Lindsey's *English After RP*.)

I am never quite comfortable with Standard Southern British as a term as, in my experience, people all over the country can speak in a version of the accent that I would term Received Pronunciation, including those in countries such as Scotland, Wales, and Ireland, but I suppose it is true to say that the majority of people who speak with this accent reside in and around London and the Home Counties.

In his foreword to Geoff Lindsey's *English After RP*, J. C. Wells states, 'The existing descriptions of standard British English pronunciation, known as RP, are outdated'. He goes on to say, 'People who speak like me now sound old-fashioned'. The simple fact is that accents are fluid and, due to many influential factors, change over time, and some of the sounds of RP, as in other accents, have shifted over time as a result of these processes. This, then, brings me back to the point I made above that some vowels, such as OO, AW, and OW, tend to be articulated differently now than when I was a young actor.

However, I think that there is still a certain kind of dramatic material that requires the actor to speak in the accent known as RP if the performance is to have a real sense of period about it and if the characters are to appear to be fully authentic. Admittedly, I think the occasions for which this accent may be required are shrinking and frequently now directors and, perhaps, voice coaches prefer actors to employ Standard Southern British – a more contemporary version of the RP accent – presumably because they feel this will seem more familiar and accessible to audiences or, indeed, versions of their own accents.

This is all a question of taste, but my personal preference is to see a revival of a play by Oscar Wilde, George Bernard Shaw, Harley Granville Barker, or even Noel Coward in which the upper-class and upper-middle-class characters speak RP for the simple reason that these plays do not take place in our own time (unless the production has been contemporised) so, to me, when actors approximate RP in these period plays (as is so often the case today), the performance rings false. It is also, sometimes, irksome to me that in a TV series such as *Bridgerton* or *Sanditon* characters who apparently speak RP are sometimes played by actors who approximate those sounds. I assume that these more relaxed versions of RP appeal to directors who don't wish their drama to be alienating to audiences, some of whom may not feel comfortable with the RP accent, but I think there is something to be said for the consistency of accent work within a drama if all the characters are supposedly from within the same social background.

Interestingly, and perhaps this is because of the importance of authenticity in current productions, when a play or film requires actors who speak RP, it would appear that native RP speakers are cast in the same way that if a TV drama is set in Liverpool or Newcastle, generally, actors are chosen for whom these accents are native or near native to them. There are exceptions – actors who are famous may sometimes be given the opportunity to acquire an accent not native to them (Meryl Streep, after all, has made a career out of playing a huge range of roles that have required her to speak in a multiplicity of different accents of English) but for the vast majority of actors, their native accent will determine how they may be cast. Personally, I would like to think that we could live in a world where any actor could still transcend personal boundaries of region, background, or class in order to play any period, style, or character that may be offered to them. This,

## The Integrated Actor

to me, is what the word 'acting' means. Whilst every actor can only draw upon their own imaginations as well as their lived experience when they play a particular role, an actor should not simply be playing a version of themselves. So, accent, and speaking authentically in an accent not their own, is part of the actor's ability to have the potential to be transformative.

# CHAPTER 21
# LANGUAGE AND TEXT 4 – SHAKESPEARE

I've implied that an ability to access the accent I am referring to as RP is a desirable asset for actors for some kinds of drama.

However, RP is not necessary in order to play many of the characters in Shakespeare, and there are all kinds of reasons for this not least the fact that the way English was spoken at the time when Shakespeare was writing was very, very different from the way it is spoken now. As far as we know, there was no RP accent of the time, although it does appear that there was a predominant accent in the court of Queen Elizabeth as contemporary comments, and jokes, are made about Sir Walter Raleigh's regional accent. However, essentially there was no generally accepted way to sound just as there was no generally accepted way of spelling a word when writing it.

The Globe Theatre has undertaken significant research in staging productions in OP – Original Pronunciation. It is not that there is anyone around today who actually knows how English was spoken in Shakespeare's time but the accent has been reconstructed through a deep examination of the extant texts of the period. One of the principal guidelines to the accent are those lines that are meant to rhyme, in plays and poems of the period, but may no longer rhyme today. A very good example is the final couplet from Shakespeare's sonnet 116, 'Let me not to the marriage of true minds/admit impediments'. The final lines are: 'If this be error and upon me proved, I never writ, nor no man ever loved' (Arden Shakespeare, William Shakespeare, Complete Works, ed. Katherine Duncan Jones, 2021). 'Proved' and 'loved' no longer rhyme, but would have rhymed when Shakespeare wrote the sonnet.

When you hear OP it is a strange experience and, initially, it is very difficult to understand what is being said, as many of the vowel sounds are pronounced differently from today. If you have a chance to listen to someone speaking OP, it is useful just to listen without trying to understand what is being said, to begin with. It is a rhotic accent, so /r/ consonants are pronounced in all positions, and you will find, I think, that it sometimes sounds Cornish, sometimes Scots, sometimes Irish, sometimes Yorkshire, and seems a strange mishmash of many accents of English, all jumbled up together. It is exceptionally expressive – somehow many of the sounds seem more open than their modern-day counterparts, and more emotionally expressive. If you have an interest in hearing Shakespeare spoken in OP, the British Library has produced a recording of speeches and scenes 'performed as Shakespeare would have heard them', entitled Shakespeare's Original Pronunciation and published by the British Library in 2012. These recordings are still available on a CD at a modest price but can also be listened to online for free.

Many of the characters in Shakespeare's plays, and those of his contemporaries, come from other regions of the UK: Harry Percy (Hotspur) in the history plays, for instance, is one example. His father is from Northumberland and Henry himself was born in Yorkshire, so it is likely he would have had an accent from the North East. If we want to be accurate in terms of accent, then it is arguable that we should think about the origins of the characters – their place of birth and where they grew up – and acquire an appropriate accent. Henry V, Prince Hal in the Henry IV plays, was born in Monmouth and fought some of his early battles in Wales, but I have never heard him played with any kind of a Welsh accent. However, he would have been brought up and educated in the court of his father, the Earl of Derby, later Henry IV, and his mother Mary de Bohun so, as with all of us, his accent may well have been the product of the way his parents spoke and of his immediate environment as he grew up.

It seems that, in order to tell these stories to audiences today, that accent is not considered to be important and I would be inclined to agree with this point of view. We rarely see productions of *Macbeth*, for instance, in which the Scottish characters have Scottish accents. However, there are Scottish and English characters (not many) in the play, and scenes that take place in Scotland and scenes that take place in England. Arguably, these should be clearly delineated for an audience. These choices are rarely made and it is, perhaps, partly because of the level of difficulty in accessing and staging these texts now for contemporary audiences that we do not add the additional layer of identifying character and place by accent.

I think, though, that if we are to continue to stage these plays, then the stories must be clearly told. The language of the plays, the grammatical constructions (many of which are archaic and no longer in use) and the fact that large sections of the plays are written in blank verse mean that they are challenging to act and also challenging for audiences to watch and to hear.

## Speaking Shakespeare

Early in this book, in *Language and Text 1*, we explored the ways in which the structures of a text need to be taken into account or responded to when we speak the text. In the poem by Yevgeny Yevtushenko, we saw that the structure was relatively free but that, nonetheless, it should not be ignored.

In a poem or play by William Shakespeare (and those of his contemporaries) the structure of the verse is somewhat more formal. It takes some considerable skill to embody both the grammar and the verse form when we speak Shakespeare and to speak it in a way that is truthful.

Again, we considered earlier in this book what we might mean by 'truth'. When we consider what is truthful when speaking Shakespeare at a very basic level, we must sound like a real person speaking. This doesn't mean, though, that we can simply speak Shakespeare ignoring the verse form, attempting to make it sound like contemporary, colloquial speech. What would be truthful about that? Shakespeare hasn't written contemporary, colloquial speech – except for those characters who use it, such as the Porter in Macbeth – so there is nothing truthful in trying to reduce the verse in a Shakespeare play to something that we think audiences might find more acceptable today. I recently saw a production of a Shakespeare play, currently touring the UK, in which the younger members of the cast seemed to be trying to do just that. They spoke the text with no sense of the verse in which it was written and opted for a very conversational way of speaking – this was aided by the fact that they were all miked. I can only say that I found this approach reductive, and the reliance on the microphones by some of the actors meant that the energy of the text, and the actors speaking it, did not in any way meet the size of the playing space or the audience.

I am not advocating here, by the way, that performances should not be enhanced by technology, but that if we are to employ amplification, it should be done in such a way that the audience still feels that the voices are being used with a sense of an acoustic use of sound. Last year, I saw *The Motive and the Cue* at the Royal National Theatre. I believe that the actors in this performance were amplified but I felt as if the actors were working for the space and I was completely unaware of the use of amplification, and this, to me, felt entirely appropriate. Theatre is an essentially live and not a recorded event.

However, my argument here is that the use of microphones in live theatre should not be a justification for actors speaking Shakespeare verse as if it is conversational prose. Cicely Berry was always very clear that if we are to play Shakespeare today, we must play it for now, but there is a way of inhabiting verse so that the actor can honour the demands of the verse whilst also owning it, psycho-physically, and speaking it in such a way that it is clearly understandable and accessible to the audience. We don't do this by attempting to reduce the language and the verse in any way but by rising to the challenge of it, finding ways to honour the verse and speaking it with immediacy and freshness.

## Blank verse

The term blank verse is a simple way of referring to verse that does not rhyme and, for the most part, Shakespeare writes his plays in blank verse. Generally, he writes his plays in both verse and prose, moving from one to the other as he feels the action of the play demands.

Some of Shakespeare's plays are written largely in verse. *Richard II*, for instance, is entirely written in verse. Some plays contain a very good deal of prose – *Much Ado about Nothing* and *As You Like It* both contain many scenes in prose – but it is usual for the majority of the plays to contain both verse and prose. There is always a reason within the drama why a scene is written in verse or prose, and sometimes a scene may begin in verse and then suddenly move to prose mid-scene. It's useful to be aware of this, and always worthwhile asking yourself why Shakespeare has moved from one to the other because the use of verse and prose gives you clues as to the nature of the dramatic action at any given point and, therefore, what may be going on within the event itself and the character you are playing.

## The Integrated Actor

There are general things to be considered: for instance, the nobility usually speaks in verse and verse itself tends to suggest that a character has been well-educated. (In *As You Like It* verse is spoken by the major characters at the opening of the play, which takes place at the court of Duke Senior, but quite quickly the characters all journey to the forest of Arden, an idyllic, but potentially dangerous, country setting, where anything goes, and the characters now principally speak in prose.) Verse is also used when the circumstances within the dramatic action of the play are heightened so, for instance, when a character is in a highly emotional state, or when two characters are in an intimate situation and need to speak of their feelings to each other. (Think of the famous balcony scene when Romeo and Juliet are alone in the Capulet's orchard for the first time – a scene written entirely in verse.) Working-class characters usually speak in prose – think of the characters referred to as 'the mechanicals' in *A Midsummer Night's Dream*; they mainly speak prose except when they are rehearsing the text of the play, to be performed for Theseus and Hippolyta's wedding celebration, which is written in a simple verse form, or the Porter in *Macbeth* who appears in one scene in the middle of the play and speaks entirely in prose.

## The nature of the verse

When I undertook my own actor training I think that most drama schools assumed that their acting students already knew a good deal about verse. At any rate, I don't recall working on verse speaking very much, though we received an introductory class or two to make sure that we understood about the kind of metric structures we would encounter. These sessions were very academic, however, and not at all a practical introduction to Shakespeare's verse.

It is my belief that intellectualizing about Shakespeare's verse form really doesn't help us speak it. I think, when we talk about it, this only renders the text less accessible for contemporary actors, so I advocate practical exercises which, when undertaken, get us in touch with the rhythms and the structures within the verse in an experiential way. Having said this, however, I will spend some time analysing how iambic verse may work for the actor here, though I will do this in tandem with some practical exploration and exercise.

Before proceeding, I must mention Cicely Berry's book, *The Actor and the Text* (Virgin Books, 2000), and John Barton's book *Playing Shakespeare* (Methuen Drama, 2009) which both offer a series of masterclasses in how to work with Shakespeare verse and prose and a wealth of very practical exercises. Patsy Rodenburg's book, *Speaking Shakespeare* (Methuen, Second Edition, 2023), is also a tremendous practical resource. Each of these texts will offer a wealth of insights if you wish to explore speaking Shakespeare texts further. Additionally, Kristin Linklater's *Freeing Shakespeare's Voice* (Nick Hern Books, 2110) is another masterwork that I would highly recommend. The early chapters on *Vowels and Consonants* and on *Words and Images* offer practical ways of embodying your voice and Shakespeare's text.

## Blank verse

First of all, the blank verse of a Shakespeare play is 'blank' because for the most part it does not rhyme. It is written in the verse form known as iambic pentameter. In its regular form, this means that there are ten syllables in a line – actually made up of five iambs: an iamb is a weak syllable followed by a stressed or strong syllable. The simplest way to understand this is to know that a line of Shakespeare verse consists of a string of five heartbeats – what could be more human than that?

Tap out a heartbeat with a soft fist on your chest and execute them in strings of five at a time. You can say Dee-Dum-Dee-Dum-Dee-Dum-Dee-Dum-Dee-Dum as you tap the rhythm out on your chest. (Or Buh-Boom-Buh-Boom ….I like Buh-Boom myself, but we're all different. Go with the sounds that you feel are right for you.)

This helps you find the rhythm but is also a bit counterproductive because when we beat the rhythm out on our chest in this way, we tend to make it a kind of downbeat and, in fact, the iambic rhythm, simply put, is much more of an upbeat.

The best way to feel this and to get it into your body is to skip around the room while you say Dee-Dum-Dee-Dum-Dee-Dum-Dee-Dum-Dee-Dum (or, if you prefer, Buh-Boom).

> ### Iambic exercise
>
> Skip, in this rhythm, as energetically as you like and then, perhaps, try the exercise with a couple of lines of Shakespeare verse, skipping while you speak them. Sonnets are quite handy for this. Try a couple of lines from Shakespeare's famous sonnet 18, 'Shall I compare thee to a summer's day? / Thou art more lovely and more temperate'. Or 'When in disgrace with fortune and men's eyes / I all alone beweep my outcast state' (Sonnet 29). While you are doing this ensure that your voice is relatively relaxed – you should be speaking around your optimum pitch – and don't worry too much about trying to keep your voice steady as this will make you unnecessarily tense. Then, try a whole sonnet. Don't worry too much about whether you understand it before you begin, just skip and speak, allowing your voice to be jogged out of you in a very relaxed way and, perhaps, try the whole thing through two or three times.
>
> When you've done this, try standing still, grounding yourself, and allow yourself to tune into your natural breath. You'll find the breath will be moving within you quite actively after several minutes of skipping and speaking. Don't try to control the breath, let the breath be, but just ensure that you are accessing a gentle low belly release in response to each breath as it drops in.
>
> Then, without skipping, speak the text. I think the chances are that you will feel as if you can speak it relatively easily and that you understand quite a bit of it without having really attempted to work on your understanding of the poem. I think you will find that the skipping has helped you to get the rhythm of the verse

> into your body, and it also helps to acknowledge something about the intrinsic nature of this kind of verse – iambic verse is a series of forward moving up-beats. After skipping the text you have a good sense of the movement and drive of it, and of this up-beat feeling within it.

At this point, it is useful to say that the five stresses in the iambic line are not equal. If you find that, after these exercises, they seem to be so, try to honour the natural cadence of the spoken thought: there are five stresses in the verse line, but they are not equally important. There may be only one or two major stresses in a verse line – there are not likely to be more, though there are always exceptions – but there will be five beats.

So far, so good. Depending on which sonnet you choose, you may find that some lines of a sonnet or a speech from a play don't seem to fit the very regular, heartbeat rhythm of the iambic line. Quite simply, some verse lines are regular and some irregular.

For the purposes of the above skipping exercise, you can make the words fit the rhythm, even when they don't. If you do this, of course, you will notice when the words don't quite fit the rhythm and this is useful because, when the rhythm is momentarily disturbed, something is happening within the thought or emotional life of the verse (and thus within you, the speaker).

Don't misunderstand me, as this is just an exercise designed to help you understand, experientially, something about the nature of the verse you are speaking. When you speak the verse for an audience, you will wish to find a natural cadence and not sound at all as if you are speaking verse in some self-conscious or artificial kind of way. Put simply, when speaking Shakespeare verse, or that of any of his contemporaries, you must sound like a person speaking.

## The English language is iambic

The natural rhythm inherent in the English language is an iambic rhythm. That is not to say that all words or all phrases of English fall into that pattern, yet it is very easy to speak simple thoughts within the iambic pattern. For example:

> I went to town to buy myself a coat.
> My mother says I shouldn't wear this blouse.
> I'd like to buy myself a brand new car.
> Then, if you say you're cross, that makes me sad.
> The night is dark, I cannot see the moon.
> I feel afraid and cannot cross the street.

These are simple, regular, end-stopped, iambic statements.

> Try making up some simple iambic statements for yourself. This is yet another way to get the rhythm of iambic verse into your body and into your way of thinking.

As you can see, English easily falls into these iambic patterns and this is why Shakespeare and his contemporaries landed upon iambic pentameter as a suitable metric form for their purposes. It's a verse form but it is only a small step away from the way we speak in everyday life, in fact. Shakespeare opts for iambic verse in a scene when something in the circumstances calls for it. A good example of this is the first scene for Oberon and Titania in *A Midsummer Nights Dream*, Act II Scene I.

**Oberon**    Ill met by moonlight, proud Titania.
**Titania**    What, jealous Oberon? Fairies, skip hence,
I have forsworn his bed and company.

(*William Shakespeare/Complete Works*,
*A Midsummer Night's Dream*, ed. Sukanta Chaudhuri, Arden, 2021)

This is the beginning of a blazing argument between the fairy King and Queen. The poetry that emerges in the course of the scene is astonishing, but the reason for the scene and the verse is that these two mighty powers are at loggerheads. Each time Shakespeare employs verse in a scene, the reasons for the verse are always different, but it is likely that the stakes are high and that the emotions of the characters within the scene are heightened. In this scene there are a number of factors that lend themselves to verse. Firstly, the characters are fairies and not human; secondly, they are the fairy king and queen, and so very high status; thirdly the stakes are high for both characters and their emotions very fully engaged in an argument.

So, we have played with the rhythms of iambic pentameter, but this reference to the argument in *A Midsummer Night's Dream* brings us to another important aspect relevant to Renaissance drama.

## Rhetoric

This will be a word that you have probably heard before. The classic definition of rhetoric is that it is the art of persuasive speaking, but basically the use of rhetoric when we speak is to promote, to advance, or to win an argument.

Put simply, the majority of scenes in a Shakespeare play are arguments – sometimes in the literal sense, as in the scene above between Oberon and Titania – but the word argument does not necessarily mean a row but, more generally, discourse: two or more people holding different points of view, frequently caring very much about what the outcome of the discussion may be, who battle it out with words.

## The Integrated Actor

When you work on a Shakespeare play, it is useful to remember this: the majority of the scenes in any play are conflicts between opposing parties. And these arguments matter to them, in the same way that, if you become involved in an argument in your own life, you also care very much about the outcome.

There are a number of approaches to argument, but there are three that occur and recur in rhetoric. These are identified as:

> Logos
> Ethos
> Pathos

Logos, as the Greek word implies, means that the basis of the arguments you employ is logical: you try to reason with your opponent. Ethos indicates that the speaker is using ethical arguments to try to win their case. Simply put, you might argue that something must be done because it is in the best interests of the greater good of the populace, for instance. When Pathos is employed, you are using emotional blackmail of one kind or another to win your argument.

It is quite useful to take a major speech from any of Shakespeare's plays and annotate, line by line, whether you think the character is employing Logos, Ethos, or Pathos at any given moment. If you know a speech by heart, get hold of a copy of it and analyse it, marking thought by thought with L (Logos), E (Ethos), P (Pathos).

Any of the speeches from the climactic scene of Julius Caesar, Act III Scene II, when Mark Antony and Brutus face the mob after Caesar's assassination, are useful for this exercise. Mark Antony's famous, 'Friends, Romans, countrymen, lend me your ears' ... for instance, or his later speech, 'If you have tears, prepare to shed them now'. But you can use any speech, in verse, made by a major character – Volumnia, Coriolanus' mother, has some brilliantly effective speeches in Act V Scene III of *Coriolanus*. 'Should we be silent and not speak ....' for instance, which starts around line 94 of the scene.

## Rhetorical devices

In order to win arguments, it is likely that rhetorical devices will be used. If you have studied literature, it is quite likely that you will think of these as *literary* devices, but they originate in, and arise from, argument and discourse and not literature. There are hundreds of them and you cannot possibly, I would argue, know them all. However, an awareness and sensitivity to the way that language can be employed to advance an argument, persuade someone to a course of action or, simply, in order to get what you want, is useful in classical drama. Some of them may already be familiar to you: hyperbole, litotes, epithet, assonance, onomatopoeia.

I won't spend time here explaining them all, but there are several rhetorical devices that Shakespeare especially likes to employ that I think are worth discussing. Some of them are quite simple, such as repetition, and lists, and he also quite likes to use personification: the attribution of a personal nature or human characteristics to something non-human. An example of this might be:

**Miranda**  The sky it seems would pour down stinking pitch
But that the sea, mounting to th' welkin's cheek,
Dashes the fire out.
*(William Shakespeare/Complete Works, The Tempest*, ed. Virginia Mason Vaughan and Alden T. Vaughan, Arden, 2021)

This is from the second scene of *The Tempest*, when Miranda tries to persuade her father, Prospero, a magician, to intervene when a storm at sea, which he has created by his magic, destroys a ship. Both the sky and the sea are here given human attributes – personification.

Key rhetorical devices that Shakespeare likes to use are the 'rule of three' and antithesis and oxymoron.

## Rule of three

The 'rule of three' is sometimes given much fancier names: a triad, a tricolon, and hendiatris. Each of these is slightly different from the other – by all means look these descriptions up if you'd like to know the difference – but essentially, you are looking for things that come in threes within an argument. It's really useful to be aware of these and to know how they advance your argument if the character you are playing uses them.

Here's a very good example of the use of 'rule of three' in operation. This is a speech of Portia from *The Merchant of Venice* made to Bassanio when he has just unlocked the casket that contains her picture, which means that he will become her husband.

**Portia**  You see me, Lord Bassanio, where I stand,
Such as I am. Though for myself alone
I would not be ambitious in my wish
To wish myself much better, yet, for you,
I would be trebled twenty times myself,
A thousand times more fair, ten thousand times more rich,
That only to stand high in your account
I might in virtues, livings, beauties, friends
Exceed account. But the full some of me
Is sum of something: which to term in gross,
Is an unlessen'd girl, unschooled, unpractis'd.
Happy in this, she is not yet so old
But she may learn; happier than this,
She is not bred so dull but she can learn.
Happiest of all is that her gentle spirit

> Commits itself to yours to be directed,
> As from her lord, her governor, her king.
> Myself, and what is mine, to you and yours
> Is now converted. But now, I was the lord
> Of this fair mansion, master of my servants,
> Queen o'er myself; and even now, but now,
> This house, these servants and this same myself,
> Are yours, my lord's. I give them with this ring
> (*giving him a ring*)
> Which, when you part from, lose, or give away,
> Let it presage the ruin of your love,
> And be my vantage to exclaim on you.
>
> (*William Shakespeare/Complete Works,
> The Merchant of Venice*, ed. John Drakakis, Arden, 2021)

See how frequently Shakespeare employs the 'rule of three' within it as Portia attempts to sway Bassanio to become her husband. (He doesn't really need much persuading, but she doesn't necessarily know that.) How many 'rules of three' can you spot in the extract from the speech above? Notice that the 'rule of three' may be explored in lists of three things, e.g. 'an unlesson'd girl, unschooled, unpractis'd', or, 'As from her lord, her governor, her king'. It may also occur in a series of three related phrases, 'But now, I was the lord of this fair mansion, master of my servants/Queen o'er myself ... ' How do you think you would make this kind of rhetorical device work in a spoken argument?

I always think it is unwise to offer answers that are too simple, as there may be a number of different ways to work a 'rule of three' in an attempt to persuade someone to your point of view, or to get what you want from someone. However, I would say that the speaker makes a point, then realizes that this statement is not sufficient, so the point is reinforced or made again, but this, too, does not seem winning enough, and so the point is reiterated. (By the way, notice in the section of the speech that contains, happy, happier, and happiest, that each clause here also creates a 'rule of three', so a 'rule of three' can be phrases that come in threes and not just single words.) Essentially, then, when you speak words or phrases that make a 'rule of three', each statement needs to make some kind of advance from the one that precedes it or, in other words, there must be some kind of growth or development within the 'rule of three' as you speak it.

Staying with this speech for a moment, it is also useful to ask yourself why this character, at this moment, speaks this way – why does Portia use so many 'rules of three' in her speech? I think there may be a number of choices here and, again, I think it is unwise to suggest that there is only one reason why Portia expresses herself in this way, at this point. However, to me there are two very important possibilities.

Firstly, this is a huge moment for Portia, and she makes this clear within the speech: that when Bassanio marries her, everything she owns becomes his, and everything she currently is ('master of my servants/Queen o'er myself') she gives up, because he will become the master of the household and of herself. (This is an Elizabethan/Jacobean reality for all women who marry.) Her speaking in threes is one of the ways in which she emphasizes the importance of what is happening. Secondly, she herself, of all her suitors (and we see three suitors attempting to choose the right casket in the play), has wanted Bassanio to be the one that makes the right choice, so she, like Bassanio, is very much invested in this moment. Simply put, she wants him, and the use of 'rule of three' as she speaks reinforces this want, this need for the outcome to be what she, herself, most desires.

If you continue to consider this speech further, you will also find other potential reasons why Portia uses 'rule of three' here, but I would say that whatever justifications you come up with for the use of a rhetorical device, they must be playable – they must help you act it. Your job, if you happen to play Portia, is not to share with your audience your literary knowledge but to embody the person and to share what drives her – her wants, needs, and desires – and what she does to achieve them.

## Antithesis and oxymoron

Antithesis is a rhetorical device that juxtaposes two contrasting or opposing ideas, within similarly constructed phrases or clauses, usually of equal length. For instance, Neil Armstrong used antithesis when he stepped onto the surface of the moon in 1969 and said, 'That's one small step for a man, one giant leap for mankind'. It's a bit like an old-fashioned kitchen weighing scale, with one idea balanced against another.

An Oxymoron is a similar kind of device but one which juxtaposes single words rather than phrases. Two words that represent things that are opposites, which normally would not belong together, are placed together in order to emphasize a deeper truth. A good, simple example of an oxymoron is the phrase, 'sweet sorrow'. Shakespeare loves to use antithesis and oxymoron and you will find examples of both in every play.

Here's a very good example of antithesis from *Julius Caesar*. 'The evil that men do lives after them, / The good is oft interred within their bones'. And, from *Hamlet*, 'give every man thine ear, but few thy voice. Take each man's censure, but reserve thy judgement'.

Below are two speeches spoken by Romeo in *Romeo and Juliet*. One is from the first scene of the play when the families of the Montagues and the Capulets have been brawling in a public place.

**Romeo**  Alas, that love, whose view is muffled still,
Should without eyes find pathways to his will.
Where shall we dine? O me, what fray was here?
Yet tell me not, for I have heard it all.
Here's much to do with hate, but more with love.
Why then, O brawling love, O loving hate,
O anything of nothing first create,
O heavy lightness, serious vanity,
Misshapen chaos of well-seeming forms,

## The Integrated Actor

> Feather of lead, bright smoke, cold fire, sick health,
> Still-waking sleep that is not what it is.
> This love feel I that feel no love in this.
> Does thou not laugh?

'Misshapen chaos of well-seeming forms', is an example of antithesis, where contrasting ideas are juxtaposed against each other, but there are many examples of oxymoron here, such as 'brawling love', 'loving hate', and, 'heavy lightness' to name a few.

The second speech is from Act III Scene III of the play, when Romeo has been banished from Verona and can no longer be with Juliet. He is begging Friar Lawrence to find a way to help him. I would argue that the use of oxymoron and antithesis is more sophisticated here.

**Romeo**  'Tis torture and not mercy. Heaven is here
Where Juliet lives, and every cat and dog
And little mouse, every unworthy thing
Live here in heaven and may look on her,
But Romeo may not. More validity,
More honourable state, more courtship lives
In carrion flies than Romeo. They may seize
On the white wonder of dear Juliet's hand
And steal immortal blessing from her lips,
Who even in pure and vestal modesty
Still blush, as thinking their own kisses sin.
But Romeo may not, he is banished.
Flies may do this, but I from this must fly;
They are free men, but I am banished:
And sayest thou yet that exile is not death?
Hadst thou no poison mixed, no sharp ground knife,
No sudden mean of death, though ne'er so mean,
But 'banished' to kill me? Banished!
O Friar, the damned use that phrase in hell;
Howling attends it. How hast thou the heart,
Being a divine, a ghostly confessor,
A sin-absolver, and my friend professed,
To mangle me with that word 'banished'?

In both examples the use of the rhetorical devices of antithesis and oxymoron helps the actor to embody the confusion, and the mental and emotional distress, that Romeo is experiencing at both of these points in the dramatic action of the play. So, when you find examples of antithesis and oxymoron in the text, make sure you play them.

# CHAPTER 22
# OTHER ASPECTS OF IAMBIC PENTAMETER

We've explored some of the aspects of iambic pentameter and an introduction to rhetoric. (If you are curious to know more about rhetoric and its workings there are some excellent resources out there. I would recommend *Dramatic Adventures in Rhetoric* by Giles Taylor and Philip Wilson, Oberon Books, 2015.)

In the previous chapter I have spent some time drawing your attention to two equally important aspects of dramatic verse: the basics of iambic pentameter and rhetoric. Both aspects need to be appreciated and engaged with by the actor as a starting point, but I'd now like to return to the verse itself and explore some of the other elements within blank verse.

## Enjambment

Early on in this book, we looked at the implications of the way the poetic text is laid out on the page and, if you spoke any of the Shakespeare extracts quoted above, you will have noticed that sometimes there is punctuation at the end of the verse line, and sometimes there is none. When there is no punctuation at the end of the verse line, the indication is that the thought continues and that, therefore, your speaking runs on. The technical term for this, where it occurs, is enjambment. However, as it is verse, I think it is important in some way to acknowledge where the line ends, even if the spoken thought continues beyond the end of the line. More about this later. If the sense of the spoken thought clearly does end at the end of the verse line, for instance, if there is a full-stop, then this is called an end-stopped line.

Before I go any further with this particular point, it is probably useful for me to say that there are at least two major approaches to the speaking of Shakespeare verse, and they are not always in agreement. One approach, which many directors favour, is that proposed by Peter Hall. Key to this approach is the notion that you should only breathe at the end of the verse line, never in the middle of it. I am not much in agreement with this approach which, to me, seems too rigid, and I favour the Cicely Berry/John Barton approach which allows for the possibility of a breath being able to be taken mid-line or at the end of the line. Personally, I am for a world in which the actor has choices and how they exercise their choice is part of the skill that the actor brings to the role. For me verse speaking for actors is about having tools, not rules.

Returning to the earlier point about verse lines where the thought runs into the next line, some interpreters of the Peter Hall approach to verse speaking insist that a breath should be taken at the end of every line. I think this is possibly a misunderstanding of what Peter Hall advocates – it seems to me a very rigid approach – but some experienced actors have explained this to me as a means of sounding as if the thought is still developing within the speaker and that if you employ this approach, breathing at the end of every line so that the thought is interrupted, the actor can make their speaking better emulate patterns of everyday speech. Certainly, some actors can demonstrate this very, very well but, again, it would not be my choice. However, I am all for choice for the actor, so by all means try the Peter Hall approach in practice and see how you feel about it.

In the Cicely Berry/John Barton approach to verse speaking, where there is enjambment, it is useful as you speak the speech to kick an object as you arrive on the last beat of every verse line. If the line is enjambed, you carry on speaking into the next line, but you remember to kick the object on the last beat of every line, nonetheless. Cicely Berry advocated kicking something like a shoe – obviously, when you kick the shoe you then have to follow it as you speak and catch up with it for the next kick, and some actors really enjoy this exercise. I prefer an object that is not likely to move much, if at all, so that it is possible to concentrate on the way the kick at the end of every line affects your speaking of the text.

### *Structure of the verse* – Exercise 1

Stand opposite a wall and speak a section of Shakespeare verse – a speech from a play, written in verse, would be a useful choice. As your voice arrives on the last beat of the line, kick the wall. If the thought runs on into the next line (i.e. the line is enjambed), continue speaking but kick the wall on the last beat of each line, nonetheless. When you've completed this exercise throughout the speech you've chosen, go back to the top of the speech and speak it again, without physically kicking the wall. How has the exercise changed your relationship with the text?

### Exercise 2

You could also undertake another version of this exercise by making a strong punching gesture with one hand and arm in front of yourself as you arrive on the beat rather than kicking something.

Earlier in this section, I asked you to speak some iambic verse and skip as you did so, and we identified that a line of iambic pentameter consists of a series of forward moving up-beats. This is part of the intrinsic nature of iambic verse – it just works that way, naturally. Kicking an object at the end of the verse line, as you speak, also helps you find the up-beat within the verse line and, also, enables you, the actor, and your audience to sense how the thought is structured through the verse writing.

I apologize as I am now doing the very thing I advocated against – I am intellectualizing about the way the verse in a Shakespeare play works – but I am trying to find ways to describe to you accurately ways in which to inhabit the verse when you speak it.

At this point, perhaps it will be helpful if we look at some of these ideas in practice, so take a look at the speech below from *Hamlet*.

**Hamlet**  To be or not to be – that is the question;
Whether 'tis nobler in the mind to suffer
The slings and arrows of outrageous fortune
Or to take arms against a sea of troubles
And by opposing end them; to die: to sleep –
No more, and by a sleep to say we end
The heartache and the thousand natural shocks
That flesh is heir to: 'tis a consummation
Devoutly to be wished – to die: to sleep –
To sleep, perchance to dream – ay, there's the rub,
For in that sleep of death what dreams may come
When we have shuffled off this mortal coil
Must give us pause; there's the respect
That makes calamity of so long life.
For, who would bear the whips and scorns of time,
Th'oppressors wrong, the proud man's contumely,
The pangs of despised love, the law's delay,
The insolence of office and the spurns
The patient merit of th'unworthy takes,
When he himself might his quietus make
With a bare bodkin. Who would fardels bear
To grunt and sweat under a weary life
But that the dread of something after death
(The undiscovered country from whose bourn
No traveller returns) puzzles the will
And makes us rather bear those ills we have
Than fly to others that we know not of.
Thus conscience does make cowards of us all
And this the native hue of resolution
Is sicklied o'er with the pale cast of thought,
And enterprise of great pith and moment
With this regard their currents turn awry
And lose the name of action.
(*William Shakespeare/Complete Works*,
*Hamlet,* ed. Ann Thompson and Neil Taylor, Arden, 2021)

### The Integrated Actor

This is Shakespeare writing at the top of his game. It is a later play, and the verse reflects Shakespeare's considerable experience as a playwright at this point, and is quite sophisticated and challenging to speak.

Notice the use of enjambment – how frequently the sense of one line runs into the next.

> ***Structure of the verse – Exercise 3***
>
> Try speaking the speech without honouring in any way the line endings, and then try speaking it, kicking something on the last beat of the line – or punching one fist straight out in front of you when you arrive on that final beat. Then try speaking the speech again without kicking or punching. Which do you prefer? It seems to me that, if we run the sense from one line to the next without finding a way to emphasize the last beat of the line, we have prose and that, when we do find a way to arrive on that final beat, landing on that word in some way, but still run on into the next line when the thought continues, we have verse.

Don't misunderstand this exercise. Some actors look for a quick fix with it, a formula, and decide that you have to lift the end of every line. This is not at all the case. There are any number of ways of arriving on the last beat of the line – you might give that word more weight, you might extend the syllable, you might change the pitch: you might do a number of things, but there is no one, 'right' way. It's not a rule as to how you give the final word of the verse line more attention but, if you wish to honour the verse, you should find a way to do it.

### Eleven (or more) syllable lines

In the monologue above from *Hamlet* you may have noticed that quite a few of the lines run to eleven and not ten syllables, the eleventh syllable being weak, and you may also notice that some of the lines are not regular in terms of where the beats fall. Interestingly, the lines that are regular, such as 'for, who would bear the whips and scorns of time', which I would argue has a very strong and insistent beat, falling in the regular iambic pattern, stand out and have particular impact. The second line, 'Whether 'tis nobler in the mind to suffer ... ' is not quite regular: the opening beat falls irregularly, and the line has eleven rather than the standard ten syllables. You'll find quite a lot of eleven syllable lines within this speech. These irregularities create disturbance within the speaker and tell the actor about Hamlet's emotions at this point. If you speak the speech and connect with it, you will begin to sense the nature of the disturbance within the thought process and the text.

It is traditional to call a regular iambic line one with a 'masculine' ending, and one that has eleven syllables, when the last syllable is weak, a line with a 'feminine' ending.

# Other Aspects of Iambic Pentameter

I'm not particularly sold on these ways of identifying this difference and would simply say that it is useful to notice when lines are regular or irregular because, again, these are clues to the character's state of mind and emotional state.

## Jazz

At this point, perhaps it is useful to share with you that I think Shakespeare verse is rather like jazz. If you like to listen to jazz, you will appreciate that it is a musical form in which the bass provides a regular and steady beat whilst the other instrumentalists, or the singer, riff, improvise, and bend the melody line in various ways against this moving bass.

So, in Shakespeare verse, the heartbeat is constantly there, at the heart of every line, and the heartbeat pulse is underneath the spoken thought, like the steady rhythm of the bass in jazz. The words spoken may, at times, be arranged in an irregular pattern, in terms of the iambic beat, but the heartbeat rhythm is always at the heart of the text. So, don't be anxious as an actor when the verse line doesn't seem to fit the regular iambic beat, because this irregularity is providing you with clues about the character's state of mind, the relationship between characters, or the atmosphere within the scene, at any given moment.

For this reason, I am not for an analysis of the text where other rhythms within it are identified. For example:

**Hamlet**  To be or not to be – that is the question;
Whether 'tis nobler in the mind to suffer
The slings and arrows of outrageous fortune
Or to take arms against a sea of troubles
And by opposing end them;

Some scholars will say, the second line consists of a troche (Whether 'tis nobler … ) and the fourth line starts with an anapaest (Or to take arms … ) for example, but if we know that the line is intrinsically iambic all we need to be aware of is that the rhythm becomes irregular and that this is a clue to something happening within the character or within the scene. I don't think this kind of analysis, which can seem very clever, helps you as an actor to play the text. The text itself is always iambic, because the heartbeat of the iambic rhythm is underneath every line.

## Other features within iambic texts

I'd like to explore some of the other features of structure within iambic verse. The first, the caesura, is hotly contended by those who follow the Peter Hall approach to verse speaking but is very much a feature of the Berry/Barton approach.

# The Integrated Actor

## Caesura

The word caesura, which comes from Greek, means an interruption or a hiatus. For centuries it has been understood to be a mid-line pause. However, some individuals who follow the Peter Hall school of verse speaking insist that there can be no mid-line pause, since a pause, which might or might not be a breath, can only occur at the end of the verse line. (And by the way, the words pause and breath are not synonymous here – a pause may be a moment when a breath drops in, or it may not: we do not have to breathe when we pause, and it depends very much on the context and the individual speaker.)

If we look again at the speech of Romeo's, above, it would appear that there are a number of potential mid-line pauses indicated in the text by full stops. Arguably, there are others marked, mid-line, by commas. If you like the idea that there can be no mid-line pause, then the theory is that where a full stop occurs around the middle of the line you change pitch to indicate a new thought is taking place, but you do not pause. You might also snatch a breath at this point but it must be so fast that the flow of the rhythm of the line does not appear to be interrupted. If this interests you, try it: though I think you will find it difficult to accomplish if you do not really know the speech. The idea behind this is that the character is so emotionally charged and so worked up that their thoughts and feelings are just pouring out of them.

**Romeo**   'Tis torture and not mercy. Heaven is here
Where Juliet lives, and every cat and dog
And little mouse, every unworthy thing
Live here in heaven and may look on her,
But Romeo may not. More validity,
More honourable state, more courtship lives
In carrion flies than Romeo. They may seize
On the white wonder of dear Juliet's hand
And steal immortal blessing from her lips,
Who even in pure and vestal modesty
Still blush, as thinking their own kisses sin.
But Romeo may not, he is banished.
Flies may do this, but I from this must fly;
They are free men, but I am banished:
And sayest thou yet that exile is not death?
Hadst thou no poison mixed, no sharp ground knife,
No sudden mean of death, though ne'er so mean,
But 'banished' to kill me? Banished!
O Friar, the damned use that phrase in hell;
Howling attends it. How hast thou the heart,
Being a divine, a ghostly confessor,
A sin-absolver, and my friend professed,
To mangle me with that word 'banished'?

This, to me, seems unnecessarily artificial and technical, though I accept that it can sometimes be a choice. But should it be a choice every time a caesura appears to occur?

Incidentally, you might also choose to re-explore the speech of Portia's from *The Merchant of Venice* that was also featured earlier in this book. This also contains a good number of potential caesuras. I have heard directors say that her thoughts and feelings here are just pouring out of her – that she is so excited at the thought that she can now be with Bassanio that she cannot control the way she expresses her feelings. Certainly, if the caesuras in this text are never pauses, it would seem that she is experiencing this moment in this kind of way. However, if you take pauses, occasionally (perhaps not every time) where some of the caesuras may be indicated by punctuation, mid-line, within the text, the interpretation of this speech will be very different: perhaps the moment is so enormous (after all, past this moment, she is no longer the head of her household and her property becomes Bassanio's) that she speaks more thoughtfully and more carefully and, perhaps, too, she does not want to appear to Bassanio to be too rash in her thinking and to free with her feelings.

I think that this discussion about caesuras is a really important one because it emphasizes the suggestion I made earlier that understanding the possibilities within Shakespeare verse is all about choices: once again, tools not rules. Also, as you can see with the example of Portia's speech, the choices you make with regard to the speaking of the verse affect what is taking place within the character and the action of the scene and can change your characterization.

# CHAPTER 23
# LANGUAGE AND TEXT 5 – SHAKESPEARE SONNETS

### A sonnet is, traditionally, a fourteen-line poem and is a love lyric

Shakespeare sonnets are such a good way of being introduced to speaking Shakespeare's verse. The skills we develop in speaking a sonnet are easily transferrable to handling the verse a character speaks in a play. I am a great believer in the sonnets as an introduction to getting the feel for iambic verse. Each sonnet is short and self-contained, and everything the actor needs to speak a sonnet is contained within the text.

The verse is different, though, in that a sonnet rhymes, where blank verse, generally, does not. However, I think the beauty of working on a Shakespeare sonnet is in the discipline it requires because, besides the rhyme, a sonnet also has a clearly defined structure which needs to be honoured in the speaking if the thoughts and feelings within it are to be communicated to the listener in the most complete way.

I am a great believer in the development of discipline within the actor, and I think working with Shakespeare's text, in sonnets and in plays, is such a good way of beginning to develop a kind of discipline within interpretive work. I indicated at the beginning of this book, with the Yevtushenko poem, that every text we interpret has a structure of some kind or another and that our job is to be able to respond to the structural clues within the text.

I believe that the actor's job is to serve: the playwright, the other actors, the space and the audience. We seem to live in a time where the expectation is that we should be self-serving. At any rate, it is my belief that actors who are entirely self-serving are self-centred and selfish. They are unlikely to work well with their fellow actors with whom they need to be generous as well as accepting but, more importantly, an actor who is self-serving, for instance, one who cares more about their own feelings than the demands of the scene itself, or the text they speak, is a poor communicator.

The wonderful thing about Shakespeare, and his contemporaries, is that the text gives you everything you need, but in order to do it justice, you need to know how to respond to all of the information – the clues, if you like – that are embodied within the text.

### The caesura

I've already declared my bias and said that I am a great believer in the possibility of the caesura as a pause – and, by the way, pauses can vary in length: they do not have to be

## The Integrated Actor

chasms within the text. Some pauses may be merely momentary – some longer. We have choices and all is dependent upon context.

Let's take a look at the possibility of the caesura as a pause by speaking a Shakespeare sonnet.

Sonnets are also personal and in the first person and so, whilst it is not a dramatic text, when spoken it can be similar to the experience of speaking a monologue or a soliloquy in a play. Shakespeare's sonnets are frequently both intensely personal and passionately expressed. In fact they summarize perfectly something that is especially Renaissance: the notion that the idea, the thought and the emotional expression of it are entirely one. There is no separation between thought and feeling, no distance between the idea and the emotional response to it.

This is easy, perhaps, to understand but not easy to realize in performance for many of us today because we are taught to separate the idea from any feelings we may have about it, so that we can discuss ideas without what some think of as emotional baggage. In academic circles, particularly, we are taught that we should be able to discuss ideas rationally and clearly without muddying the waters of discourse with too many feelings. This is not at all Shakesperean and, I believe, would have been counter-intuitive to an Elizabethan.

Sonnet 18

Shall I compare thee to a summer's day?
Thou art more lovely and more temperate:
Rough winds do shake the darling buds of May,
And summer's lease hath all too short a date:
Sometime too hot the eye of heaven shines,
And often is his gold complexion dimmed;
And every fair from fair sometimes declines,
By chance, or nature's changing course, untrimmed.
But thy eternal summer shall not fade,
Nor lose possession of that fair thou ow'st,
Nor shall death brag thou wander'st in his shade
When in eternal lines to time though grow'st:
  So long as men can breathe or eyes can see,
  So long lives this, and this gives life to thee.

*(William Shakespeare/Complete Works,* ed. Kathrine Duncan-Jones, Arden, 2021.)

You are going to use this sonnet to experiment with the notion of a mid-line pause when you speak it.

I would advocate skipping this sonnet a few times before you experiment with the mid-line pause, just to help yourself be more familiar with it before you experiment; however, you can attempt the mid-line pause exercise without really knowing the sonnet, if you prefer.

You will find the iambic verse in this sonnet almost entirely regular, so skipping the sonnet does not offer any real challenges in terms of realizing its rhythm. Some of you may feel that you have to speak, 'Sometime', at the beginning of the fifth line in the contemporary way. It's worth trying it with the stress on 'time' which is where the stress would fall if the line is honoured as an iambic line. I think you will find that this still makes sense and, in a strange way, I feel honouring the iambic beat here actually renders the thought more active, in the moment. However, these are both viable choices, so it is up to you, as you speak it, to make the choice which makes more sense to you. 'Nor shall death brag ... ' is another line where the line could be regular or irregular, depending on your choice. I would recommend allowing this line to be spoken as a regular iambic line but, again, there is a choice.

I am going to spend some time exploring punctuation and the implications for the speaker in the next chapter, but it is worth my mentioning here the line, 'By chance, or nature's changing course, untrimmed.' Contemporary speakers are frequently taught somewhere along the way in their education that a comma is an opportunity to pause and/or a place where a breath can be indicated. In my view, there is only one punctuation mark that indicates a pause and, indeed, the need for a breath, and that is a full-stop. A full-stop indicates that one thought has ended and that a new thought is beginning and, when a new thought drops in, a breath also drops in. I would advocate, therefore, saying this line with short pauses at the commas, and then saying the line without pauses, as an experiment. I think you will find that the spoken thought works very well without two pauses and that if you do place two pauses in this line the emotional drive of the thought is lost. I also think, quite simply, that the integrity of the iambic line is compromised if two pauses are placed within it.

So, you may then ask, if I am not keen on pausing at commas, as a rule, and if the integrity of the iambic line matters, why pause at all? Generally, in this sonnet, you will find that a mid-line pause can work and it is just something intrinsic to the way iambic pentameter works that a mid-line pause often seems both possible and plausible.

### Caesura exercise

So, you are going to speak the sonnet doing your best to place a pause in the middle of each line. Don't be too strict about this – I am not asking you to count the number of syllables so that the pause falls exactly in the middle of the line: the place where you pause needs to make some kind of sense and so may not always fall after the fifth syllable. For instance, if you place a mid-line pause in the very first line, it would have to be after 'thee', which is after the fifth syllable – the spoken thought doesn't make sense if there is a pause placed anywhere else in it. However, as we have already seen, in the line, 'By chance, or nature's changing course, untrimmed', a mid-line pause really doesn't work. Experiment: I think a pause is possible in this thought, possibly after the word 'chance', but perhaps this thought is best spoken without pauses.

## The Integrated Actor

In the end, I am fairly sure that you will find that in some verse lines a mid-line pause really isn't warranted and isn't helpful, but in some lines it will feel absolutely right. All I really want you to have a sense of from this exercise is that a caesura is a possibility – a possible choice. I am not at all suggesting that we should look for a caesura in every line as a general rule, but when the opportunity genuinely arises we should respond to the possibility. Again, I reaffirm that this work is always about tools, not rules. What we choose to do when we find the possibility of a caesural pause is not a rule – we may take the pause or we may not: we have a choice. This is down to interpretive choice, but we should always make the choice that enables us to communicate the thought to its fullest potential. We serve the text, as actors we do not (or we should not) serve ourselves.

### *More about sonnet structure*

Before launching into this section of the book, let me say that structure is only relevant to the speaking of a sonnet because it is key to thought and to the development of the argument within it.

Earlier in this book, we have considered rhetoric and its implications for actors – how every major scene in a play by Shakespeare, is some kind of argument or discourse – but a sonnet, too, poses an argument.

If you look at the rhyming scheme of a sonnet, it will tell you a great deal about the way the thoughts within the argument are developed. The way the sonnet rhymes divides it into four sections: the first four lines provide an introduction to the main subject, idea or problem; the next four lines develop this idea further; the four lines that follow then, usually, look at the problem from a very different perspective and can introduce a new idea; and the final rhyming couplet provides a summary or conclusion to the problem.

This structure can be very clearly seen in a Shakespeare sonnet as the rhyming scheme (i.e. which lines rhyme with which) is easily observed and is: A,B,A,B,C,D,C,D,E,F,E,F, G,G. The poem falls into three groups of four lines and a final couplet. Clearly, then, there are thought shifts after the fourth line, the eighth line, and the twelfth line and the speaker must be able to realize these shifts in the way they respond to this structure when they speak it.

The groups of four lines are usually referred to as quatrains just as the final two rhyming lines are referred to as a couplet.

Let's explore now Sonnet 29.

Sonnet 29

> When in disgrace with fortune and men's eyes
> I all alone beweep my outcast state,
> And trouble deaf heaven with my bootless cries,
> And look upon myself and curse my fate,
> Wishing me like to one more rich in hope,

Featured like him, like him with friends possessed,
Desiring this man's art and that man's scope,
With what I most enjoy contented least;
Yes in these thoughts myself almost despising,
Haply I think on thee, and then my state,
Like to the lark at break of day arising,
From sullen earth sings hymns at heaven's gate;
    For thy sweet love remembered such wealth brings
    That then I scorn to change my state with kings.

*(William Shakespeare/Complete Works,* ed. Kathrine Duncan-Jones, Arden, 2021)

There are perhaps some fairly obvious things to notice about it before you explore the sonnet structure. For instance, in the way that Katherine Duncan-Jones has edited it, the ideas are expressed in one very long sentence. There are also not many opportunities for enjambment, where the sense runs from one line to the next – nearly all verse lines here are end-stopped. This is worth experimenting with when you know the sonnet better: for instance, the first two lines offer the possibility for enjambment and, I would argue, the line, 'Like to the lark at break of day arising,/from sullen earth sings hymns at heaven's gate;' which could be spoken as if end-stopped, or could be spoken as an enjambed line. These possible choices render the meaning of the thought here somewhat differently.

If you do skip and speak the sonnet through a few times you will notice that some lines are irregular. However, I'd like to suggest that if it does not corrupt the sense of the spoken thought, you allow the line to be regular if it can be. I am thinking here about the opening two lines, 'When in disgrace with fortune and men's eyes / I all alone beweep my outcast state', where it may seem odd to place the first stress on 'in' – you may prefer to make, 'When', the first stressed word and this is almost certainly what we would do in contemporary speech. However, I think if the first stress is placed on, 'in', the spoken thought still works and becomes more active, and, if this is your choice, you have also honoured the iambic rhythm.

Speak this sonnet through, then, and notice how the thought shifts as you move from line four to line five. As you move into line five you are still continuing to discuss the same subject, but in the second quatrain the expression becomes more detailed and more personal – examples of the reasons why the speaker feels down and dejected are provided. Notice how, as you move into line 9 (immediately after the second quatrain), there is a complete change of subject. Simply put, the narrative states, when I am feeling so dejected, if I think of you, my spirits lift – they, literally, soar heavenwards. The final couplet then sums everything up – the emotional journey through the sonnet – with great clarity, of both thought and feeling.

The Integrated Actor

## *The rhyming couplet*

As previously discussed, a sonnet always ends with a conclusion summarized in the final rhyming couplet.

A rhyming couplet has a particular drive and energy and makes an impact on the listener, largely because the two lines rhyme and this is something that has not occurred previously in the sonnet. The way you speak the rhyming couplet matters insofar as it must feel like a conclusion or a summing up when you say it.

I'm spending time to say this because rhyming couplets also occur in the plays. In some of the earlier plays (*Richard II* is one example) you find speeches that end with rhyming couplets – not often the case in the later plays – and, more importantly, scenes usually conclude with a rhyming couplet. Simply put, it's the way of signifying something has come to an end. Rhyming couplets at the ends of scenes, however, were particularly important to the Elizabethan audiences of the time. The plays were originally played in daylight, so there could be no blackouts, and so the rhyming couplet signified the end of the scene very clearly for those original audiences, and signals the start of the next scene – so it also signals a change of scene.

The rhyming couplet is also useful to actors because the energy of the final couplet of a scene is what takes the actors speaking offstage and brings the next group of actors onstage. If you play a final rhyming couplet with a flat, falling or negative energy, it simply cannot help you get off stage nor will it help the next group of actors entering to come on.

## *The volta*

To return to Sonnet 29. It is very evident when you speak it that there is a major thought shift after the eighth line and in the vast majority of the sonnets you will find a similar shift, in the thought and in the emotions embodied by it, at this point. This is sometimes known as the 'volta'. (At the time, the volta was also a famous dance – a favourite of Queen Elizabeth 1, in which the male threw his female partner into the air. The success of your volta was judged by how high you could ascend in that assisted leap.)

It is not really important that you remember this as a term but that you understand that, when you speak the sonnet, this major shift of tone – imaginative and vocal – must be realized as you move into the third quatrain.

Here in sonnet 29, having expressed at some lengths what it is like to feel isolated and low in spirits, at the volta the speaker remembers how much they treasure the person they love and their thoughts move quite dramatically – again, this must take place in the speaker both imaginatively and in their vocal expression.

I think sonnet 29 is one of Shakespeare's best – the range of emotions is quite seismic – and it is worth spending time to speak it and find ways to embody the journey through it. For instance, the imagery and the language of the lines, 'Like to the lark at break of day arising, / From sullen earth sings hymns at heaven's gate', is especially powerful. The lark, hovering close to the ground, suddenly ascends (they do this in a, more or less, vertical line) to a point high above the speaker, and they seem to be singing joyously at heaven's gate.

There's really quite a lot to unpack here if you really want to make deep contact with the poem because Shakespeare is referencing things that, to many of us today, do not seem so significant – either they do not have the impact today that they would have had to Shakespeare (the lark itself, for instance) or because we may not believe in heaven. However, the speaker of this sonnet does see the lark as significant and does believe in heaven and hell, which are real possibilities.

Can I unpack this for you further? Shakespeare is writing at a time when nothing can be airborne, besides a bird – man cannot fly, there are no aeroplanes. The fact that birds can fly is, therefore, wonderful to a Renaissance person and the lark itself is extraordinary within the bird kingdom because its ascent, from hovering close to the ground to shooting to a position way, way above our head in one very swift, vertical movement, appears almost magical and inexplicable. The lark then sings, and larks do have the most glorious kinds of song available to them – rich and complex – so this is also wonderful. The lark also flies so high that it seems to be at 'heaven's gate', so it sings for God, or for the glory of God. So from complete dejection, when the speaker thinks of their loved one, their spirits lift and 'sing' and heaven is once again possible and attainable.

So, is it possible when you speak this sonnet to allow your imagination to inhabit these images and for this process to affect your internal experience in such a way that your voice expresses what lies within this text?

I'd like to spend some time, finally, with two further sonnets: 116 and 129, which couldn't be more different from each other or more contrasting. Both present great challenges for the actor. Please take some time to have a look at them.

Sonnet 116

Let me not to the marriage of true minds
Admit impediments; love is not love
Which alters when it alteration finds,
Or bends with the remover to remove.
O no, it is an ever-fixed mark,
That looks on tempests and is never shaken;
It is the star to every wand'ring bark,
Whose worth's unknown, although his height be taken.
Love's not Time's fool, though rosy lips and cheeks
Within his bending sickle's compass come;
Love alters not with his brief hours and weeks,
But bears it out even to the edge of doom.
    If this be error and upon me proved,
    I never writ, nor no man ever loved.

## The Integrated Actor

Sonnet 129

Th'expense of spirit in a waste of shame
Is lust in action; and till action, lust
Is perjured, murderous, bloody, full of blame,
Savage, extreme, rude, cruel, not to trust;
Enjoyed no sooner but despised straight;
Past reason hunted, and no sooner had,
Past reason hated, as a swallowed bait,
On purpose laid to make the taker mad;
Mad in pursuit, and in possession so,
Had, having, and in quest to have, extreme;
A bliss in proof, and proved, a very woe;
Before, a joy proposed, behind, a dream.
    All this the world well knows, yet none knows well
    To shun the heaven that leads men to this hell.

I am not going to spend too much time analysing these texts, I'll leave that job to you. They really are worth working with and for a multiplicity of reasons.

Sonnet 116 is one of the greatest poems about the nature of love ever written – perhaps, the greatest. There's a lot to unpack here if you are to own it fully when you speak it. What is a 'wandering bark', for instance? And what is the relevance of a star to the 'wandering bark'? Do you hold the image in your mind of Time? What is time's sickle and what does it do? And what is 'doom'? You need to be able to image all these things and to experience strong, internal responses to them, as you speak this text. Remember that this is a matter of the imagination working behind the words on the page, the image being dropped into your centre when the breath drops in, and of you allowing (or trusting) your emotional reactions to the images to then take place. And all of this needs to take place within the structure of the sonnet form as you speak it.

Remember, the form is not a straight jacket – it is a challenge. There are hundreds of ways to map your way through this sonnet, but there are choices that you can make as an actor that will not work, or will work less well, and there are others, stimulated by the form, the structures within it, and the imagery, that will honour the text and help you to communicate it. In a way, it is a great puzzle, but one that will bear great rewards if you are prepared to do your homework in order to own it when you speak it.

Sonnet 129 was Cicely Berry's favourite, though perhaps it is unfair of me to suggest that she had a favourite, but it is the one she always brought out in workshops and it is the one that she herself recorded on the DVD *Shakespeare Sonnets*. (Produced by Henry Volans and Max Whitby, directed by John Wyver, published by Touch Press and Faber and Faber in partnership with Illuminations and The Arden Shakespeare, 2012. This is also available as an iPad app.)

For the most part this sonnet is incredibly regular, and the iambic beat, emphasized by many of the consonants – /p/, /s/, /m/ and /b/ in particular – is insistent and driving.

It's a sonnet in which you cannot afford to hold back when you speak it. In many ways this sonnet is very straightforward. That's not to say it is easy to understand – you have to know what Shakespeare means by the word 'spirit' for instance – and it has to be grappled with in order to be owned, but it speaks for itself if you can spend some time to get your imagination around some of the grammatical structures and the lists.

I've included it here because it makes particular demands in terms of sustained imaginative and emotional drive, vocal energy, and in terms of breath. It is also an unusual sonnet in that, arguably there is no volta – the conflict from the outset continues to the very end of the sonnet.

# CHAPTER 24
# PUNCTUATION

If you look at Sonnet 29 above everything is stated in one very long sentence – a sentence that spans the full fourteen lines of the sonnet. Similarly, if you look at Sonnet 129 again, you can see that this sonnet contains only two sentences – one very long, that spans lines 1 to 12, inclusive and the rhyming couplet.

First of all, in both the plays and the poems, the punctuation is quite frequently not Shakespeare's and it is also true to say that punctuation was used differently within Shakespeare's time than it is now. I think, for this reason, it is always worth considering that there may be other options in terms of how the text is punctuated.

Don't misunderstand me. The editor of the edition of the sonnets I quote here, Katherine Duncan-Jones, has done a masterful job in editing the cycle and in considering how best punctuation can be used to help to reveal the meaning of each sonnet. I don't think the punctuation is arbitrary or that we have a free-for-all as interpretive artists to play fast and loose with it. Occasionally, though, if we struggle with the punctuation offered, it can be interesting to look at another edition to see if there's an alternative, or simply to play with an alternative ourselves.

I mentioned earlier that I believe that the only punctuation that indicates the need for a breath to drop in is a full-stop. If we were to apply this as a rule to Sonnets 29 and 129, that would be quite a challenge to rise to, and anything that is going to make the actor unduly tense is going to be counterproductive, so my advice is that it is possible to breathe elsewhere in a long sentence so long as the listener knows that the breath taken does not suggest that the speaker has finished the thought. Such a breath would probably need to be quite rapid and, preferably silent, so as not to draw attention to it. So we are speaking here about a good deal of skill being available to you, the actor.

**The gasp breath – Allowing the breath to drop in rapidly**

Should you need to allow for a rapid intake of breath, you can practice gasping.

Earlier in this book, if you have been practising the exercises, you may have found that time has been needed to allow the breath to drop in, when you have perceived the need for it. You may have experienced this need to take time for any number of reasons, not least in order to allow the lower abdominal area, the area between belly button and pubic bone, to release.

However, it is possible to release the belly quickly, and when sustaining complex spoken thoughts, you may find yourself working to the end of the breath and needing to allow a new breath to drop in quickly because you are in the midst of, and need to sustain, a long or complex spoken thought.

This need to allow a breath to drop in rapidly can occur in a Shakespeare text or, indeed, any text from a bygone age – Elizabethan, Jacobean, Restoration, Georgian, Victorian, Edwardian – and even some modern and contemporary texts where characters are particularly articulate.

You may find the exercise below may help with this.

### The gasp exercise

### Exercise 1

Allow your jaw and lips to be relaxed and neutral so that the mouth is slightly open. Imagine that you hear or see something shocking and gasp. You should find that you experience a very fast low belly release as the breath rushes into you through your mouth. It may not feel to you as if you have taken in very much air but, in fact, you have. Avoid attempting to top up with any additional air and try speaking a long phrase or thought. You will probably find that you can.

### Exercise 2

Some actors find this exercise quite problematic to achieve. If you find this is the case, imagine as you gasp, that the air rushes into you via imaginary nostrils at the base of your spine, or in your pubic bone. This is also quite a good way of visualizing a quick inrush of breath so that the intake is less noisy.

In an ideal world, an in-breath should not really be audible. If we are constricting in the vocal tract, or if the musculature in the upper chest is overly engaged, then breath will not, in fact, 'drop in' but will be drawn in effortfully. This kind of in-breath will be quite noisy. If you are retracted in the vocal tract and if you achieve low belly release, even if you need a rapid intake of breath – the gasp breath described above – you should find it to be almost silent.

If you find this exercise tricky to achieve, you should find that it will become much easier with practice.

## Punctuation, phrasing and long sentences

On the subject of long sentences in Shakespeare (and there are plenty of them in the plays, too), I will share an anecdote once told to me by American speech and accent master teacher Deborah Hecht when we were both working at the Julliard School in the 1990s. She trained with master teacher Edith Skinner and at the end of the first year of their training they were required to speak a Shakespeare sonnet on one breath. If they were unable to do this, they failed the year and had to repeat the year or leave the course. I absolutely wouldn't advocate for this as a requirement for speaking Shakespeare, but what is interesting is that, according to Deborah, everyone in her class was able to do it.

However, this seems to me to be too rigid a demand – tools not rules, remember – but I would recommend that it is worth spending time experimenting with whether it is possible to sustain some of these long, Shakespearean thoughts on one breath. There are any number of reasons why you may find this difficult, but it is always worthwhile to see if it is possible to challenge existing habits and push back one's own boundaries, in the best interests of serving the text you wish to speak.

In contemporary everyday speaking, we tend to think and speak in short sound bites. With the advent of digital media and the text, I would say that this tendency has become even more prevalent. In conversational speaking we also, now, tend to speak in ways that are fairly uncommitted. It is just not 'cool' to declare our feelings too obviously or to sound as if what we say matters. For many of us, then, the longer more complex thoughts of Shakespeare can be difficult to handle and sustain.

### Breath – Shorter thoughts and longer thoughts

We're going to come back to Shakespeare's text shortly, but for the next experiment can I suggest that we go back to the Yevtushenko poem on Page 54.

---

**Phrasing exercise 1**

It is useful to try this exercise with a partner so that you have an objective observer, but it can work equally well if you explore this on your own. Take the opening four lines, which are actually a sentence. You experimented with ways in which the structure of the text might be honoured when you first explored this text as an exercise. For the sake of this exercise I'd like you to speak the first four lines, perhaps breathing at the end of each line. Don't be too rigid about applying this – you possibly will not want to breathe after, 'When your face … ' – but find a way to phrase this opening thought and place a breath or breaths within it, at the line endings.

When your face
appeared over my crumpled life (breath)
at first I understood (breath)
only the poverty of what I have.

## The Integrated Actor

While you explore these possibilities it's important that you are thinking through the text and, ideally, experiencing inner responses in relation to the thought. It may be that it is completely counterintuitive to explore the text by allowing the breath to drop in at these points and, of course, if this is the case, you wouldn't make this choice. However, I am guessing that quite a few of you experimenting with this will feel comfortable taking one or two breaths during this thought.

> ### Phrasing exercise 2
>
> Now see if you can speak the thought on one breath. It is possibly easiest to approach this gradually:
>
> When your face
> appeared over my crumpled life (breath)
> at first I understood
> only the poverty of what I have.
>
> Then try the four lines on one breath. You still need, I would maintain, to find a way to respect the line ending in one way or another. Remember, it is very important that you are thinking/experiencing through the text as you speak it, and if you do not take a breath at the end of the verse line, this does not mean that you cannot pause – it is possible to pause mid-thought without breathing.

If you have a partner listening to you as you explore this, it is interesting to hear how the text affects them as they listen: a version with one or two breaths and a version with no breath interrupting the thought of the first four lines. (If you are not working with a partner, then record the different performances and then listen to them back.)

You may be surprised to find what can result from this simple exercise, in terms of both how you feel and what someone else may experience as they listen. There are two things that are particularly useful to observe, however. You may feel that speaking the four lines on one breath is less comfortable than allowing time for the breath to drop in at places within the four lines. This tells you something about your own habit and if you find it more of a challenge to speak the four lines on one breath, it is worth considering why this may be and whether it is possible to change this habit.

The second thing to notice is how the listener feels when the thought is interrupted by breaths and when the whole thought is spoken on one breath. It may not feel very different to you when you speak it if you allow a breath to drop in after the second line, for instance, and if you don't – especially if you pause at the end of the second line, without a breath dropping in at this point. You may feel the two performances are not very much different. The listener is likely to feel, simply put, that they continue to listen to the thought when the four lines are spoken on one breath in a different way than when you breathe at the ends of lines.

As a result of this exercise, you might want to go back to the Yevtushenko text and work it through again, exploring whether it is possible to sustain each thought on one breath and how this might alter your performance of it,

I think this exercise has implications, then, for handling longer more complex thoughts in Shakespeare.

> **Phrasing exercise 3**
>
> Perhaps return now to Sonnet 29 which is written as one very long sentence. I am not advocating that you attempt to speak this sonnet on one breath, though some of you may be able to do this comfortably, but if this is one long thought, how is it possible to keep the thought afloat if you breathe within it?
>
> When in disgrace with fortune and men's eyes
> I all alone beweep my outcast state,
> And trouble deaf heaven with my bootless cries,
> And look upon myself and curse my fate,
> Wishing me like to one more rich in hope,
> Featured like him, like him with friends possessed,
> Desiring this man's art and that man's scope,
> With what I most enjoy contended least;
> Yes in these thoughts myself almost despising,
> Haply I think on thee, and then my state,
> Like to the lark at break of day arising,
> From sullen earth sings hymns at heaven's gate;
>     For thy sweet love remembered such wealth brings
>     That then I scorn to change my state with kings.

Always remember that a breath dropping in is a change of thought or, at least, a shift within the thought. I would say that it is fairly obvious that a breath can drop in at the volta, when the thought shifts markedly, and the emotional response with it, but it is likely that you will have felt the need for a breath before this point.

Given the structure of a sonnet – three quatrains and a rhyming couplet to finish – it makes sense that a breath could drop in at the end of lines four, eight and twelve, as thought-shifts take place at these points. However, you may still, feel that you need further opportunities for breath to drop in, even within the four lines of a quatrain.

This possibly will seem to you unnecessarily technical and it is important to say that the actor speaks as the character (or should do so) when they have the need to speak. If you can find the need that justifies speaking four lines of iambic verse on one breath, then you will find that it is possible to accomplish this.

I confess, this is all a bit chicken and egg because if you do not attempt to push the boundaries of your imagination, and with this the boundaries of your breath, you are unlikely to find the deep need to speak these thoughts. On the other hand, if you feel you are unable to breathe when you feel you must, you will not own the words of the text and your performance of it will be unconvincing. However, these technical considerations and explorations now can help you to change your own internal patterns in order to meet the demands of the text you have to speak better.

I'd like to illustrate these matters further by referring you to a recording of the Michael Parkinson show first shown in 1973. (It's shown fairly regularly on BBC 4 and can be sampled on YouTube.) The three guests are the actors Maggie Smith and Kenneth Williams, and the poet John Betjeman. Smith and Williams speak one of Betjeman's poems, *Death in Leamington*, towards the conclusion of the interview. They are actually reading, but nonetheless give a coherent and touching shared performance of the text. I would argue that both actors impress and have a strong shared understanding of the text they speak. Do you notice, however, that Williams tends to breathe at the end of each verse line and that Smith does not? Initially, Smith speaks her first verse all on one breath. You'll notice in the rest of the poem she varies where she may take the breath but, overall, she speaks much longer thoughts than Williams. I think both performances are convincing so, again, I am not trying to force a 'rule' upon you as an actor about breath and phrasing but if you are able to sample this performance, do you feel one actor is more persuasive than the other? If both performances are equally successful, why is that? What is it each actor is able to do that justifies where they breathe and the way they interpret the text?

I think the corollary of what I am attempting to get you to think about is why should we settle for what is merely comfortable for us and easy? Why should we impose our own habits upon the text we speak, or a character we play? Should we not endeavour to meet the character to meet the text, on their own terms?

All of this work is painstaking and takes concentration, focused working and time. Should we not be prepared to undertake this kind of work, though, if we are ambitious to interpret a playwright's work and to engage and entertain audiences?

## Further work with punctuation

I have mentioned before that the punctuation in a modern edition of a play or poem by William Shakespeare is most likely not all his, so you may wonder why I am taking time to get you to think about, and work around, matters connected with punctuation.

First of all, as mentioned above, the Shakespeare play or poem you read will have been edited by a contemporary writer. They have considered very carefully how the text should be punctuated: they will probably have retained Shakespeare's punctuation but may also have made some amendments or additions for a modern reader, bearing in mind that the way punctuation worked at the time when Shakespeare first wrote the plays was different from today. So, it is always worth working with the punctuation that is given you, at least to begin with, because the editor will have thought long and hard about how to make the text accessible to you today.

Take any of the classical texts on offer in this book or find a printed copy of a monologue in verse by Shakespeare that you may already be familiar with. The two exercises offered below are both adapted from the work of Cicely Berry, but I offer these versions here because I think they are tremendously helpful to actors and they help you to experience the kind of clues that punctuation give you in terms of the experience of embodying a text.

### Punctuation exercise with chairs

Place two chairs – they need to be the same size and shape – opposite each other about a metre apart. Sit in one of the chairs. With a copy of the printed text in your hand, speak the text – when you arrive at the first punctuation mark, pause and move as quickly as possible to the chair opposite. Only when your behind is touching the seat do you continue to speak the thought. When you arrive at the next punctuation mark, move to the other chair, as quickly as possible. Continue through the text in this way, speaking to the next punctuation mark and then moving, until you reach the end.

It's important that you think the thought you are speaking – don't just gabble the words. It's easy to get caught up in this exercise without really thinking about what you are saying, but it is still your job to internalize the thought as you speak. In the moments when you pause to change seats aim to keep the thought moving forward in your mind – don't just stop speaking: keep the thought active in the silence when you move.

Actors do not always enjoy this exercise, and I think it may be because there is a discipline in it. It takes an enormous amount of concentration to engage, at the fullest level, with it. What does this exercise do for the text? If you feel as if you have not gained very much from undertaking the exercise, I recommend doing it again, with the same text, as you may find more the second time.

There are any number of experiences that can arise from this exercise with the chairs. You may find the rhythm of the thoughts and the internal rhythm of the character. You may experience the forward movement of the thought, as it develops. With some texts, usually ones in which there is a lot of punctuation, this exercise can help you experience the emotional turmoil of the character. There may be other things, too, that arise within you as a result of this exercise. The key observation, though, is that each punctuation mark is some kind of turning point within the spoken thought: that is to say, the thought shifts, deflects or turns when a punctuation mark occurs.

## The Integrated Actor

### Walking the text

This exercise is similar to the last and is also based on an exercise from the work of Cicley Berry. It's quite simple, and my experience is that many actors really enjoy this exercise, though my personal preference is for the chair exercise because of the discipline of it. This next exercise can easily run out of control and the actor may not be aware that this has occurred.

> **Punctuation exercise 2**
>
> Looking at a printed copy of your text and, again, monitoring the punctuation as it occurs, speaking the text, start to walk forwards, with purpose. At the first punctuation mark do not make any kind of a pause but turn and walk in a different direction. At the next punctuation mark, again, turn and keep walking, and so on. If the punctuation mark you arrive at is a full-stop, you may pause, momentarily, before changing direction and moving off on the next line, but only pause at a full-stop. Work through the text in this way until you reach the end of it.

It's very easy with this exercise just to get caught up with turning and moving and actors often start to move faster and faster around the space. As with the previous exercise, it is absolutely essential that you are thinking the thought you are speaking as you speak it and not just gabbling words and rushing about the space.

> **Punctuation exercise 3**
>
> Repeat the exercise of walking the text. This time, when you reach a punctuation mark turn and, at the same time as you turn, change your pitch. Choose a pitch slightly higher, or slightly lower, than the pitch on which you were previously speaking.

Again, with this exercise, you begin to appreciate how the punctuation indicates a shift or turning point within the way the thought thinks. It is also easy with this exercise to feel the forward moving upbeat of the iambic rhythm and the drive forwards within each thought.

In life, when we change direction within our spoken thought we frequently change pitch. These changes might be quite subtle, but they are there. The changing pitch version of the exercise may seem unduly technical, but it may awaken an awareness within you that changes of pitch are a natural part of expressive speaking.

## Summary

Punctuation, then, is not principally about a place where you might breathe, it is about the way a writer encapsulates the journey of the thought, the twists and turns within it. That's not to say that a punctuation mark can't be a breath – a full-stop almost certainly will be as it indicates a completely new thought – but don't make it a rule to allow a breath to drop in at a punctuation mark, such as a comma.

# CHAPTER 25
# INTEGRATION: IMAGINATION, BODY, BREATH, VOICE

### Tools from the Stanislavski System

Before guiding you through the next exercise, I would like to take some time to outline those aspects of the Stanislavski System that I think are particularly important in the process of becoming an integrated actor.

If I had more time and space, I would outline these in a much more detailed way than I am able to do here but, of course, there is a wealth of other books that can take you through the tools of Stanislavski's system and provide you with exercises to help you embody them.

In many schools in the UK the approach to the creative processes of acting can be quite reductive – some schools placing emphasis on the Objective, some on playing an Action and so on. The Stanislavski System is, in fact, a much more rigorous system than this kind of approach would imply.

When working on a play, I think the following concepts, all from the work of Konstantin Stanislavski, are important and need to be explored in training: Relaxation, Given Circumstances, Magic 'If', Objective (sometimes referred to as Intention), Obstacle, Super-Objective, Tactics, Sense Memory and Substitution.

I have spent a considerable amount in the early section of this book outlining ways to access a relaxed but focused state through an application of applied Alexander principles. Nothing creative, or really truthful, can happen for you in your acting without being able to work from a place of ease in which you are not physically defended. Tension is a form of defence and self-protection – an excessively tense body and tense musculature do not facilitate the radiation of inner life to an audience or enable you to be expressive. More simply put, when you are unduly tense your thoughts and feelings cannot be communicated. Actors who work from tension tend to push, in an attempt to be understood so that, in the end, a tense actor overworks.

For the purposes of the integration exercise that follows you will spend time preparing yourself to be relaxed and open. The other main focus of this exercise is focusing on your Intention, in the UK frequently referred to as your Objective. This, of course, is what the character you are playing wants, and I much prefer the use of the word 'want' to any of the other words that can be used to identify this important acting

## The Integrated Actor

tool. The key to this final exercise that leads to your ability to integrate imagination, body, breath and voice is the want. This is the want of the character, of course, but it must become your want if you are to embody it.

> The key questions, then, are:
> What do I want?
> What brings me (your character) to this place?
> When I speak to the character I meet there (or the audience), what do I want from them?
> And the question that then follows is what will I do to get what I want?

To stay with the notion of 'the want' for a moment, identify the fact that when you really want something this is very much like the feeling of a physical need. It's a sense of yearning from deep within you. There will be times in your life when you will have felt this strong sense of wanting – perhaps it was similar to a feeling of hunger, perhaps it almost felt like a pain in your stomach, perhaps it came close to the feeling of wanting to be sick – but wanting is a physical sensation located in your gut, so when you think about your want it is essential that this does not remain an intellectual concept. By imagining what you want and connecting your imagination to your breath, and through your breath to the centre, you will then begin to find that sense of wanting that fuels your objective or intention.

You will need a text, and it is probably best to focus on a monologue from a play. You could, arguably, use a poem, such as *Colours*, or a Shakespeare sonnet, but to do this you would need to create some given circumstances for the text. A monologue from a play is ideal, therefore, as the context in which it takes place, the given circumstances, are provided for you in the play itself.

Assuming that you have spent time working through all of the imaginative, physical and technical challenges presented to you so far in this book, we finally come to the process that I call integration. This is what occurs when at least some of the physical and technical work has been explored and absorbed by you, when you can further explore the ways in which the imagination, the breath and the body work as one. For this final exercise. in which I hope all the elements so far undertaken will come together, you need to return to Floor Work 3, which begins on page 70 of this book. This prepares the way for the final challenge.

## Floor work into text and character

I can summarize the preparatory process again for you here, but you will find a more detailed description of the preparatory work in the earlier section, so do refer to it if you feel that you are still unfamiliar with the process that leads to physical freedom.

## Recap of semi-supine preparation

Lying in semi-supine, with a couple of books to support your head, spend time to allow your back to lengthen and widen against the floor. Remember that your knees feel as if they want to float directly up to the ceiling above you, and imagine the knee joint, behind the knee cap, as a space. The tail of your spine wants to lengthen in the direction of your heals – direct it to do this. Your neck spine wants to lengthen away from the tail. Imagine your spine, particularly the tail and the small of your back, wanting to make contact with the floor. (You do not need to push your spine down, or force it to the floor – imagine the spine relaxing towards it.) Your right shoulder wishes to float away to your right and the left shoulder to the left. Imagine the space between your shoulders, behind you, widening as you allow your shoulders to float in opposite directions away from each other, and you allow your upper back to spread across the floor.

Place your mind in your spine and imagine it lengthening out along the floor, the spaces between the vertebrae (where the discs are) gradually opening up: each vertebra trying to float away from the one below it, with the tail bone wanting to move in the direction of your heels. Say to yourself, as your attention comes to the top of your back spine, 'Let my neck be free to let my head move forwards and upwards.' (Or forwards and out.)

As your back lengthens and widens across the floor, become aware of the fact that it is not necessary to hold on to any of the musculature in the front of your body. Think of the breastbone and the solar plexus (the area of muscle immediately below the breastbone) softening and think of the belly area also being able to soften.

As your neck lengthens out of the top of your back spine, remind yourself of the relationship between your lengthening neck and the freedom of your lower jaw. Your lower jaw wants to float down and away from your upper jaw so that there is a natural space between your lips. Imagine tiny springs between your upper and lower molars in the back of your mouth – the imaginary springs lift the back upper molars away from the lower molars and move the lower molars down and away from the upper molars.

At this point, tune in to the breath. It's useful to focus on the out-breath, noticing that it falls out from your centre like a sigh of relief and without any control – as the breath falls out there is a tiny sensation that your breastbone falls back towards your spine. At the end of the out-breath, wait for the moment when the body wants to allow the next breath to fall in and allow this to touch down at centre. Every breath is going to fall out of you like a sigh of relief, and on each replacing breath release the musculature in the lower belly area a little bit more – how deeply are you able to release here: the sense of release is likely to be subtle, but can be as low as the pubic bone.

## Release work into text

### Stage 1

Take your imagination, now, to the text you have chosen. When the character speaks this speech, what do they want? This simple question is dependent on many other things but, for now, let's focus on that particular question. For the speech you have chosen, if it is spoken to another character, are they an obstacle to what you wish to achieve, or is what you want something that the other character can give you? Is the monologue you have chosen spoken to the audience (it might be a soliloquy from a Shakespeare play, for instance)? If it is, what do you want from your interaction with the audience?

Picture what it is you want as you let your breath fall in and out of you. How much do you want it? If you are able to get what you want, what will that do for you? How will it change you or your circumstances? Your visualization of what you want should affect your breath – drop these images of your desires or drives into your centre with your breath and let your responses to those desires fall out of you with your breath. It's possible that the rhythm of your breathing may be affected – it may even become erratic. Allow this to happen, maintaining your sense of low belly release as it does. As your breath falls out of you, your whole being lets go: simply put, your spine lengthens in two directions, your shoulders and your back spreads, but you may also start to experience a sense of the feelings that are stimulated by your want also releasing through your body. (Don't worry if you don't – this may, or may not, be something you experience, but the sense of release from within and through your spine on the out-breath is something you will be familiar with.)

### Stage 2

As you explore your want in this way, allow your imagination to go to a moment in your monologue where the thought or the language most expresses your want. This is not going to be more than two, three or four lines, if it is a classical text, or a longer phrase or sentence if it is a contemporary text.

Start to taste the words in the section you have chosen, touching them off as sounds from centre and tasting them on your tongue, lips, teeth and soft palate. How do these words, the sounds of these words, help you to express what you want? Or how can the way in which you say these words help you to get what you want?

Occasionally, you can say to yourself, 'Let my neck be free to let my head move forwards and upwards'. Notice that this thought enables free movement of the lower jaw. If any tension in your jaw joint arises as a result of your exploration of your want and the feelings that are stimulated by wanting it, let this tension release and place your focus deeper within your being, to your centre which is the root of everything.

> Spend some time exploring the vowel sounds that you move through in the section of the speech you are working on – which ones are more open, which ones are rounded. How do these enable you to express the way you feel about your want?

All of this exploration can take some time. At times, you should sense that it is almost as if you are learning to speak, so that you are sometimes playing with the sounds as you explore them. Throughout this exploration, keep your imagination active by visualizing your want, and the potential consequences of your being able to fulfil it, in different ways. Your want is not a fixed thing – each time you attempt to visualize it, the images may come to you in a different way and you can allow these visualizations to be quite random, for instance, they may be colours and amorphous shapes and do not have to be specific objects or people. If you were able to achieve your want it might also be that you, or your circumstances, would be changed in some way – what might that look like and how might you feel about yourself, and the world around you, if these changes were to occur?

All of these imaginative explorations can be explored in relation to the physical exploration, and inner experience, of the sounds you are making. Once you have explored the phrase or sentence as fully as you feel you can, simply speak it, touching the thought off from centre as you do and allowing it to fall out of you.

You can spend time to work through the whole monologue in this way, or you can move on to the next stage.

### Stage 3

You're still in semi-supine. Relax on your exploration of the spoken text and let go of any feelings that have been stimulated by the previous exercise. Tune into the breath and your natural breathing rhythm, and remind yourself of your directions – lengthening the spine, allowing the back to spread across the floor and allowing the floor to support your weight. Know, also, that if you allow your imagination to focus again on your want that you will be able to return to that work easily.

You are going to bring yourself to standing, finding how you are grounded over your feet. You are going to do this with a minimum amount of effort and with a maximum sense of ease. The easiest way to accomplish this is to roll onto one side, allowing a turn of the head to lead you, keeping your back long and wide, into a semi-foetal position. You can rest in this position for a moment or two, allowing the breath to drop in and out of you naturally – you may notice some movement of your lower ribs against the floor as you breathe. From here you will bring yourself onto your hands and knees maintaining a flat back: your knees are an easy distance

## The Integrated Actor

apart and your face is parallel to the floor, maintaining the length of your neck. Again, spend some time to breathe in this position, noticing how there is a sense that your belly is heavy in relation to gravity and that, as breath drops in, the belly wants to give towards the floor beneath you.

You can take a moment or two to remind yourself that your head wants to move forwards and upwards off your spine – 'Let my neck be free to let my head move forwards and upwards.' You are not moving yet, you are still on all fours, tuning into the breath, but you can allow these directions to take your focus. Also notice, in this position, that the tail of your spine wants to move in the direction of the floor beneath your knees. The tail lengthens away from the neck and the neck lengthens away from the tail so that, in your imagination, the spine is still lengthening in two directions.

Take a moment or two to focus again on your want. You're not going to spend a great deal of time with it, but allow yourself to visualize what you want again, keeping your belly free in this position. Notice how what you want may affect your experience of your breath. Your want is going to motivate you to come into standing – your head, will lead you as one knee moves forwards and upwards until the sole of the foot is in contact with the floor. From here, you should be able to find an easy way to bring yourself into standing – you're looking for an economy of effort and, as you come up, you may find yourself uncurling through the spine into standing. Feel the weight of your pelvis hanging off your spine as your knees release, sensing how your weight is grounded through your feet which are firmly in contact with the floor. Your neck is lengthening away from the tail as your head (and it is head, not chin) wants to float forwards and upwards. Your shoulders want to move in opposite directions away from each other as your back spreads or widens behind you, in the space. Your belly muscles have remained soft and, when breath drops in, it is as if the breath arriving deep within you also grounds you.

### Pause for thought

At this point it is important to say that if your belly muscles are held or are gripping as you stand, you should probably go back to the semi-supine work and not move forward with this exercise. There are other ways to release the belly, however, so if you sense that your belly is held, which can be a response to bringing yourself back to standing from semi-supine, then spending time with the 'gathering water' exercise or, simply, dropping down and building up through the spine, ensuring that you release the lower belly and that it stays released may be beneficial at this point.

Low belly release is crucial not only to your experience of breath and then of making sound but also to your ability to experience your inner emotional life and to express it.

## Stage 4 – Movement into speaking

Stand in an aligned and grounded position, allowing the breath to fall in and out of you easily and freely, take your imagination back to the circumstances in which the monologue you have chosen occurs.

Imagine, for the sake of this exercise, that you have not yet arrived at the point in the play where the events that give rise to the thoughts in this monologue occur.

As you stand in alignment and breathe, freely and easily, put your imagination into the events of the play that take place just before this monologue occurs. It may be that a number of events have led you to this point – you may have to re-imagine the major things that have occurred up to this point – or you may only need to think about what has occurred just before. Where were you? What things happened around you and to you? Let your imagination wander freely through these events and breathe them – allow them to affect your experience of the breath.

Now take yourself on an imaginary journey – this may not exist within the events of the play, but you will undertake this imaginary journey in order to facilitate this exercise. The journey is going to take you to the place and point in the play where you speak this monologue.

You are going to start walking around your rehearsal space – why are you going to the place you're headed and what is it that you expect to find there and what do you want?

At this point you need to take your attention to both your body and movement and also to what you want. The objective is for your body to remain released and open, free and easy, and for you to be able to make a connection between this released state and your want.

As you pursue your want, moving through the space, be aware that it is your head that leads you – it naturally wants to move forwards and upwards: remember that it's your head that leads and not your chin. Each knee also wants to move forwards and upwards as you walk – the knee floats forwards and upwards bringing the foot away from the floor and, as you step forwards, the heal of this foot goes down as your other knee floats forward and upwards for the next step. Your back is long and wide – the tail of your spine wants to move in the direction of the ground below you, while your neck lengthens away from your tail bone in the opposite direction.

As you move around the space, keep pursuing your want and notice that your experience of this is very much connected to your breath. Your breath moves freely within you, but remains rooted and, crucially, your lower abdominal muscles are free to respond to the movement of the breath. Let your breath respond to whatever is in your imagination that is connected to your want. There are no rules about the rhythm of your breathing, or the way your body responds to it – for instance, you may feel the breath connecting with your pelvic floor, or beginning to engage the bottom of the ribs or you may feel it opening your back, or you may not sense these elements – but you will feel you have a sense of breath being centred within you and of the low belly release which is a response to the breath dropping in.

You can explore directions in response to your want. As your want takes you forward in the space remind yourself that it's your head that leads you. As you visualize your want, direct your neck to be free, or sense that your back is long and wide. As you pursue your want, allow your knees to float forwards and upwards as you make each step, and so on.

You can spend a considerable amount of time coordinating this process, which is all led by your imagination, both in relation to what it is you want and the sense of efficiency of movement, freedom and physical release. Ultimately, though, focus on your want, allowing yourself to visualize this in different ways – don't let your imagination get stuck. Allow your want to become more urgent and feel the need to pursue it more intensely – you may be walking faster in response to this, you may even break into a light jog. If you do find yourself jogging, allow chest, belly and shoulders to be loose and for breath to be loosely jogged out of you.

Keep pursuing that want – you are almost at the place in the play where the monologue occurs. Arrive, grounding yourself as you do. If you have maintained the freedom in your lower abdominal muscles, don't worry about your breath – your body knows what to do in order for you to achieve your want – let the breath drop in and speak your monologue sensing how the words you speak are connected to your attempt to get what you want. If you are speaking to another person, a group or an imaginary audience, explore how you will use your words to get what you want, and how the muscularity of the words is one of the ways in which you can affect them.

### Reflection

Once the speech is over, relax and take time to reflect on this experience. You may be able to consider quite specific details within what you have just experienced, to do with your body, your breath or your imagination, or you may only have a more general sense of what happened, or of what you felt. It is all valuable to you and if you undertake this exercise again, with the same speech, the experience will be different and you will probably notice different things within it on each occasion.

It is good, obviously, to note for yourself what feels different, in a good way, and whether anything new happened for you, either within yourself or within the speech. If you worked with a partner or with a small group of people, then feedback from them is also tremendously useful as they may have seen or experienced something that you were not aware was happening.

# CHAPTER 26
# WORKING WITH ENERGY – CHARACTER EXERCISE

The exercises below relate to the previous integration exercise but offer an introduction to working with energy as an approach to character.

I wrote in an early section of this book about a friend who referred to 'attunement' as a skill an actor needed to acquire, and I spent some time to try to describe what I understood she meant. I think of this now as an awareness of, and an ability to work with, energy.

Some of you may feel that working with energy, as described below, is a step too far – then don't go further in this book. You may come to this work later or may never feel the need for it. However, this work is very much concerned with the potential of energy and our awareness of it. I believe we are working with energy all the time – in life as well as in acting. Each of us radiates energy, for instance, and there is an exchange of energy between people when they share a space and when they communicate.

Places, too, have energy – sometimes when you stand within an empty theatre or in a church you have a sense of the energy of the space. (You might have previously thought of this as 'atmosphere'.) As an actor you can also have a sense of the collective energy of an audience. If an actor, or a group of actors, is able to tune into the collective energy of the audience in a live performance they can work with it, and I would argue that many great performers do this on an instinctive level.

### Exercise for tuning into energy

Standing, or sitting, in a grounded and aligned position, your feet in contact with the ground, your knees released and your head floating forwards and upwards, bring the palms of your hands together and rub them rapidly against each other for a minute or so. Then place your hands, palms facing each other, perhaps, eight inches apart from each other (20 centimetres). Allow your breath to drop in and out but focus on what you sense is occurring between your palms. You may need to place your hands slightly closer together, but not touching, and if you do not sense very much, then you may need to rub your hands together for longer before placing them opposite each other.

It is difficult to describe what you may sense occurring between them but the sensations you are tuning into we are going to call energy. (By the way, you may be able to sense this movement of energy between your hands without having

> to rub them together first.) Close your eyes – can you find a way to visualize the energy moving between your hands? It might have a colour, for instance, or you could imagine it as light energy, electricity or laser energy. Any kind of image that helps you to visualize the sensations you are feeling between your hands will be useful.
>
> So your hands are radiating energy and hopefully it is only a short step away from this exercise with your hands to be able to imagine that energy is radiating out of your body in every direction. Standing (or sitting), allowing breath to drop in and out of you in an easy, relaxed way, attempt to visualize an energy field around the whole of your body, from your feet to your head. Again, this might be coloured in some way, and you may visualize it as electricity, laser energy, or it might be gaseous or some kind of liquid.
>
> Go back to the exercise with your palms facing each other, about six or eight inches away from each other. See what happens to the feeling of energy between your hands when you move your hands further away from each other or bring them closer together. The quality of the energy usually changes in some way depending on whether they are closer or further apart and some of you will feel that, when your hands are some considerable distance apart from each other, that you lose the feeling of energy passing between them. (If you have lost that sensation of energy passing between them, then go back to the initial exercise of rubbing your palms vigorously together for a minute or two. After this, you will probably find that the sense of energy between your hands has returned.)

Our energy fluctuates, so you will find the experience of this exercise different each time you do it – certainly on a day-to-day basis. I think it is quite important to acknowledge this – it has implications for acting. I used to think, as a young actor, that my job was to arrive at a coherent performance through the process of rehearsal so that I could give this on the opening night and then repeat it, performance after performance, with each performance being more or less identical to the one I'd arrived at through the rehearsal process. I now know this to be quite an uncreative, and not a useful, concept.

First of all, why should the actor ever assume that the work is at an end when the play opens: every time you play the character and go through the journey of the play with your fellow actors, there is the chance to continue to make discoveries. Secondly, each performance cannot be the same because the experience of your energy, day to day, fluctuates and changes, so does that of your fellow actors and, in addition, each audience brings a different collective energy to the experience of participating in the performance. We have to learn to work with these changes in energy, focusing on the creative processes of acting in such a way that we can re-experience the character we play, the relationships we explore with our fellow actors, and the events within the play, and to do this as if for the first time each time we perform the play. Tuning into, and working with, energy can be one of the creative tools we draw upon to enable us to do this – along with the other creative processes we know, such as living within the given circumstances of the character and the world of the play, pursuing our want, tackling the obstacles that present themselves and so on.

## Being grounded and aligned, and energy

One of the reasons why I believe being able to work from a place of being grounded and aligned is important is because when we compromise our alignment in some way, the channels for energy within the body will be, at least partially, blocked.

We can argue about the fact that when we act we may be playing someone other than ourselves, and that the character we play may be blocked in some way. I think this is to misunderstand the processes of acting. Rather than debate this at length here, I would simply say that as you are the actor creating the character, you must be able to start, at least, from a place where you are at your most at ease and free, and not pre-judge the character you are to play before you commence the process of creating them. In addition I would like to say that if your ultimate goal is to be transformative in your acting – that is to say, appear to become someone other than yourself – do not assume that the main way of achieving this is by assuming a different physical identity, particularly not one that is going to compromise your psycho-physical function. In my experience, actors who start from the outside-in and begin by making changes to the way they stand, walk, hold their spine or their head and so on, simply exaggerate one or more of their own physical habits and then claim they are playing a character. So my advice is to be wary of this as an approach.

However you go about the business of 'transforming' in order to become the character, if you are to remain healthy and be able to continue to give a performance night after night and week after week, then you must be able to use yourself in a way that allows you to work organically and healthily. I believe, therefore, that the transformation that is most valuable to us is an imaginative, internal, psycho-physical one. This may result in some shifts in our physical embodiment but it is wise, for the reasons just discussed, not to start with the external.

## Your own energy

Before we consider moving towards becoming a character, let's consider your own experience of energy a little further. We can, and do, generate energy, within ourselves – for instance, the food we eat feeds our energy levels, and getting deep and healthy sleep (and enough of it) affects our energy levels. However, energy can also come into us or be received by us in various ways.

> ### Exercise to further explore energy
>
> When we sit or stand in a grounded position, energy can come into us through the soles of our feet. (If you are sitting, you may also experience a sense of energy coming into you through the base of your spine.) Spend a moment or two, standing or sitting in a grounded and aligned position, to imagine this possibility. Again, if it helps, you can give an image to your experience of energy – if standing, imagining that you are somewhat like a tree or a plant that draws water out of the ground may be helpful, for instance.
>
> We have explored the idea that the hands give out, or radiate, energy but they can also receive it. Spend a few moments thinking of radiating energy from your hands, and then imagine that the air around you is filled with atoms (energy) and that you can draw this in through the palms of your hands.
>
> Imagine that you can draw energy in through your feet, your hands and through the top of your head, and that it gathers and releases within you. The act of allowing breath to drop in and out of you is, itself, potentially, energizing and, as mentioned at the start of this book, breath is energy.

I would like to suggest that, as an actor, we should be constantly radiating energy when we are acting so we should be willing to be generous with it, though not profligate. So, giving is, perhaps, more valuable to us than taking. I believe that actors who radiate a considerable amount of energy have what is sometimes called 'star quality' – an audience simply feels compelled to watch them. Dame Judi Dench is such an actor, as are Sir Derek Jacobi and Sir Ian McKellan, and amongst the younger generation of actors Andrew Scott, Jonathan Bailey and Jody Comer all have the ability to appear 'magnetic' and charismatic.

Acting tools help you to generate energy, too – so pursuing a strongly felt want, for instance, helps to generate and sustain energy, or finding tactics with which to overcome an obstacle.

## Sharing energy and being attuned

I wrote about 'attunement' earlier in this book. If you are working in a group session, you might like to try this exercise. The group can be of any size but probably shouldn't be smaller than five or six people – ten or twelve people is an ideal number.

## Working with Energy – Character Exercise

### Simple exercise to experience attunement

#### Stage 1

Standing in a circle, with a small space between each member of the circle, with each member in the circle taking a moment to ensure that they are grounded and aligned, each person in the circle should repeat the exercise of vigorously rubbing their hands together for a couple of minutes. At this point, everyone in the circle should join hands, and each person needs to imagine that they are generously sending their energy into the hands of the person on either side of them. Ensure that you remain at ease and that your breathing is relaxed and organic, and really concentrate on being as generous with your energy as possible, sending it out from your hands. Your objective is to give as much energy as possible out of your hands.

Then decide to be really selfish with your energy. Simply think of taking energy from the partners' hands on either side of you. Focus on gathering as much energy as possible from your partners, through your hands.

A useful discussion can follow. What was the difference between these two activities, in terms of what you felt and experienced? The chances are that you felt most energized when you were focusing on being as generous with your energy as you could – that when you focused on taking energy it felt to you as if you received less energy and that when you concentrated on giving out energy, you seemed to receive more.

#### Stage 2

Repeat the exercise, rubbing your hands together for between one and two minutes before you join hands with your colleagues in a circle. Ensure that your breathing is easy, relaxed and centred.

This time think of sending the energy around the circle, in both directions, to your left and to your right when your hands are joined.

Then, gently, let go of your partners' hands and allow your hands and arms to relax by your side, simultaneously trying to maintain the sense of the energy travelling around the circle. In your imagination, you stay connected to the partners on either side of you and sense the shared energy between you.

Now, let everyone widen the circle by taking one step back so that there is a greater distance between members within the circle. Is it possible to still sense the shared energy between you?

# The Integrated Actor

Now, breathing deeply and freely, begin to walk around the space, each member changing direction from time to time. Is it possible to still sense the shared energy with the group? As you walk and you pass someone else, explore the sense of energy passing between you – you might pause as you pass each other, sense the energy and then move on.

Finally, come back into the circle and join hands again for a few moments, before coming out of the exercise.

At this point, a useful discussion might follow. What came out of this sequence of exercises for you? Did this help you to have a stronger sense of what we might mean by 'energy'? What did you experience, or notice, at various stages within this sequence?

If you were able to maintain a sense of the shared energy of the group, either in the circle when the hands were relaxing by your sides, or when you began to walk around the space, you are beginning to experience being attuned to the group and to your fellow actors.

### Energy centres – Character exercise

I have discussed previously within this book the idea that I think the most significant transformation that needs to occur in the actor in order to seem to become another character is internal and is principally an imaginative one. We may not need to move very far away from ourselves in order to assume the character we play – and in the world of theatre and film today we are probably going to be cast to type. However, we may find ourselves playing someone who is very different, imaginatively, socially, culturally and physically, from who we are. Hopefully, whether the character feels close to you or more removed from you, the next exercise will be helpful.

The Chakras are part of esoteric ideas and concepts about physiology and psychic centres that have emerged across Indian traditions. In Sanskrit, within Hinduism and Buddhism, the word chakra means

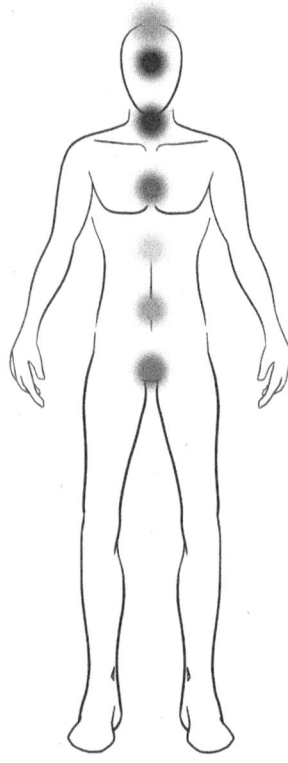

**Figure 3** Chakras
This diagram indicates the general location of the various chakras, or energy centres, in the body. This is to enable you to visualise them if you wish to explore the work in the final chapter of the book. A colour version of this diagram is available in the website that accompanies this book.

## Working with Energy – Character Exercise

'disk' or 'wheel' and is used to refer to the seven energy centres within the body. If you regularly practise Yoga, you will probably be familiar with the concept of chakras or energy centres.

I find that imaginative work with the chakras is useful as a stimulus in relation to character work and it is in this spirit that I offer the exercise here. Of course, if you are interested in exploring a deeper, spiritual understanding of chakras then you are free to undertake further research of your own.

The seven energy centres are identified for you on the diagram. Each centre is identified by a different colour and is associated with particular human qualities or attributes.

Within Eastern philosophy, each chakra has both a mundane and a higher spiritual level on which it operates. However, for the imaginative application that is being suggested here, we will only consider the mundane level. If you are interested to learn more about chakras and about applications of the Alexander Technique, there are a number of books that you can consult. A book that I have always found extremely accessible, and which explores in a fuller way the chakras, is *The Art of Changing: A New Approach to the Alexander Technique*, by Glen Park, published by Ashgrove Press in 1989. (This appears to be currently out of print, but there is an Audible Audiobook available through Amazon entitled 'The Art of Changing: Exploring the Alexander Technique and Its Relationship to the Human Energy Body', also by Glen Park.) Other excellent books about the Alexander Technique are detailed in the bibliography.

First of all, when trying to visualize the chakras, it is possible to think of them either in relation to your spine or in relation to various organs within your body. For the purposes of the exercises here, I suggest that you think of them in the way that is easiest for you. Each chakra or energy centre is associated with a different colour, and you may find thinking of each colour another helpful way to stimulate your imaginative awareness of them.

The root chakra, which is located at the base of the spine and/or in the sexual organs, is associated with the colour red. At its most basic level, this energy centre relates to grounding and it relates, principally, to our survival instincts – our need for shelter and food, for instance. When the root chakra is open, we feel confident to stand on our own two feet, and to withstand challenges. When blocked, we feel threatened, as if standing on unstable ground. It is also associated with sexual energy and sex drive.

The sacral chakra is associated with the colour orange and is located about an inch or so below the belly button and/or in the centre of the sacrum, where it is attached to the spine. This energy centre relates to pleasure and to our ability to experience emotionally, and it relates to the root chakra in that while we need shelter for survival we can also take pleasure in making the place where we shelter a home, and we need food to survive but we can also take great pleasure in the food we eat.

The solar plexus chakra, which you can also locate in a corresponding position along your spine, is concerned with power and control. The colour to work with here is a golden yellow. This energy centre, then, is associated with self-worth, self-confidence and self-esteem, and is concerned with a sense of feeling in control of your circumstances – or not. I often think that this is quite an important energy centre in relation to the characters we play, as a character is almost certain to believe themselves to be in control of the world they inhabit or not at all. Think of Macbeth's (or Lady Macbeth's) journey in Shakespeare's play, who begins, arguably, very much in control of their circumstances, but ends the play feeling they have lost all sense of control.

The heart chakra is located in the centre of your chest (or a point on your spine directly behind it) and is the next one to consider. It may surprise you that the colour to work with here is a rich green – the green of nature. As you might expect it is concerned with the ability to give and receive love. At its highest level, this energy centre is concerned with unconditional love – something many of us have never experienced, but it is closest to the kind of love a mother feels for her new born child. It is as much about our ability to love ourselves as it is to loving others and, arguably, if we are unable to love and accept who we are, we are not then able to love another.

The throat chakra is located in your throat, or on a point on your spine immediately behind it, and is concerned with self-expression – not just your relationship with your voice and with language, but also with any form of activity through which we express ourselves: for instance, playing an instrument or the ability to paint a picture. The colour to work with here is blue.

The brow chakra – sometimes referred to as 'the third eye' – is located in the centre of your forehead. The colour to work with here is indigo or a shade of purply-blue. As you might expect it is concerned with how we see things, perception and how we perceive the world around us. Can we see things for what they are, or do we only see what we want to see? This energy centre also relates to psychic ability and to a sense of seeing into the future or connecting with spirit. This may not be something you believe in, but some of the characters you might play may well possess psychic abilities. However any character who is strongly intuitive or who has a rich imaginative life would be strongly developed in this area.

The final energy centre is the crown chakra. It sits on top of your head or can be located in the space just above this area. The colour to work with here is either violet or white – go with whatever your imagination connects with most strongly when you try to imagine the place where this chakra is located. This is concerned with a connection to whatever we believe to be a higher power, so in traditional thinking, God. When this energy centre is highly active, then this person would have a strong connection with God – or it might be the cosmos, or whatever higher power they might believe in. I think this energy centre can be a difficult one to imagine for many Westerners today, but it can be a useful imaginative tool when playing a character from another time: for instance, almost every character in a Shakespeare play has some concept of God, of heaven and of hell. They may or may not be strongly connected to the higher power they believe in but, for instance, if you were to play Richard II, you can easily argue that he believes himself strongly connected to God – he mentions at several points in the play that he rules by divine right, i.e. it is God who has placed him as a ruler above his countrymen.

## You and the character you play

To familiarize yourself with the chakras, it's probably worth your while to explore them in relation to yourself first of all. I am not going to talk you through this preparation in a detailed way beyond saying that, if you lie in semi-supine and spend some time, first of all, to lengthen and widen through the back, then allow yourself to be with your breath allowing it to drop in to your centre and then fall out from your centre, this makes a good preparation for the imaginative work that follows.

If you have an opportunity to work with a friend or a colleague, it might help if they talk you through the process, but you can also undertake a mindful exploration of your own.

### Visualizing the chakras

Start at the root chakra, working with the colour red – you can imagine a red disk spinning here, or a red flower slowly opening, petal by petal or a red light, pulsing. Think about the qualities this energy centre governs – your survival instincts and your sex drive.

Then move to the sacral chakra where the colour is orange and explore in your imagination those things you find pleasurable or that you do in order to experience pleasurable feelings.

Take your attention, then, to the solar plexus chakra where the energy is a golden yellow, and the focus is on power and control. Do you feel in control of your circumstances or do you tend to feel you have no sense of control?

Now move to the heart chakra where the colour to work with is the rich green of nature and think about love and your relationship with it.

From here, move to the throat chakra. The colour to work with here is blue. Think about the ways in which you express yourself in the world. How important is your voice to you? What is your relationship with language? Do you play an instrument? Do you like to draw or to paint?

Now take your attention to the brow chakra. The colour to with work here is indigo and consider whether you are someone who sees things or whether you are less perceptive. Also, are you sometimes intuitive and sense what someone is thinking or what will happen next?

Finally, take your attention to the crown chakra – go with the colour violet or white – some people find that pink also works quite well here.

## The Integrated Actor

Try not to prejudge any of these energy centres and their associated qualities as you work on them, by the way. So when you bring your attention to the crown chakra go, first of all, with the image of a white (violet or pink) disc spinning, or flower opening, petal by petal, or a white light glowing or pulsing, and concentrate on this for some time before you then think about exploring what this might mean to you. If there is a higher power in your thinking, do you feel, in this moment, connected to it, or is this area not at all active or responsive?

When meditating on the seven chakras, it is possible that some of them will seem easy to visualize or that they will feel active within you as you focus your imagination on them, and some of them you may find hard to imagine or they may just feel inactive. There are also energy centres in your hands and feet, as mentioned earlier, so if you find it hard to visualize one or more of these energy centres and their associated colours, place the palm of one hand just above the centre concerned and imagine the colour getting brighter and brighter just there – a disk spinning or a light pulsing are possibly easiest, or a flower opening, petal by petal. Think, too, about the attributes associated with that particular energy centre and how you relate to these personally and within your life. If a particular energy centre seems difficult to imagine, it is possible that the elements associated with it are not very important or you or not very developed within you. It might be useful to notice, and to reflect, on that.

## Approaching a character

I recommend starting this work either in semi-supine or fully supine as this offers you the opportunity to be at your most relaxed, aligned and available to the work. You could, if you prefer, work in a seated position, so long as this offers you the opportunity to be grounded through the feet, and aligned, as a starting point. Towards the end of this exercise sequence, you will move into standing and walking.

Take time to allow the weight of your body to be supported by the floor and imagine your back lengthening and widening across it in the usual way. You could use Semi-Supine 1, 2 or 3 from earlier in this book as a starting point. Remember to imagine the tail of your spine moving in the direction of your heels and think, 'Let my neck be free to let my head move forwards and upwards.' (Or out.)

Remind yourself not to hold on to the muscles in the front of your body – upper chest, solar plexus, belly. Take your attention to your outbreath allowing it to fall out from your centre with no control, sensing the breastbone soften or slightly fall as the breath falls out. Wait for your body to need the next breath and when you allow the next breath to drop in, release in the lower abdominal area.

While you are engaged in the process of lengthening and letting go, take your attention to the character you wish to play. This could be linked to a monologue but, ideally, you have some understanding of the character's journey through the play and are not only familiar with the monologue you wish to focus on.

## Approaching the character

### Stage 1

Allow your imagination to explore the things that you think are important to the character. These will largely be identified by key events within the play. What drives the character? What is their main drive, or want? (There may be more than one want, but to begin with, try to identify what you think is their chief or overriding drive.) Which chakra or energy centre would be dominant in relation to this drive?

Focus on that area in your body, the organ associated with the particular energy centre rather than the place on the spine where it might occur. If you decided, for example, that the main drive of the character was a sexual one, it would be better to focus the root chakra within the area of the sex organs rather than focusing on the tail of the spine, and if they are hedonistic and enjoy a range of pleasures you will also focus on the orange energy of the sacral chakra, but perhaps place it in the belly rather than in the sacrum. If, on the other hand, you decided that the character was motivated by unconditional love for their child, they would be heart centred. Again, focus on the area in your body where the heart resides rather than on a point on the spine.

Work with the colour associated with that energy centre and imagine that colour growing stronger, glowing brighter, and beginning to fill the whole area. So, for instance, if the character is heart centred, imagine the centre of your chest filled with green light, or a large green flower opening petal by petal on your chest, but then begin to imagine the whole area being dominated by that colour. If imagining a green light pulsing, stronger and stronger, works for you it is, perhaps, easier to imagine that green light beginning to fill the whole of the chest cavity, or sometimes it helps to imagine that it is green smoke or a green-coloured gas that begins to fill that area. As another example, if you thought the character was dominated by an ability to seek out the truth and to see things – their circumstances, events and other people – clearly, your focus would be on the brow chakra and on the indigo energy of that area. You would imagine the upper part of your head, gradually, filling with this indigo colour.

You need to take time with this work – don't rush it. Remember that if you feel the energy centre you wish to focus on doesn't seem to be responding or feels inactive, placing the palm of one hand on, or over, that centre may help to stimulate your experience of it. Just the heat of the palm of your hand in that area can be helpful (and heat, itself, is energy, of course) but you can also remember that the energy centres in the palms of your hands have the potential to be energy giving, too. If you do place the palm of one hand on an energy centre, then also continue working, imaginatively, with the colour associated with that area, giving that colour a form, such as a spinning disk, a glowing or pulsing light, a flower that is opening.

### Stage 2

When you feel confident that you have worked on a particular want or drive associated with a specific chakra, take time to consider if the character has other drives or another dominant characteristic. For instance, the solar plexus chakra associated with power and control, can be an important one – many of the kings or warriors in Shakespeare's plays are likely to have a strong relationship with this centre. In Richard II, for example, King Richard himself is quite obsessed, on one level, with exercising his power or with being seen by others as powerful, and in the same play Bolingbroke, who usurps the throne, too, is very concerned with achieving power.

So you may find that a character is dominated by one particular energy centre, or you may find that two or three chakras are important within their lived experience. It may also be worth considering if there are energy centres that are not very active within particular characters. You will not work on those, but it may be useful to know that a character is not interested in pleasure (the sacral chakra), for instance, or that they have no ability to perceive things (the indigo energy of the brow chakra), or that they do not believe in a higher power and that their crown chakra is inactive.

### Stage 3

After you have completed all of this imaginative exploration, spend some time thinking of how you gather and release energy and how it travels through your body. This sounds somewhat esoteric, but it is quite a simple and practical focus.

First of all, if you return to focusing on your breath, as breath falls in and out of your body, this is a gathering and releasing of energy. You can also imagine that energy comes into your body through your feet, travels up your legs, into your centre, and then falls out (with the breath) up the length of your spine, leaving you through the face and the head. Again, as before, it is helpful to give an image to your concept of energy – water energy, light energy or laser energy: whatever you feel works for you instinctively. As you imagine the energy travelling through your being, imagine it collecting or intensifying within those energy centres that you have decided are important to the character you are working on.

You may find that this particular way of focusing on your experience of energy within your body affects your breathing, in terms of rhythm, and it may seem to you as if your breath drops in deeper or not so deep. In relation to this, there is always a relationship of breath dropping in to centre, though that centre could be a bit higher or lower. (Avoid allowing breath to become entirely chest centred. It is true that, in life, some individuals do breathe almost entirely in the chest area and are unwilling to release the lower abdominal area to allow the breath to drop in but allowing your own breath to become restricted in this way will not help you use yourself efficiently as an actor, so a degree of shift, higher or lower, in your experience of centre can be part of your experience of the character, but that shift cannot be so great that it will compromise your ability to be free and flexible with your larynx and within the vocal tract.)

Stay in touch with the breath and allow your attention to return to the key energy centres that you feel dominate your character as you bring yourself up to standing. As in the early stages of moving from the floor to a standing, grounded position, you should take your time with this, allowing your head to lead you, and moving to a semi-foetal position, then to all fours, and then to standing, at each stage working with the various energy centres of your character and checking that you are still allowing breath to fall in and out of you without clenching or tensing in the lower belly area.

Once standing, explore your relationship with the ground for a few moments. If your character is dominated by the root chakra and/or the sacral chakra (red and orange energy), you should find you have a strong relationship with the ground beneath your feet, and you should sense that your weight is low in your body, probably concentrated in the belly and the hips, with your knees feeling very released. However, it is also possible that your character may not be dominated by these centres at all – they could be heart and crown centred (green and indigo energy), for instance – and then your relationship with the ground is less important to you and your sense of weight will be somewhat higher in your torso. As with the breath, which needs to maintain a relationship with your own centre, as an actor you will still need some sense of how your character is grounded through the feet – if you recall, this is part of your support system – but your sense of groundedness could be lighter and less powerful for the character you play.

## Stage 4

Once you have sorted out your relationship with your body and with the ground in standing alignment, allowing your head and knees to lead you, begin to walk around your rehearsal space. You may find, after the chakra work in semi-supine, that you already feel different within yourself. Continue to explore how the various energy centres dominate the experience of your character and, as you walk, think about the way you now see the world around you.

As in the previous integration exercise, focus now on a particular moment in the play – if you have chosen a monologue to work on then it will be the moment just before this monologue occurs. Start to connect with the want of the character – this may also help you stay connected to one of the particular energy centres you have worked on – and explore how this want moves you around the space: your want is driving you to get to where you want to go and to say what you need to say. It is up to you how you pursue this part of the exercise, but it is very important that you feel your want very strongly and that the urgency of this want connects with your experience of your breath and is what motivates you to move through the space.

Arrive and speak your monologue – believe in and invest in the circumstances of that moment. Where are you? Who is there with you? Who are you speaking to? And, of course, what do you want from them and how do you use your words to get what you want from them?

## Reflection

As with the integration exercise, once the speech is over, relax and take time to reflect on your experience. You may be able to consider quite specific details within what you have just experienced, to do with your body, your breath, your voice, or your imagination, or you may only have a more general sense of what happened, or of what you felt. If you are able to harness some, or all, of this experience, it will be valuable to you.

It is good, obviously, to note for yourself what feels different, in a good way, and whether anything new happened for you, either within yourself or within the speech. Hopefully, you will feel that you have found something out about the character and the way you can use yourself to embody them. If you worked with a partner or with a small group of people, then feedback from them is also tremendously useful as they may have seen or experienced something that you were not aware was happening at a particular moment and their feedback may help you identify what you experienced.

You may find this way of working difficult to monitor, at least to begin with, as you are working strongly with your imagination, working in collaboration with your breath and your body, and you can be so focused on your internal experience that you later find it hard to assess it or quantify it. If you feel the benefit of it, in some way, then the more you take yourself through these processes the more familiar they will become to you, and the better you will know yourself and be able to identify what is useful to you as an actor.

# CONCLUSION

I set out at the start of this book to share key elements from my particular way of working with actors. If you have worked your way through the book, then you will appreciate that this is by no means a complete approach to acting, or to body, breath and voice work.

I have attempted to identify those elements that I think are key in relation to how the actor uses themself and how the actor's imagination can work to unlock both healthy physical and vocal use and their imaginative resources. I have also attempted to debunk elements of traditional practice that I believe are unhealthy or counterproductive.

I hope you leave this book with a clear sense that if the actor is to be able to integrate their experience they must have a fertile imagination, both in relation to themselves and their own use, and in relation to the character they will play and the world in which that character 'lives'. The inner life of the character the actor plays is dependent upon a powerful connection between the actor's imagination and the breath, and that inner life can only radiate (i.e. communicate to the camera or the audience) if the actor is sufficiently grounded, centred and at ease. Breath is at the centre of everything and needs to be organic, which is to say responsive to the actor's thoughts, feelings and inner life. In order to do this, the breath must be free – not held, 'directed', 'controlled' or restricted – and central to this sense of freedom in the breath is a low belly release which is, in fact, entirely natural but not available to you when you are unnecessarily tense or self-conscious.

'Authenticity' resides in the actor's ability to both know themselves and to accept themselves as they are as a starting point, and then in their ability to place themselves, imaginatively, in the shoes of the character they play – the actor's ability to stand, imaginatively, in the world in which the character lives, and inhabit it. The work in this book that is rooted in principles drawn from the Alexander Technique is a basis for bringing you to yourself through being able to let go of mannerisms and habitual use that will not be of use to you as an actor, if you want your acting to be truthful and honest. Through physical release – you may prefer to think of this as a place of ease – you are then ready to connect your imagination to your voice through the process of centring the effort for sound, and to language.

Language, and the structures within written text, provides tremendous stimuli for the actor's imagination and the actor's ability to turn words into living thoughts as part of their inner life. The actor also needs to develop a discipline in response to language and in their ability to respond sensitively to the structures that the writer provides.

### The Integrated Actor

I hope this book may have inspired you to think about acting and acting processes differently, or that it has offered you perspectives about acting that might challenge your existing ideas about it.

There is also a video recording that accompanies this book and if some elements within my writing seem obscure or are difficult to grasp, I trust that the evidence in the video can clarify these for you. (https://www.bloomsburyonlineresources.com/the-integrated-actor)

# FURTHER READING

The list below is not exhaustive. Several of the practitioners listed here have written many books – not all are listed. I have chosen to highlight below the books I have found the most useful, informative and inspiring, a number of which are directly referenced within the text of *The Integrated Actor*.

## Acting

**The Technique of Acting,** Adler, Stella: Echo Point Books and Media, LLC, 2024
**Acting Stanislavski: A Practical Guide to Stanislavski's Approach and Legacy,** Gillett, John: Methuen Drama, 2014
**A Challenge for the Actor,** Hagen, Uta: Simon and Schuster, 1991
**Respect for Acting,** Hagan, Uta: Jossey-Bass, 2023
**The Year of the King,** Sher, Anthony: Nick Hern Books, 2004
**An Actor's Work,** Stanislavski, K./Jean Benedetti: Routledge Classics, 2016

## Alexander Technique

**Introduction to the Alexander Technique: A Practical Guide for Actors,** Connington, Bill: Methuen Drama, 2020
**The Alexander Technique,** Liebowitz, Judy/Connington, Bill: Souvenir Press, 2011
**The Art of Changing,** Park, Glen: Ashgrove Publishing, 2000
**Alexander Technique for Actors,** Penny O'Connor: Nick Hern Books, 2021

## Fight or Flight

**Bodily Changes in Pain, Hunger, Fear and Rage,** Cannon, Walter B.: Cannon Press, 2013

## Polyvagal Theory

**Polyvagal Exercises for Safety and Connection,** Dana, Deb: W. W. Norton, 2020

## Anatomy and Care of the Voice

**The Performer's Voice,** Bunch Dayme, Meribeth: W. W. Norton, 2006
**Care of the Professional Voice,** Davies, Garfield D./Jahn, Anthony F.: Methuen Drama, 2004
**The Owner's Manual to the Voice: A Guide for Singers and Other Professional Voice Users,** Gates, Rachel/Arick Forest, L./Obert, Kerrie: Oxford University Press, 2013

The Integrated Actor

## Voice and Speech

**Voice and the Actor**, Berry, Cicely: Virgin Books, 2000
**Voice into Acting**, Gutekunst, Christina/Gillett, John: Methuen Drama, 2021
**English after RP**, Lindsey, Geoff: Palgrave MacMillan, 2019
**Freeing the Natural Voice,** Linklater, Kristin: Nick Hern Books, 2006
**The Moment of Speech,** Morrison, Annie: Methuen Drama, 2021
**The Actor Speaks,** Rodenburg, Patsy: Bloomsbury, 2023
**The Estill Voice Model: Theory and Translation**, Steinhauer, Kimberley, McDonald Klimek, Mary, et al.: Estill Voice International, January 2017

## Speaking Shakespeare

**Playing Shakespeare**, Barton, John: Methuen, 2009
**The Actor and the Text**, Berry, Cicely: Virgin Books, 2000
**The Dramatic Text Workbook and Video,** Carey, David, Carey, Rebecca Clark: Methuen Drama, 2019
**Tackling the Text,** Houseman, Barbara: Nick Hern Books, 2008
**Freeing Shakespeare's Voice,** Linklater, Kristin: Nick Hern Books, 2010
**Keeping It Active, A Practical Guide to Rhetoric in Performance,** Nelson, Jeannette: Nick Hern Books, 2022
**Speaking Shakespeare,** Rodenburg, Patsy: Methuen, 2023
**Shakespearean Verse Speaking,** Rokison, Abigail: Cambridge University Press, 2011
**Dramatic Adventures in Rhetoric,** Taylor, Giles/Wilson, Philip: Oberon Books, 2015

# INDEX

Note: Page numbers in *italics* refer to figures and tables.

abdominal release exercise 41
accent 157–8
   actor 158–9, 166–8
   Received Pronunciation 166–7
   resonance 141–2
   Shakespeare 169
acting 125
   centre 56
   creative processes 209
   emotions 58–9
   intuitive elements 10–11
   job 2
   nature of 3–4
   processes 3
   technique 69
   truth 9
actors
   accent 142
   acting, nature of 3–4
   audience 11
   being grounded 24, 26–8
   being present 34–5
   breath 20
   character making 219
   communicate, spoken thought 143–4
   discipline 205, 231
   energy 35–6, 218–20
   engagement, physical 111
   experience 1
   fight *vs.* flight response 4, 5
   freedom in performance 10
   grounded and aligned 219
   intuitive ability 10–11
   mind and body 6
   muscular engagement 16
   optimum pitch 62
   organic nature 2, 3
   physical characterization 102
   radiating energy 220
   representing thoughts 71, 75
   self-image 24
   serving the text 93
   technique 69–70
   thought processes 15
   training 1, 3, 10, 14, 23
   transformation 10
   voice work 127

work and therapeutic benefits 23
working with Shakespeare's text 189
air-flow exercise 91
Alexander, F. Matthias 47
   principles 102, 209
   technique 2–3, 14, 28, 47, 223, 231
alignment 24–6
   component parts, body 25
   concept of 43
   head/neck relationship 43
   larynx 43–5
   support 26
alternative pair work exercise 117
alveolar consonants 100
alveolar ridge 128, 161
anger 58
antithesis 179–80
articulate/articulation 114
   English 157
   exercises 164–5
   organs of *160*, 161
   soft palate 153
aspirate onset 67–8
attractor state 32, 34
attunement 10–11, 217, 220–2
aural sense 13–14
authenticity 231
autonomic nervous system 5

Barton, John 181–2
   *Playing Shakespeare* 172
Berry, Cicely 55, 56, 171, 181–2, 196, 205, 206
   *The Actor and the Text* 172
   *Voice and the Actor* 165
Betjeman, John, *Death in Leamington* 204
blank verse 171–3
body 6–7
   breath 41, 105
   gathering water exercise 110
   potential exercise 90
   swings 105–9
Boston, Jane 165
box breathing 89
breath/breathing 199, 215–16
   being grounded 28
   body 41
   and body potential exercise 90

# Index

capacity 59
centre 56, 59
concepts of 17
control 20
as energy 17–18
energy centres 228–9
exercise 17–18, 37–40, 91, 200
facts 18–19
form of energy 17–18
gasp 199–200
imagination 73–4
inspiration 18
latissimus dorsi 115–16
management 21, 87–9
movement 149
muscle groups 20, 87
natural and organic 18–19
optimum pitch 63
overworking 21
presence 37
psycho-physical act 20
reflex 20, 37
relationship with 2
rhythm 19
semi-supine position 49, 52–3, 97
standing 30, 32–3
support 21, 26, 112
thoughts 87–8, 94, 201–4
vocal folds 21–2
whispered 'Ah' exercise 99
breathy tone 22
brow chakra 224

caesura 186–7, 189–92
   exercise 191–2
Cannon, Walter Bradford 5
centre
   acting 56
   awareness of 57
   breath 56, 59
   concept of 55–6, 60
   for each person 56
   of gravity 57
   language expressions 57
chakras 222, 222–5
   character, approaching 226–30
   visualizing 225–6
channel for sound
   constriction 101
   soft palate 152–6
   space 149
   tongue 150–2
chanting 147–8
character 10, 14–15, 59, 69, 210–14
   approaching 226–30
   energy 217, 219–20

exercise 222–5
   inner life 231
chest resonance 124–6
chin 27, 44, 45, 48, 138, 139, 148, 215
Colson, Greta 166
comma 94, 186, 191
connected speech 68, 143
consonants 100, 146, 150, 157, 159–61, 164, 165, 196–7
   clusters 165–6
   repeated voiced 113–14
   voiced 159
   voiceless 159
constriction 101, 149–50
creak 68–9
creative freedom 10
crown chakra 224

Davis, Bette 9
Dayme, Meribeth Bunch, *The Performer's Voice* 20
Deb Dana, *Polyvagal Exercises for Safety and Connection* 6
deep fascia 6
Dench, Judi 11
diaphragm 18, *19*, 22, 59, 87, 124
driving air 22
Duncan-Jones, Katherine 193, 199

education 1, 13
embodiment 111, 120
emotions 58–9
energy 35–6
   centres *222*, 222–5
   chakras *222*, 222–5 (*see also* chakras)
   character 217, 226–30
   exercise 36, 217–18, 220
   fluctuations 218
   radiating 218, 220
   sharing 220–2
enjambment 181–4, 193
Estill, Josephine 63, 65, 88, 115, 125, 146
Estill Voice Craft 63, 65, 125, 146
Ethos 176
Eyre, Richard 11

false vocal folds 101
fascia 6
fight *vs.* flight response 4–5
figure of 8 exercise 164–5
freedom 9
full-stop 94, 181, 186, 191, 199, 206

gasp breath 199–200
gathering water exercise 110
glottal onsets 66–7, 89
   exercise 65–6

# Index

glottal stop 66–7
Grace, Sally 141
grounding, act of 24
   breath 28
   exercise 26–8
   seated position 26–8

habits
   grounding, act of 24, 26–8
   self-image 24
   sitting 31
   standing 29, 30, 32–3
   therapeutic benefits, actors' work 23
   traumatic experience 23
Hall, Peter 181–2, 185
hard palate *19*, 152
head
   books for support 48, 50, 77
   fixing 44
   neck relationship 43
   poise of 27, 28, 38, 44, 136
   sinus resonance 129
heart chakra 224
Hecht, Deborah 200–1
humming 132–3, 135

iambic pentameter
   caesura 186–7
   eleven (or more) syllable lines 184–5
   English language 174–5
   enjambment 181–4
   exercise 173–4
   jazz 185
   verse 191
identity 62
imagination/imaginative 7, 13–16, 69–71, 212–13,
     216, 231
   aural sense 13–14
   breathing 73–4
   free rein 13, 14
   muscularity 16
   physiological and emotional responses 13
   power of 7
   responses 13
   sensory exercise 15
   visual sense 13–14
imaging exercise 73
inner emotional experience 17
inspiration 18
integrated actor 1–3. *See also* actors
integration 2
   character 210–14
   exercise 209
   movement into speaking 215–16
   reflection 216
   semi-supine position 211, 214

text 210–14
   the want, notion of 210, 214
intellectual prowess 1
intercostal muscles 87
intuition 10–11
Irving, Henry 13

jaw 127, 161, 212
   freeing 161–3
   lower 34, 52
   upper 52
   whispered 'Ah' exercise 98
jazz 185

Langham, Michael 17
language expressions 57
larynx 59, 63, 112, 123, 129, 154
   depressing 45
   movement 44
   observation of 44
   optimum pitch 61
   shortened neck 45
   structure of 43
latissimus dorsi 115–16
   exercise, seated position 116–17
Lindsey, Geoff, *English after RP* 166–7
Linklater, Kristin 6, 20, 72–3
   *Freeing Shakespeare's Voice* 172
   *Freeing the Natural Voice* 20, 72–3,
     89, 154
lips 34, 52, 100, 127–8, 133, 135–8, 151, 162, 211
lived experience 9–10
living thoughts 100, 114, 120, 148
Logos 176
longer thoughts 69, 88, 201–4

Marshall, Lorna 105
meaning 68, 95–6
microphones 16, 33, 68, 159, 171
middle constrictor 101
mind 6–7
Moscow Arts Theatre School 11
*The Motive and the Cue* 171
muscularity 16, 114, 163

nasal resonance 128
nasal sinuses 128, 137
neck spine 27–8, 38, 49, 78, 83–5, 139, 211
   semi-supine position 52
neurodivergent individuals 71
neutral position 59, 61, 63
neutral vowel 127, 128, 133, 151, 162

occipital joint 14, 27, 39, 78, 121
Olivier, Laurence 9
optimum pitch 61, 143, 144

# Index

dependent factors 61
exercises 63–5
gender stereotypes 62
speech quality 63
vocal identity 62
way we sound to ourselves 62
oral cavity 123, 124, 128, 149, 152, 154, 163
oral resonance 126
Original Pronunciation (OP) 169
oxymoron 179–80

palpate 44
parasympathetic nervous system 5
parietal fascia 6
Park, Glen, *The Art of Changing: A New Approach to the Alexander Technique* 223
Parkinson, Michael 204
partner work 117, 136
Pathos 176
pelvic floor 117–18
    exercise 118–19
pendulum swing 105–7, 109
performance anxiety 37
pharynx 61, 123–4, 129, 140, 149, 152
phrases/phrasing 93–4
    exercise 201–3
    punctuation 200–1
phrenum 164
physical centre 55. *See also* centre
Pisk, Litz 36, 105
pitch 64
    larynx 44
    uses of 143
polyvagal theory 5–6, 57
Porges, Stephen 5
potential range 61
psoas muscle 40
psycho-physical exercise 72–3
psycho-physical processes 10
psycho-physical responses 1, 13, 14
punctuation 191, 204
    concept of 199, 207
    exercise with chairs 205
    modern edition, Shakespeare play/poem 204–5
    phrasing 200–1
    rules 94
    Shakespeare sonnet 199
    walking the text 206

Qigong/Chi-gung 110

Raleigh, Walter 169
range 44–5, 61, 63, 64, 68, 69, 144–5
    chanting exercise 147–8
    exercise, begin to access 145–6

extend range, exercises 146–7
gliding, highest to lowest note 146–7
Received Pronunciation (RP) 141, 166–7
recoil breath 99
regular/irregular verse lines 174, 184–5, 191
relaxation 9, 16, 55
resonance/resonant 67, 123, 148
    accent 141–2
    adaptation of 137–8
    balance of 129–30
    body 123, 138–9
    chest 124–6
    exercises 131–6
    face 139
    head 129, 139
    lower 139–40
    nasal 128
    oral 126
    qualities 61
    sinus 128
    spaces 123
    true and sympathetic 124–5
    vibrations 124, 126–8
    working with partners 136
retraction 150
rhetoric
    definition of 175–6
    literary devices 176–7
rhyming couplet 194
rhyming scheme 192
ribcage *19*, 22
ribs 20, 59
rib swing 88
Rodenburg, Patsy 4, 56, 115
    *The Actor Speaks* 4
    *Speaking Shakespeare* 172
*Romeo and Juliet* 17
root chakra 223
Ross, Maggie 56
Rowles, Jan Haydn 141

sacrum/sacral 51, 78
    chakra 223, 225, 227
self-consciousness 13
self-image 24
self-serving 189
semi-supine position 75, 87, 97, 101–3, 211
    Alexander Technique 47
    alignment and release 77, 79
    all-fours position 84
    books, support for head 48, 50, 77
    breastbone 78
    breath 49, 52–3
    definition 47
    exercise 48–53

# Index

fingers and hands 80–1
on the floor 77–8
habitual tensions 50
head and neck 80
knees and feet 81–2
pelvis 79
ribcage 82
shoulder 83
spine 78–9, 83
standing and speaking 83–6
working in 47–8
senses 13–15, 35, 37, 71, 74, 125
sensory exercise 15
Serota, Carolyn 2
Shakespeare 43
    accent 169–70
    antithesis 179–80
    blank verse 171–3
    caesura 186–7
    eleven (or more) syllable lines 184–5
    enjambment 181–4
    *Hamlet* 179, 183–5
    iambic exercise 173–4
    jazz 185
    *Julius Caesar* 176, 179
    *Macbeth* 172
    *The Merchant of Venice* 177–9, 187
    *A Midsummer Night's Dream* 172, 175
    *Much Ado about Nothing* 171
    oxymoron 179–80
    *Richard II* 171, 224, 228
    *Romeo and Juliet* 179–80, 186
    rule of three 177–9
    Scottish accents 170
    speaking 170–1
    structure, verse 182
    verse, nature of 172
    *As You Like It* 171–2
Shakespeare sonnets
    caesura 189–92
    emotional expression 190
    enjambment 193
    punctuation 191
    rhyming couplet 194
    rhyming scheme 192
    Sonnet 18 190
    Sonnet 29 192–4, 203
    Sonnet 116 169, 195
    Sonnet 129 196
    speaking 189
    structure 192–3
    volta 194–7
Sharpe, Edda 141
Shaw, Maxwell 55
Shelley, Rudi 69–70

Sher, Antony, *The Year of the King* 43
side swings 108–9
simultaneous onset 67, 68
sinus resonance 128
siren 146–7
sitting exercise 31
Skinner, Edith 200–1
Smith, Maggie 204
social pressure 29
soft palate *19*, 152
    articulation 153
    /g/ sounds 153
    /k/ consonant 154–6
    oral space 154
    Shakespeare play/Greek tragedies 156
solar plexus chakra 223–4
sound
    breath 40
    English articulation 157, 159–60
    experiments with 34
    of speech 163–4
speech 68
    accent 157–8
    actor 158–60
    articulation 157
    clarity of 159
    jaw 161
    playing with/imitating sounds 157
    quality 63, 65
    sounds of 163–4
Speed, Anne Marie 21
spine 38, 57
    semi-supine position 48–53
    standing 32
stage performances 9
standing 29
    breath 30, 32–3
    exercise 29–31, 34, 36
    forward momentum 30
    grounded 105–6, 120, 229
    for grounding 31–2
    key factors 29
    sound exercise 34
    speaking 83–6
Stanislavski, Konstantin 3–4, 37, 73, 209
    Stanislavski System, tools 209–10
stress 68, 174
'stroking the jaw down' exercise 161–3
structures
    conveying the thoughts 95
    exercise 93–5
    Shakespeare sonnet 192–3
    Shakespeare verse 182
superficial fascia 6
supine 90, 226

# Index

support
    abdominal muscles 111–12
    breath/breathing 21, 26, 112
    concepts of 111, 120
    definition 112
    exercise 120
    for head 50, 77
    latissimus dorsi 115–17
    pelvic floor 117–20
    subtle/gentle sensations 121
    system 26
    transversus abdominus 113–14
swings 105–7
    momentum of 108
    pendulum swing 105–7, 109
    side swings 108–9
syllabic stress 143
sympathetic nervous system 5
sympathetic resonance 124

tail bone 27–8, 30, 32, 53, 84, 90, 211, 215
tapping 134–5
technique 69–70
teeth 98, 114, 126–8, 131, 138, 139, 151, 153, 154, 161, 162
tensions 209
    balance of 16
    habitual 50
Terry, Ellen 13
text 210–14
    actor 93
    meaning 95–6
    phrases 93–4
    structure exercise 93–5
thoughts
    breath 87–8, 94, 201–4
    emotional responses 74
    exercise 71
    visualization 71–2
throat chakra 224

tongue 164
    root 58, 150–2
    simple vowel exercise 152
    tip 128, 157, 161, 164
touch 14, 34, 35, 53, 55–6, 71, 73–4, 97
    breath 79, 80, 107, 229
    of sound 53, 71, 114, 116
transformation 10
transversus abdominus 113–14
true resonance 124
truth 9–11, 69, 170
Turner, Clifford, *Voice and Speech in the Theatre* 165

vagus nerve 5–6
vertebrae 14, 25, 38, 51, 52, 102, 139, 140, 211
visceral fascia 6
visual sense 13–14
vocal folds 65, 88–9, 112, 123, 149
    approach to 22
    breath 21–2
    false 101
    onset 67–8
vocal freedom 145
vocal health 68
vocal identity 62
vocal range 61
vocal tract *19*, 21, 41, 43–5, 63, 97–8, 101, 124, 140, 148–53, 163, 200
volta 194–7
vowels 65–7, 116, 149, 151, 159, 165
    simple exercise 152

Wells, J. C. 166, 167
whisper 33, 67
whispered 'Ah' exercise 97–101, 150
Williams, Kenneth 204

yes/no nod 27–8, 38–9
Yevtushenko, Yevgeny 72, 170
    *Colours* 72, 95